# Access to Higher Education

**Palgrave Teaching and Learning**
*Series Editor:* **Sally Brown**

Access to Higher Education
Coaching and Mentoring in Higher Education
Facilitating Work-Based Learning
Facilitating Workshops
For the Love of Learning
Fostering Self-Efficacy in Higher Education Students
Internationalization and Diversity in Higher Education
Leading Dynamic Seminars
Learning, Teaching and Assessment in Higher Education
Learning with the Labyrinth
Live Online Learning
Masters Level Teaching, Learning and Assessment

*Further titles are in preparation*

**Universities into the 21st Century**
*Series Editors:* **Noel Entwistle and Roger King**

Becoming an Academic
Cultures and Change in Higher Education
Global Inequalities and Higher Education
Learning Development in Higher Education
Managing your Academic Career
Managing your Career in Higher Education Administration
Research and Teaching
Teaching Academic Writing in UK Higher Education
Teaching for Understanding at University
Understanding the International Student Experience
The University in the Global Age
Writing in the Disciplines

**Palgrave Research Skills**

Authoring a PhD
The Foundations of Research (2nd edn)
Getting to Grips with Doctoral Research
Getting Published
The Good Supervisor (2nd edn)
Maximizing the Impacts of University Research
The PhD Viva
Planning Your Postgraduate Research
The PhD Writing Handbook
The Postgraduate Research Handbook (2nd edn)
The Professional Doctorate
Structuring Your Research Thesis

*You may also be interested in:*
Teaching Study Skills and Supporting Learning

For a complete listing of all our titles in this area please visit
**he.palgrave.com/study-skills**

# Access to Higher Education

## Understanding Global Inequalities

Edited by Graeme Atherton

Editorial and selection matter © Graeme Atherton 2017
Individual chapters © their respective authors 2017

All rights reserved. No reproduction, copy or transmission of this publication may be made without written permission.

No portion of this publication may be reproduced, copied or transmitted save with written permission or in accordance with the provisions of the Copyright, Designs and Patents Act 1988, or under the terms of any licence permitting limited copying issued by the Copyright Licensing Agency, Saffron House, 6–10 Kirby Street, London EC1N 8TS.

Any person who does any unauthorized act in relation to this publication may be liable to criminal prosecution and civil claims for damages.

The author has asserted his rights to be identified as the author of this work in accordance with the Copyright, Designs and Patents Act 1988.

First published 2017 by
PALGRAVE

Palgrave in the UK is an imprint of Macmillan Publishers Limited, registered in England, company number 785998, of 4 Crinan Street, London, N1 9XW.

Palgrave is a global imprint of the above companies and is represented throughout the world.

Palgrave® and Macmillan® are registered trademarks in the United States, the United Kingdom, Europe and other countries.

ISBN: 978–1–137–41189–1 paperback

This book is printed on paper suitable for recycling and made from fully managed and sustained forest sources. Logging, pulping and manufacturing processes are expected to conform to the environmental regulations of the country of origin.

A catalogue record for this book is available from the British Library.

A catalog record for this book is available from the Library of Congress.

Printed and bound by CPI Group (UK) Ltd, Croydon, CR0 4YY

# Contents

List of figures and tables vii
Contributors viii
Series editor's preface xiv

**Introduction** 1

1 Canada – Access at the Crossroads 13
  *Diana Wickham*

2 Marching in the Rain: The TRIO Programme and the
  Civil Rights Legacy in the United States 29
  *Ngondi Kamatuka*

3 Access and Retention in Higher Education in Colombia:
  The Case of the Children's University EAFIT 43
  *Isabel Cristina Montes Gutiérrez and Ana Cristina Abad*

4 Changing the Mindset: How Germany Is Trying to Combine
  Access and Equity 55
  *Julia Mergner, Shweta Mishra and Dominic Orr*

5 Extending Equity in Higher Education in an Equitable Society:
  The Finnish Dilemma 68
  *Ari Tarkiainen*

6 The United Kingdom: The Access-to-Higher-Education Nation? 77
  *Graeme Atherton*

7 Access to Post-secondary Education in Malaysia: Realities
  and Aspirations 94
  *Glenda Crosling, Mien Wee Cheng and Ruma Lopes*

8 Expanding Higher Education in India: The Challenge
  for Equity 109
  *Manasi Thapliyal Navani*

9  National Access Policies for Higher Education in China: Creating Equal Opportunities in Education    121
   *Baocun Liu and Yang Su*

10 Access to Higher Education in South Africa: Addressing the Myths    137
   *Ncedikaya Magopeni and Lullu Tshiwula*

11 Making Commitment Concrete: Policy and Practice in Access to HE in Ghana    151
   *Joseph Budu*

12 Evolution or Revolution: The Three Ages of Access in Australia    164
   *Margaret Heagney and Fran Ferrier*

13 Conclusions: The Age of Access    182

References    192
Index    212

# List of figures and tables

## ▶ Figures

3.1  Children's University  47
6.1  Proportion of 18-year-olds Accepted for Entry to HE by Cycle and Country of Domicile  78
6.2  Eighteen-year-old Entry Rates for Disadvantaged Areas (POLAR2 Q1) by Country of Domicile  80
6.3  Expenditure on Office for Fair Access–related Activities 2006–07 to 2016–17  89
6.4  Percentage Point Difference of the Outcome from the Sector-adjusted Average, Split by POLAR3 Quintile  91

## ▶ Tables

3.1  Professional Projections for the Future  51
3.2  Student Future Employment Projections  51
6.1  Total Student Numbers and HE Institutions in the United Kingdom 2013–14  78
6.2  HE Financial Support Available in the United Kingdom  79
7.1  Student Enrolments in HE Institutions in Malaysia (2008–12)  96
8.1  GER among Religious Groups  111
8.2  GER (18–23) and Inter-caste Disparities  112
8.3  Location-wise Distribution of Institutions  112
10.1  Science Foundation Programme Models in South Africa  140
10.2  Gross HE Participation Rates by Race (2005–11)  144
11.1  Type of Tertiary Education Institutions in Ghana  152
11.2  The CAMFED Model  156
12.1  Operational Definitions of Each Target Group and Indicators for Measuring Progress Were Established by 1994 (the 'Martin Indicators')  169
12.2  Number of Students in Equity Groups as a Proportion of Domestic Onshore Students and as a Proportion of Australian Population; and Ratio Proportion of These Groups in HE in 2012 to Total National Population 2007 and 2012  176

# Contributors

▶ **Canada: Access at the crossroads**
*Diana Wickham*

Diana Wickham is a strategic planner with experience spanning the public, private and not-for-profit sectors. From 2002–10 she was Executive Officer of the Canada Millennium Scholarship Foundation. In 2008, she launched the Canadian Post-Secondary Access Partnership with YMCA Canada and other community-based organizations, to inspire and assist youth facing barriers to pursuing higher education. In 2009, she partnered with the Toronto-based Institute Without Boundaries to organize the 1st Community Access Challenge, which mobilized multisectoral teams from across Canada to come up with local strategies to broaden access to post-secondary studies. In 2012, Diana was the volunteer chair of GAPS 1st World Congress on Access to Post-Secondary Education, held in Montreal.

▶ **Marching in the Rain: The TRIO Programme and the Civil Rights Legacy in the United States**
*Ngondi Kamatuka*

Dr Ngondi A. Kamaṭuka is Director of the Achievement & Assessment Institute's Center for Educational Opportunity Programs at the University of Kansas, and has been with the University in many capacities since 1987. He has also taught at the University of Kansas for 15 years. Dr Kamaṭuka continues active engagement in his global community by serving on several local and national committees, as well as advising European universities and organizations on educational access and success issues. He has served as chair of the Council for Opportunity In Education Board of Directors and is the recipient of the Walter O. Mason award.

▶ **Access and Retention in Higher Education in Colombia The Case of the Children's University EAFIT**
*Isabel Cristina Montes Gutiérrez and Ana Cristina Abad*

Ana Cristina Abad Restrepo did her undergraduate studies in social communication and journalism in the Universidad Pontificia Bolivariana, Medellín-Colombia. She is a specialist in semiotics of interactive communication at

Universidad EAFIT, Medellín-Colombia. Her Master's degree in advanced communication studies, with an emphasis in science communication, was earned at Pompeu Fabra University, Barcelona-España.

Ana worked as Communication and Culture Department Chief in EAFIT University for 11 years. She has worked as a cathedratic professor in the organizational communication area of social communication in the undergraduate program of EAFIT University. She has been working as General Coordinator of EAFIT Children´s University program since 2005.

Lina Maritza Vásquez Guzmán (lvasqu18@eafit.edu.co) earned a BA in philosophy at Universidad de Antioquia; she received her master's in humanistic studies at Universidad EAFIT, Medellín-Colombia. Currently she works as a strategic assistant in the EAFIT Children´s University program.

Ana María Londoño Rivera is a product design engineer and has a master's in humanistic studies from Universidad EAFIT, Medellín-Colombia. She has been working for EAFIT Children's University since its creation in 2005, and she has been the strategic coordinator of this program since 2008.

Isabel Cristina Montes Gutiérrez is a PhD student in the program of Educational Leadership & Policy Analysis at University of Missouri–Columbia. She did her undergraduate studies in economics at the Universidad EAFIT and earned a master's in science of administration at the same university. She worked for eight years at Universidad EAFIT, Medellin-Colombia, as a planning director and teaching director in educational researches and reports.

▶ **Changing the Mindset: How Germany Is Trying to Combine Access and Equity**
*Julia Mergner, Shweta Mishra and Dominic Orr*

Dr Shweta Mishra is Head of the Research Unit for the Students and Graduates Organization at the International Centre for Higher Education Research (INCHER), Kassel, University of Kassel.

Her research interests focus on the social dimension of higher education, social network analysis and under-represented groups in higher education. In 2012, she received her PhD in social work from the University of Minnesota, USA. In the United States, her work primarily focused on examining the educational outcomes of children with a concentration on child protection involvement in the state of Minnesota. Dr Mishra formerly worked as a researcher at the German Centre for Research on Higher Education and Science Studies (DZHW) in Hannover, Germany. At DZHW, she was involved with the EUROSTUDENT project, which compares the socio-economic backgrounds and living conditions of students in higher education systems in Europe.

Julia Mergner works as a research assistant in the research group StuFHe at the University of Hamburg. StuFHe investigates the development of academic competence with regard to the effects of institutional support and student diversity.

Ms Mergner holds a BSc degree in psychology and a MSc degree in public administration from the University of Twente, Enschede (NL). Currently, she is a PhD student at the Centre for Higher at the Technical University of Dortmund. Her dissertation focuses on organizational change in German higher education institutions as a response to political demands in the context of the widening participation agenda.

Dr Dominic Orr is senior researcher at the FiBS Institute for Education and Socioeconomic Research, Berlin. Previously he worked for over 13 years at DZHW in Hannover (German Centre for Higher Education Research and Science Studies). There, for nearly ten years, he led the project EUROSTUDENT, which collects comparative data on the social dimension of higher education from nearly 30 countries. He has also worked as an external senior policy analyst for the OECD's Centre for Educational Reform and Innovation and has contributed to UNESCO's Global Education Monitoring Report on the topics of access and affordability in tertiary education.

▶ **Extending Equity in Higher Education in an Equitable Society: The Finnish Dilemma**
*Ari Tarkiainen*

Dr Tarkiainen is Senior Project Manager at the Karelia University of Applied Science. He has almost 30 years' experience in RDI project management on the national and international levels in issues like demographic change, guidance and counselling in higher education, science education, well-being and ICT technology and the development of social and health services. His PhD thesis (2009) focused on the introduction of Finnish innovation policy in the 1990s and 2000s. He has also lots of practical experience in usability research and evaluation linked with RDI. Tarkiainen has supervised a number of master's theses; worked as a researcher, publishing many articles and reports; and participated in numerous international conferences and seminars.

▶ **The United Kingdom: The Access-to-Higher-Education Nation**
*Graeme Atherton*

Dr Graeme Atherton has been working in widening access to higher education (HE) since 1995. After reading philosophy, politics and economics at Trinity College, University of Oxford, he completed his doctorate at the University of Liverpool. He founded and leads both AccessHE and the National Education Opportunities Network (NEON). AccessHE is a network of over 200 schools, colleges and higher education institutions (HEIs), working in London to widen access to HE. NEON is the national professional organization for widening access to HE in England, with over 80 university members. He holds Visiting Professorships at London Metropolitan University; Amity Business School; and Sunway University, Kuala Lumpur, Malaysia. He has produced over 120 conference papers and publications in this field.

▶ **Realities and Aspirations: How Access to Higher Education is Contributing to Nation-building in Malaysia**
*Glenda Crosling, Mien Wee Cheng and Ruma Lopes*

Professor Glenda Crosling is an academic expert currently based in Malaysia. She is Dean of Quality at Sunway University in Malaysia, with responsibility for programmes to enhance the student educational experience and outcomes, and is a recipient of a Jeffrey Cheah Institute Harvard University Asia Institute award. Glenda has been invited to be MQA Expert Panel Chair and Member engaged in the development of national Guidelines for Good Practice. She is on the Register of Experts for the Australian government Tertiary Education Quality and Standards Agency (TEQSA, formerly AUQA); and has participated on numerous Australian university audit panels. Glenda is an active member of the Malaysian Australian Business Council (MABC) Executive Committee. Glenda has researched and published widely through books, book chapters and journal articles. She has been Visiting Professor at universities in Thailand, China, Hong Kong and Singapore.

Ruma Lopes is currently Director of the Sunway Foundation Programme, which prepares students for study at the tertiary level in business, liberal arts and Science courses. Her extensive teaching experience at the secondary level includes the UK School system, the Western Australian Higher Certificate of Education and Monash University Foundation Year Programme. Over the past six years, she has shaped the curriculum for Sunway College Foundation Programme, to prepare students from the Malaysian Education System for a challenging curriculum. Her strength is in understanding the gaps in the learning experience of students from urban and rural backgrounds as they prepare for tertiary study.

▶ **Expanding HE in India: the challenge for Equity**
*Manasi Thapliyal Navani*

Manasi Thapliyal is Assistant Professor with the School of Education Studies, Ambedkar University Delhi (AUD), India. Her doctoral work at the National University of Educational Planning and Administration (NUEPA), Delhi, is a case study of academic reforms in the University of Delhi. Her research attempts to address questions of politics of access and quality assurance in universities in India.

▶ **National Access Policies for Higher Education in China: Creating Equal Opportunities in Education**
*Baocun Liu and Yang Su*

Dr Baocun Liu is a professor of comparative education and the director of the Institute of International and Comparative Education (IICE) at Beijing Normal University (BNU). He also serves as the president of Comparative Education Society of Asia and vice president of China Comparative Education Society. With his specialization and research interests in comparative education, higher education, education policy and management, he has been involved in a wide range of national and international research and consultancy projects, and has published more than 150 journal papers and ten books.

Yang Su is a Master's candidate at the Institute of International and Comparative Education, Beijing Normal University.

▶ **Access to Higher Education in South Africa: Addressing the Myths**
*Ncedikaya Magopeni and Lullu Tshiwula*

Professor Lullu Tshiwula is former Deputy Vice Chancellor – Student Development and Support at UWC. She has a PhD in social work and an MA in social development and planning from the Nelson Mandela Metropolitan University, and a BA with Hons in social work from Fort Hare University. Her experience includes lecturing and practising social work. Her research outputs include book editing and some refereed articles.

Dr Tshiwula served on committees such as the African Union's the Rights and Welfare of the Child, Centre for Justice & Crime Prevention; co-chaired a research capacity building partnership between South Africa and the Netherlands; and chaired the national Joint University Committee on Social Work.

▶ **Making Commitment Concrete: Policy and Practice in Access to Higher Education in Ghana**
*Joseph Budu*

Mr Budu has over 30 years' experience in University administration in Ghana, starting his career at the University of Ghana in 1977, where he worked up to 2013, apart from a period of five years as registrar of the Akrofi Christaller Institute in Ghana. His career has been solely at the University of Ghana, and ended there on 31 July 2013. In September 2013, Joseph started a two-year consultancy assignment with the Ghana Institute of Management and Public Administration (GIMPA) as registrar. He is also convener of a committee appointed by the National Council for Tertiary Education (NCTE) to consider and make recommendations on the diversification and differentiation of tertiary education institutions in Ghana.

▶ **Evolution or Revolution: The Three Ages of Access in Australia**
*Margaret Heagney and Fran Ferrier*

Margaret Heagney is a student equity consultant and researcher with a background in national and institutional policy and practice. An ambassador (Australasia) for the World Congress on Access to Post-secondary Education and a co-editor of *Widening Participation and Lifelong Learning Journal*, UK, Margaret's primary research projects have resulted in publications on the access and retention of students from groups under-represented in higher education, attrition from higher education, equity for postgraduate students and the impact of globalization on students from under-represented groups.

# Series editor's preface

▶ **Palgrave Teaching and Learning**

I am delighted to include this truly international edited collection on a key topic for the twenty-first century into the Palgrave teaching and learning series. The series, for all who care about teaching and learning in higher education, is designed with the express aim of providing useful, relevant, current and helpful guidance on key issues in learning and teaching in the tertiary/post-compulsory education sector. Widening participation and fostering fair access is an area of high importance globally and one which is addressed helpfully in this volume, with ample practical advice for practitioners and managers across the globe, particularly through the case studies throughout the book.

Higher Education pedagogy is an area of rapid change, with higher education institutions reviewing and often implementing significant alterations in the ways they design, deliver and assess the curriculum, taking into account not just innovations in how content is being delivered and supported, particularly through technological means, but also the changing relationships between academics and their students. The role of the teacher in higher education needs to be reconsidered when students can freely access content worldwide and seek accreditation and recognition of learning by local, national or international providers (and may indeed prefer to do so). Students internationally are becoming progressively more liable for the payment of fees as higher education becomes seen as less of a public good and more of a private one, and this too changes the nature of the transaction. In many nations, the proportion of the population undertaking higher education is increasing, with consequent rethinking required on levels of independence and autonomy we can expect from sometimes formerly disadvantaged student. Texts in this series address these and other emergent imperatives, with a deliberately international focus.

I warmly welcome this scholarly and mind-provoking contribution to the series and trust readers will find reading it as productive as I did.

Sally Brown
August 2016

# Introduction

It appears that rising participation in post-secondary education is unlikely to abate at the global level in forthcoming decades. It is estimated that 260 million students will be in post-secondary education across the world by 2025 (OECD, 2011). But who will these students be? Although there have been huge efforts in recent years to increase participation in primary education across the world for those from all social backgrounds (it was one the United Nations Millennium Development Goals up to 2015 (United Nations, 2000), it is less clear that efforts are being made to do this at the post-secondary level. However, increasing primary and secondary participation, without addressing participation at the post-secondary level, is akin to what has recently been described as building a 'pyramid without a roof' (Kirkland, 2015). The impact of universal primary or secondary education is limited unless it comes with a commitment to extending access to education across all levels. Moreover, many countries are at close to universal levels in primary and increasingly secondary education. It is legitimate to claim then that the truly global educational challenge in the twenty-first century is not access at the primary or even secondary level, but at the post-secondary level. This provides the route to higher earnings both at the individual and societal levels. Drawing on the work by the Organisation of Economic Co-operation and Development (OECD), Tremblay and Mangeol argue that '[a]dults with a tertiary degree earn 75% more compared to workers who have only completed upper secondary education or post-secondary non-tertiary education, on average across the OECD. This holds true for both men and women'. The evidence also suggests that it underpins higher levels of well-being including better health, lower crime and greater civic participation (BIS, 2014; Tremblay and Mangeol, 2014).

Participation in post-secondary level education is no cure-all or panacea to be sure. It has been argued that many policy makers and researchers have been too quick to pronounce the dawn of a new economic era driven by knowledge and information requiring more and more graduates (Brown et al., 2008; Cowen, 2013; Wolf, 2002). Lower-skilled work that does not 'require' post-secondary education is not going to go away. Research by the McKinsey Global Institute in 2012 argued that there were nearly 1 billion low-skilled workers in the world (McKinsey Global Institute, 2012). Nor, as Brown et al. (2008) argue, are graduates guaranteed high-skilled or high-paid work.

As important as these reality checks are as concerns the power and role of education, they do not, as such, represent an argument against the expansion of participation in education. Educational qualifications are a positional good, which enable sorting in the labour market at the macro and micro levels. It is unlikely that this will change (and the alternative here may well be a cronyism that is even less desirable). But neither should an alternative necessarily be sought. If there is to be a better way of dealing with the challenges associated with increasing well-being globally or reducing inequality, then it is unlikely that it will involve less education. Rather, it is important to develop the policies and practices which emphasize that the content and purpose of post-secondary education should be to endow its recipients with the attributes necessary for fulfilment across non-economic as well as economic spheres in the twenty-first century.

However, although the available evidence supports the case for extending access to post-secondary, and especially higher, education, we do not know enough about the nature of the challenge faced in extending such access in different countries. If the global educational challenge of the twenty-first century is to be addressed, we need to understand where we are starting from early in the century. This book aims to contribute to this understanding. It brings together case studies of countries from each continent in the world, and voices from inside and outside academia, to examine how inequalities in participation primarily in higher, as opposed to post-secondary, education differ, and why. They describe how policy makers are supporting (or not supporting) equitable access in higher education, (HE) and also what HE institutions and non-governmental organizations are doing to further this goal.

These case studies paint a picture characterized by contrast and commonality, but highlighting the importance of context. Access and equity in HE participation is tied intimately to the social, cultural and political nature of an individual country. However, the importance of context in understanding access does not imply that attempts to gauge the extent of inequalities in participation are not possible or worthwhile. They are in fact essential if the issue is to take its place as one of the 'global challenges' of the twenty-first century.

The rest of this chapter looks briefly at the available international evidence on inequalities in participation in HE by social background, an area where this book adds value to the existing literature in the field, before finally summarizing the 12 case studies in the book.

## ▶ Who participates?

Inequalities in participation by socio-economic background appear to transcend the size, location, education system or political complexion of different countries. The OECD collect data on participation in what it describes as tertiary education for 18 of its member countries (OECD, 2014). These data show that although there are distinct differences between countries in participation by level of parental education; in every country those whose parents had participated in tertiary education are more likely to progress than those whose parents did not. Across all countries for which the OECD collects data, 66 per cent of those who have at least one parent who has tertiary education obtain a tertiary qualification, whereas only 22 per cent of those whose parents do not have such a qualification obtain one themselves.

In terms of other transnational bodies, the United Nations Educational, Scientific and Cultural Organization (UNESCO) collects data on participation by gender that encompasses 149 countries. Their *World Atlas of Gender Equality in Education* (UNESCO, 2012) contains within it a visual representation of HE participation by gross enrolment ratio (GER). It shows that in the majority of countries in the world, more women than men enter HE. In 93 of the countries in the study, women comprise the majority, whereas in only 43 countries do men occupy this position (with 10 being 'in parity'). This creates an interesting platform for discussion regarding which gender should be viewed as the rightful beneficiary of any attempts to support greater access and equity. It also reinforces the point that access to HE is something grounded in the specific nature of each individual country.

The World Bank has produced a number of reports (www.worldbank.org/) in recent years, attempting to map patterns of post-secondary education participation by lower socio-economic groups in 68 countries, and also a set of regional reports on this topic. The European Union have attempted to bring together the available data from their partner nations to identify participation differences by socio-economic group. Again, despite the contrasts between the countries in the union, what unites them is inequity in access to HE. Even Finland, examined in more detail in Chapter 5, with an education system renowned for combining equity and excellence, cannot buck this trend, nor can Germany, which, despite being the powerhouse of the union and recently reducing its tuition fee level to zero, still suffers from the inequity contagion (European Commission/EACEA/Eurydice, 2014). Perhaps the conclusion that causes most concern from this report is that only a minority of European countries have defined attainment targets for different groups and that the collection of data on participation by different groups is very variable, with much valuable data appearing not to be collected or available. The report argues that '[t]here is therefore a long way to go before a convincing, evidence-based, European-wide picture of progress in widening access is possible to obtain' (2014: 9).

Outside of data collected by regional and global research organizations, that assembled by researchers continues to show that although access by socio-economic group varies by country, it is still unequal everywhere.

The excellent research by Koucký and Bartušek, 'Who Gets a Degree? Access to Tertiary Education in Europe 1950–2009', draws on a survey of over 160,000 respondents by combining national data sets from 25 European countries. Koucký and Bartušek argue:

> The overall results of the analysis of the Inequality index development in all participating European countries reveal that, over the last six decades, the level of inequality in access to tertiary education in Europe has been gradually decreasing, although this trend is not particularly strong.
>
> (Koucký and Bartušek, 2009: 26)

Koucký and Bartušek were particularly interested in trying to unpack the relationship between expansion and equity. They found that although there had been a reduction in inequality in countries where HE could be described in Trow's terms as 'mass', this relationship was not a particularly strong one, and it appeared to have been diminishing since the 1950s. The final point of interest to note from Koucký and Bartušek's work was the reflections on the changing nature of inequality in participation. The authors argue that there has been a *'change in character of inequalities'*. As tertiary education has entered mass and later even the universal phase, inequalities have become more subtle and less discernible as their focus has changed 'from quantitative to qualitative characteristics' (2009: 33). Inequality is becoming more than just an issue of access to HE; it is also shaped by institution, success in HE and graduate outcome. Koucký and Bartušek point to the existence of 'maximally maintained inequality' (MMI). The MMI theory argues that until all the more privileged groups obtain a level of education, inequality will pertain. When those from less privileged groups do gain access to that level, however, the marker of status or the pecuniary gain from education then moves to the next level. This relative stability in the different level of participation in HE by social group is described by Shavit, Arum and Gamoran (2007) as 'persistent inequality'. Building on the 1993 work by Shavit and Blossveld, they look at 15 countries from the 1960s to the 1990s (including three from Asia: Japan, Korea and Taiwan), and their work supports the MMI theory illustrating that inequality is persistent despite systems expanding. The countries where they saw a decline in relative inequality were those where expansion was rapid or 'saturation' approached. What they do argue, however, is that expansion itself can be inclusive. Even if relative differences remain, the impact of absolute increases in participation by those from less privileged groups cannot be completely discounted. Some of the benefits of HE participation documented above can still be realized by attendance per se, even if many others are realizing them (they could be described as potentially non-rivalrous).

The broader benefits of HE participation in terms of well-being are those which are potentially more available to all. However, we do not know nearly enough about the transmission mechanism as concerns these benefits, or how they relate to things like course, institution, country or region.

The studies listed above are valuable, but they focus primarily on European/Western and richer non-Western countries. Furthermore, they do not go far beyond access by socio-economic group. Usher attempted to widen the lens to include a slightly broader range of countries and also to develop a more rounded idea of how to understand relative differences in access to post-secondary education between countries. Building on his 2004 publication *A New Measuring Stick: Is Access to Higher Education in Canada More Equitable?*, Usher looked at 14 countries in *Global Higher Education Rankings 2010* (Usher and Medow, 2010) and built indices for 'affordability' and for 'accessibility'. The accessibility ranking included the overall participation rate for young people, attainment when in HE, their own Educational Equity Index (EEI) which measures the extent to which those with parents from lower socio-economic groups are over-represented in HE and a gender parity index. Interestingly, Finland, one of the countries featured in this book, appears at the top of these rankings.

Usher and Medow's work is a significant contribution to the literature here. It is, however, only able to look at socio-economic background and gender in a number of in mainly richer countries. Going beyond the socio-economic, and examining countries outside the more industrialized ones generally requires looking at more country-specific literature. There are a number of studies that attempt to do this (for example Brunner et al., 2006; Bloom, Canning and Chan, 2005; Grubb et al., 2006) as well as studies that look to capture the issues in a particular region rather than differences in extent per se. The Asian Development Bank has commissioned a series of studies in this area (Asian Development Bank 2012a&b). In their 2012 report *Access without Equity? Finding a Better Balance in Higher Education in Asia*, they examined participation issues in over 20 Asian countries. The report argued that

> while access has certainly improved considerably, it is still being confined to a limited group of citizens; many others who have been historically marginalized continue to be left on the sidelines for many reasons ranging from the known (economic, underpreparedness) to the unknown (social status, self-esteem, language inabilities).
>
> (Asian Development Bank, 2012a: 47)

It is clear from even the brief overview above that the drawing of the global access to post-secondary map is still at its early stages. Although the chapters in this book do not specifically deal with issues of measurement, they do highlight the huge differences in the availability of data, their quality and what data are deemed important to collect in different countries. Information whose collection is taken for granted in certain countries is just not collected for a combination of both infrastructural and ideological reasons in others.

## ▶ What this book does

This is not the first volume in recent years to look at access and equity in HE in the global context. Murray and Klinger bring together a number of perspectives, including how to engage students as actors in the access discourse, the needs for pedagogical change and case studies of different countries, in an effort to illustrate the case for a global movement bringing these different stakeholders together (Murray and Klinger, 2013). Tapper and Palfreyman's 2005 work *Understanding Mass Higher Education'* looks at the issue of equity in participation internationally, with a particular interest in the impact of HE systems in different countries of increasing participation, including contributions from Europe, Australia and the United States. Meyer et al. (2013) blend a detailed exploration of the philosophical debates around the nature of fairness in HE, with a range of contributions from Africa, Asia, Europe and the Americas, which explore the policy approaches in particular in different countries. Meyer seeks, through the book's contribution to the public discourse on the issue of fairness in access, to bolster the debate on the moral and normative basis for the claim that expanding access is justified. They conclude with an assessment of how to construct finance systems for HE that can support equitable participation.

The volumes described above combine with the articles and reports examined below to form a growing body of work that looks at access and equity in HE participation in an internationally comparative way. This book has three particular features that together add value to it.

### *A systematic global approach*

What is attempted in this volume is a global analysis of post-secondary participation (as much as one can do in a case study approach) by deliberately trying to look at countries from each continent as opposed to selecting by thematic focus or on the basis of theoretical standpoint. The merit of this approach is that it starts the work overtly from the position of an attempt to form a global understanding, as opposed to trying to reach this goal via the conduit of a theoretical frame or belief, for example a concern with the importance of finance. This latter approach will clearly add to our understanding of this issue but is inevitably partial. The main argument presented in this book is that the issue of access to post-secondary education is far too broad to be reduced to a question of one issue – be it finance or any other.

## An exploration of the meaning of access

This book, by explicitly trying to develop a 'global' understanding, enables a more grounded, contextually and culturally nuanced approach to what access means. The focus on differences in participation by socio-economic background dominates the global research agenda. However, the participation in post-secondary education of specific groups has different resonance across countries and regions. This book takes its lead from the work of Clancy and Goastellec in 2007 and Santiago et al. in 2008 in seeking to develop a deeper understanding of the role that context plays in understanding access. Clancy and Goastellec argue that each society has 'one legitimised category', which dominates in shaping the understanding of what HE equity means in policy and practice. The roots of how these identities are arrived at can only be found in the social, economic and cultural history of different nations. Santiago et al.'s report for the OECD in 2008 brings out extremely well how these 'legitimised categories' manifest themselves through policy, comparing and contrasting who is supported by special financial arrangements, positive discrimination in admissions and specific attainment development programmes in 25 different countries.

Differences in participation by socio-economic group do act as a form of common denominator internationally. The work by Santiago illustrates this, as does the annual OECD Education at a Glance reports, alongside the work from Eurydice and others described below. However, it in no way captures the entirety of the issue. The challenges facing South Africa in addressing the differences in participation by ethnic group, as documented in Chapter 8 of the book, is an obvious example of the context-driven, multifaceted nature of the access question. The importance of context is not confined to countries with such distinctive, individualized histories where social inequality is concerned. All the chapters in this volume show that each country has a specific history in terms of inequality which in turn shapes the patterns of post-secondary educational participation.

Neither can understanding differential participation be achieved by analysis of cost differentials alone. A number of comparative studies have shown that the relationship between tuition costs and participation is itself complex (Orr, Usher and Wespel, 2014; Santiago et al., 2008). Orr et al.'s 2104 study of nine different European countries argues that increasing the cost of HE seems to have little overall impact on demand. Although they acknowledge that the data available is weak, they also argue that

> changes in fees i) have no effect with respect to the gender composition of the student body (female numbers rose faster than males in all nine countries), ii) have little to no effect on the proportion of students drawn from lower socio-economic backgrounds, and iii) have little to no effect on the ethnic composition of the student body.
> (Orr et al., 2014: 12)

The 'price' of entry on its own gives only a partial view of the financial support structures where higher education participation is concerned in different countries. These structures themselves reflect both national and local differences in how HE is viewed and the wider social and economic forces at play in that country.

What the chapters in this volume show is that access is intimately linked to the individual narrative and identity each country (or in some cases part of it) wishes to construct. Although these individualized narratives can be interpreted through broader theories regarding participation, they remain, as Clancy and Goastellec argue, rooted in the historical and socio-economic fabric of that country. The exploration of the access question from this empirical standpoint actually enables more over-arching theoretical frames to be utilized more effectively as explanatory tools. It means the question of 'Why access?' cannot be separated neatly into 'for economic benefit at the individual level' or 'social benefit at the collective level' or thick and thin access. The two rationale's are intertwined in terms of philosophy, practice and policy.

## *A concentration on equity*

The third way in which this book adds value is that it concentrates on the issue of access to post-secondary education among those from groups whose social background has been an impediment to such participation. This focus on the progression of such groups is not the same as focusing on the percentage of any given population that is participating in education at post-secondary level. Any continued expansion in participation will have, at some point in time, to include those from particular social backgrounds, but this participation itself needs contextualizing. An increase on participation overall in a particular country does not necessarily imply that participation among a given group has increased. Trow's work in classifying the differentiation between elite, mass and universal HE systems has been taken by many as a marker of how progression in access to HE is understood (Trow, 1974). However, even when a system is classified as 'universal', participation rates are only at 50 per cent (Trow, 2005).

This still leaves potentially half of all a given cohort who are not participating even in a 'mass' system. Concentrating just on this overall data tells us only a limited amount about who is participating or not and why. It is true to say that in many countries, especially those outside of the richer nations in the OECD for example, increasing participation per se is the goal. This process will bring in many of those from groups more disadvantaged in that society. This does not, however, diminish the need to understand the HE participation trajectories of such groups. It may well be even more important to do this in such countries. Younger systems may be more amenable to the integration of policies and practice to extend access, such as those documented in this book, than those countries where forms of mass system are already in place.

## A focus on the how

The final distinctive contribution this book seeks to make is to bring together in one volume examples of how inequalities in access to post-secondary education are actually being addressed in different countries, and then relating these to how access is grounded in the socio-economic structures and identity of nations. The nature of the work being undertaken to widen access internationally has been examined before. Thomas and Quinn (2003) bring together examples of work from a number of different countries, aimed at widening access for older and mature learners. Several of the chapters in Murray and Klinger look at policy and practice in different countries to extend access to HE. A range of publications and journal articles also look to capture the efforts made, both political and practical, to extend equity in participation in individual countries.

Attempts to capture such efforts systematically across countries are less common. In particular, attempts to achieve greater equity through additional or supplementary work undertaken by HE institutions to support learner progression at the secondary level is under-theorized and examined. Researchers have preferred to focus on the role of cost (as Meyer et al. do above) and, when straying into practice, the part played by admissions practice.

What forthcoming chapters illustrate is that there are commonalities in the examples of how inequalities are being addressed practically across countries. Yet, as with how the who and why of access, the 'how' reflects the extent to which this issue is embedded in the socio-economic structures and cultures of different countries.

## ▶ The structure of the book

The majority of the rest of the volume is given over to the individual country chapters before a final chapter that attempts to bring out the key themes from the volume and offer ideas on the way forward for research, policy, practice and theory in this field.

We begin by looking at North America, where participation in HE ranks relatively highly in the political agenda of governments and HE backgrounds. Chapter 1 looks at Canada, one of the countries that appears consistently at the top of comparative tables in HE participation globally. There has been a historical commitment from policy makers in Canada to addressing inequalities in participation among under-represented groups, in particular those from lower socio-economic/indigenous backgrounds. However, this commitment has wavered in recent years. This chapter from Diana Wickham considers the range of ways in which efforts to take access to HE forward in Canada manifest themselves in the early 2010s, pointing to the engagement of community-based organizations and HE institutions building on the legacy of past investment. She concludes by arguing that Canada is at a crossroads where access is concerned. Access to post-secondary education in the United States is as tied intimately with the American concept of nationhood. Kamatuka points to how investments made in work to extend access find their roots in the desire of politicians to shore up the concept of the American Dream. The TRIO programmes described in detail in the chapter began in the 1960s in the midst of the civil rights movement and the growing pressure for more opportunity for black people in the United States. They have grown to encompass students from all ethnic groups. Kamatuka describes the principles which underpin this work of TRIO today and what has been learnt from over 40 years of sustained investment in work to make HE entry more equal.

Turning to South America, we have only one chapter here from Colombia. The question of access in the Colombian context is tied up with a combination of geographic, academic and economic barriers for what is a relatively young country. Although there has not been the state investment in co-ordinated cross-sectoral work to address inequalities in participation in Colombia that was evident in North America, this chapter includes one of the best examples in this volume of innovatory practice led by HE institutions themselves. Montes Gutierre and Abad describe how the work of the Escuela de Administración, Finanzas y Tecnología (EAFIT) Children's University, with its structured system of additional support over the school career, has been associated with improved progression into post-secondary education for learners and employment for learners from lower socio-economic groups.

The book contains three chapters from Europe. The chapter from Mergner, Mishra and Orr on Germany examines how the dual system of education, with its rigid divisions between academic and technical education, although at the heart of the German economic model and admired throughout the world, creates significant challenges where access to HE is concerned. Looking in particular at 'second-chance learners', they argue that the system mitigates against their participation by creating structural barriers based on historical perceptions on ability and skill. They point, though, to significant activity in Germany led by the state, the university sector and the voluntary sector, which aims to overcome inequalities in participation by socio-economic background.

The Finnish education system is renowned across the world for being, relatively speaking, highly equitable. Ari Tarkianen's chapter takes a reflective position and looks at how, even given Finland's deserved reputation for equity in education, access to HE has always been the preserve of some, not all. He outlines the recent attempts made in Finland to try to open up HE to older learners in particular and also the challenges the country is facing in recognizing a much greater range of ethnic identities in its population. He concludes by placing Finland's challenges in the context of the globalization of economy and society. The final chapter on Europe looks at the United Kingdom. There has been huge investment in widening access to HE in the United Kingdom since the early 2000s. However, although this has led to similarities where access is concerned across the four nations of the United Kingdom, there are also distinct differences. This chapter examines this story of convergence and divergence and how it is a function of the changing political landscape of the country in the early twenty-first century.

Where Asia is concerned, two very contrasting cases are examined. Crosling et al.'s chapter on Malaysia outlines how the internationalization of the HE system interacts with the particular ethnic dynamics in this Asian country to produce a distinctive and unique equity story. The other Asian chapter is quite different in approach, looking at the challenges facing India in both expanding its system to meet the demand of a fast-growing economy while also dealing with deep-rooted divisions within the society which transcend socio-economic or ethnic parameters.

Magopeni and Tshiwul's chapter on South Africa looks at how both government and HE institutions are confronting the challenge of widening access to HE, in the post-apartheid context. The chapter tackles the myths about access and presents a reality where reform of the schooling system is as important as anything that happens in HE if access, and crucially success, of learners from different racial groups is to improve in South Africa.

Ghana is another country where the government has expressed clear commitment to access to HE, enshrining it in its 1992 constitution. However, the challenges faced in increasing participation are stark. The capacity and infrastructure at the post-secondary level, as in so many African countries, need to catch up with student demand. Budu's chapter also points to the limitations in the schooling system as well as the social and cultural barriers many females encounter in entering and achieving in the school system.

Finally, we turn to Australia, where there has been exceptional commitment to equitable access. Ferrier and Heagney's chapter on Australia subjects their policy approach to access and equity to thorough and systematic examination. They examine three different policy frameworks that have structured the equity landscape since the 1970s as the system has evolved and participation increases. However, they end on a point of pessimism, as recent reforms threaten to undo much of what has been learnt in previous decades.

The book concludes by arguing that the contributions in the volume, taken together, force us to consider access to HE within its broader social and economic context. It is a phenomenon not just produced by a set of socioeconomic and cultural relationships, but shaping and reflecting national identity. This approach moves us forward in the articulation of access as one of the big global challenges of the twenty-first century. Overcoming inequality in HE participation is not just an economic imperative that binds nations; it is part of how they define equality, freedom and success to themselves and the world.

# 1 Canada – Access at the Crossroads

Diana Wickham

## ▶ Introduction

Efforts to improve access, participation and attainment in higher education (HE) in Canada have been ongoing for decades. They span both the elementary and secondary levels of the school system, include both national and provincial policies/programmes and work at the national, provincial and community levels. These policies and programs have been designed for Canada's highly diverse population. In the most current census, Canadians reported more than 200 ethnic origins and 200 first languages (Statistics Canada, 2011). This population includes groups and individuals that face a range of challenges in their efforts to access post-secondary studies and achieve success at the post-secondary level. These challenges consist of interacting barriers that may be academic, cultural/ethnic, financial, information-based and social in nature. This chapter looks at who participates in HE in Canada, who is under-represented and how the Canadian HE system is structured. It then explores how one province has managed to extend access to different groups, before outlining some of the challenges Canada faces going forward in the area of access to HE.

## ▶ The Canadian HE System

### *Education and the Canadian Constitution*

Canada is a federation of ten provinces and three territories. Under the Canadian constitution, provincial governments have exclusive responsibility for all levels of education (Constitution Act, 1867). There is no ministry or department of education at the federal level. Canada's three territories, Yukon, Northwest Territories and Nunavut, do not have the same constitutional status as the provinces, but they have delegated responsibility for education and, in turn, cooperate with the provinces to deliver post-secondary programs (CMEC, 2015; CICIC, 2015).

## Canada's Post-secondary Institutions

Post-secondary institutions in Canada are public or private. Most public colleges were established in the 1960s in response to a need for vocational and technical training. In this same period, the province of Quebec reconstituted some 200 classical colleges, 'instituts familiaux', and several technical institutes, creating a single system (the CÉGEP system) (SRAM, 2015). Canadian degree-granting institutions are largely universities and university colleges, while colleges and other institutions are primarily non-degree-granting institutions (conferring diplomas, certificates and attestations). In an increasing number of cases, however, the same institution is both degree granting and non–degree granting. There are now nearly 100 public universities and roughly 200 public colleges, degree granting and other institutions across the country (CICIC, 2015).

HE institutions in Canada set their own entry requirements, which may vary according to the institution, faculty and course. The Pan-Canadian Protocol on the Transferability of University Credits is a Canada-wide, non-mandatory protocol governing transfers among academic institutions in Canada that recognizes academic autonomy of HEIs.

Many Canadian institutions have access and success programs at the secondary (outreach programs in the post-secondary pathway) and post-secondary levels. While, in some cases these programs form part of a larger institutional strategy, they have often evolved in response to local community needs and/or provincial government policy (see the case of Ontario below).

## The HE Student Body

In 2012/2013, there were 2,023,191 students enrolled in Canadian colleges and universities (Statistics Canada, 2014). Of these, there were 1,283,229 university students (956,154 full-time and 327,078 part-time) and 739,959 college students (533,385 full-time and 206,574 part-time). Furthermore, 57.2 per cent of graduates were female in 2012, continuing a long trend (Statistics Canada, 2014).

In 2011, foreign-born Canadians represented 20.6 per cent of the Canadian population, the highest proportion among the G8 countries. This diversity is also reflected on campus. While there is significant variation across both provinces and campuses, on average 14 per cent of students on campus are from visible minority groups. Canada's most ethnically diverse universities report that nearly half their undergraduate students are visible minorities (e.g. the University of Toronto, at 47% [Birgeneau, 2001] and the University of British Columbia, at 48%), well above the national campus average.

Small universities tend to be the least diverse (9%), compared with the large, research-intensive schools (15%) and mid-size campuses (21%).

Although children of new immigrants have outperformed Canadians in post-secondary participation in recent years, with a few exceptions among specific ethnic groups (Statistics Canada, 2005), concerns about the children of recent waves of new immigrants is being voiced (Community Foundations of Canada, 2006).

## Patterns of Tertiary Education Participation in Canada

Among the 37 OECD and G20 countries with available data, Canada ranks first in the proportion of 25- to 64-year-olds (51%) with a tertiary education. The proportion rises to 56 per cent for adults aged 25 to 34 (the OECD average is 38%), whereas among adults aged 55 to 64, the proportion (at 42%) is almost double the OECD average of 23 per cent (2012). Canada ranks first among all of the OECD countries in the proportion of adults with a college education (tertiary type 5B), at 24 per cent, and eighth overall in the proportion of adults with a university education (tertiary type 5A), at 26 per cent (OECD, 2012).

Yet, despite this leading position in HE participation globally, the gap between the participation rates of lower and higher income quadrants in Canada remains significant and important access barriers persist for so-called 'first-generation' students, for certain communities and most notably Indigenous youth (First Nation, Métis and Inuit) and for some specific ethnic groups. The Canadian system also experiences challenges in ensuring that learners from under-represented groups achieve comparable outcomes once they have successfully entered HE (Parkin and Baldwin, 2009; Finnie, Childs and Martinello, 2014).

## ▶ Who Participates in HE in Canada

### Canadian Students 'Under-represented' in Canada's HE Institutions

Using data from the Youth in Transition Survey, *Cohort A*, a recent report by Finnie, Childs and Wismer (2011a) looks at the most recent trends in post-secondary participation in Canada. Groups showing notably lower rates of participation in post-secondary education (college or university) include Aboriginal youth (a 24.3 percentage-point gap compared to non-Aboriginal youth); youth whose parents had not pursued a post-secondary education (a 19.8 percentage-point gap with those youth whose parents had attended); and youth from families in the bottom third of the income distribution (annual incomes under $50,000) compared to youth from families with higher annual incomes (a 12.8 percentage-point gap). Smaller gaps also exist for youth from rural areas compared to youth from population centres (a difference of 10.0 percentage points) and for youth from single parent families compared to those from two parent families (a difference of 7.5 percentage points).

By contrast, first-and second-generation children of immigrants had higher rates of participation in post-secondary education than non-immigrant youth. This was largely a factor of the former's university participation rates; 20.0 percentage points higher for first-generation children of immigrants and 16.0 percentage points higher for second-generation children of immigrants compared to non-immigrant youth (Finnie and Mueller, 2012).

### The Special Case of Canada's Aboriginal Students

Canada's Aboriginal population (First Nations, Métis and Inuit) grew by 45 per cent between 1996 and 2006, compared to the non-Aboriginal population that grew by 8 per cent (Statistics Canada, 2011a). Aboriginal identity refers to those persons who reported identifying with at least one Aboriginal group or those who reported being a Treaty Indian or a Registered Indian as defined by the Indian Act of Canada, or those who reported they were members of an Indian band or First Nation (Statistics Canada, 2014).

There were 1.2 million Aboriginal people in 2006 – 30 per cent of them under 15 years of age, compared to 18 per cent under 15 in the larger population. Despite educational achievement gains in recent decades, large educational achievement gaps persist, notably for First Nations youth living on reserve (Giroux, 2012). In 2000, the auditor general of Canada, in an audit of Aboriginal Affairs and Northern Development Canada (AANDC) elementary and secondary education programs, reported a 28 per cent gap between the high school completion rate on reserves and that in the Canadian population as a whole. More than one third of Aboriginal people have not completed high school (over 50% on reserve). Most recently, the 2011 Auditor General's Status Report found that between 2001 and 2006 the gap had widened to 36 per cent (Office of the Auditor General of Canada, 2011).

Statistics Canada reported in 2011 that nearly half of Aboriginal people — 48.4 per cent — had some kind of post-secondary qualification, up from the 44 per cent reported in 2006. Only 9.8 per cent of Aboriginal people, however, have a university degree (an increase from the 2006 proportion of just 8 per cent), a figure that is substantially below the 26.5 per cent of the non-Aboriginal population that have a university degree. And the gap between aboriginal and non-aboriginal has definitely not narrowed when it comes to university education (Statistics Canada, 2011b).

At the college level, however, the gap is quite small. About 20.6 per cent of aboriginal people have a diploma, compared to 21.3 per cent of non-aboriginal people. And the proportion of aboriginal people with a trades certificate actually surpassed that of non-aboriginal people slightly (Statistics Canada, 2011b).

Educational attainment is reflected in social and economic outcomes. Unemployment in the Aboriginal population was 14.8 per cent in 2006 compared to 6.3 per cent in the general population (Statistics Canada, 2011b).

▶ **Policies and Practices to Support HE Progression**

*Educational System Financing in Canada*

Public post-secondary institutions in Canada derive most of their direct funding from provincial, territorial, and federal governments. Over the past ten years, total government spending on post-secondary education placed Canada among the top three countries internationally for public investment in post-secondary institutions (PSIs). Per student funding for teaching and research was about $21,000 CAD in Canada in 2008–09. This compares to $29,000 CAD in the United States; $20,600 CAD in the United Kingdom; and $20,000 CAD in Australia (Universities Canada, 2009).

In 2007–08, universities and university colleges had revenues of over $36.7 billion, with 45 per cent derived from provincial governments, 9.3 per cent from the federal government, 21 per cent from tuition fees, 14.6 per cent from sales of goods and services, 2.7 per cent from investment income and 7.4 per cent from other own-source revenues, including donations. The 2005–06 revenues of colleges and institutes was $7.6 billion, with 53.2 per cent coming from provincial and territorial governments, 2.1 per cent from federal funding, 24.3 per cent from tuition fees and 20.4 per cent from contract revenues, interest payments and other private sources (Universities Canada, 2009).

Although tuition fees vary by province/territory and discipline of study, in 2013–14, the average cost of tuition in Canada was $5772, with tuition costs for law ($10,942), medicine ($12,438) and pharmacy ($10,039) significantly higher. In Quebec, however, provincial residents do not pay fees to enrol in a public college (or CÉGEP) on a full-time basis (Statistics Canada, 2015).

With one notable exception, the funding made available for Aboriginal education, Canada's federal government plays an *indirect* role in funding post-secondary education through federal transfer payments to the provinces and territories. Employment and Social Development Canada (ESDC) is responsible for the Canada Student Loans Program, funding that students are able to access through their provincial offices of student financial assistance (SRAM, 2015).

Elementary, secondary and tertiary education funding for Canada's First Nations is provided by the federal government (Aboriginal Affairs and Northern Development Canada [AANDC]) based on an outdated formula contained in the Indian Act (Drummond and Rosenbluth, 2013). Federal PSE funding supports about 24,000 Aboriginal students attending college and university per year (AANDC, 2015a). Funding has been capped at 2 per cent per year since 1996, whereas at the post-secondary level, tuition has increased at an average of 4.4 per cent per year in Canada since 1998. Inadequacies in funding at all levels are currently the focus of court challenges and have been the focus of a major campaign by the Assembly of First Nations, the national advocacy group for Canada's First Nations. A number of high-profile national studies and panels examining gaps in First Nations education in recent years have failed to lead to a consensus on addressing the issues (Drummond and Rosenbluth, 2013). The federal government's latest reform proposal has led to an impasse with First Nations chiefs (AANDC, 2015b).

In the late 1990s, the federal government made a series of 'legacy' investments in education to mark Canada's entry into the millennium, among them the creation of the Canada Millennium Scholarship Foundation in 1998 as a private foundation at arm's length from government, with $2.5 billion of government funding and a ten-year mandate to improve access to post-secondary studies. In 1998 and 2004, the federal government also introduced policy measures designed to encourage families to save for their children's post-secondary education and training prior to enrolment. In 2004, the federal government created the Canadian Council on Learning (CCL), whose mandate focuses on research and knowledge mobilization (CCL, 2015).

### *Canada Millennium Scholarship Foundation*

Interpreting its mandate broadly, the Canada Millennium Scholarship Foundation distributed over $3.14 billion in need-based bursaries (nearly 1 million individual bursaries) and merit scholarships; spent $57 million on access-related research and experimentation; and published a major body of research on access and success policies and practices (over 84 individual reports). It also organized 16 policy and research conferences, two major policy summits and two international conferences on HE access (see *Legacy*, Canada Millennium Scholarship Foundation Annual Report 2009–10). Although CMSF's mandate was not renewed in 2010, a federal government assessment of the role of CMSF over the period argued that 'the CSMF had made a great impact on the landscape of student financial assistance[1] in Canada' (Government of Canada, 2012).

## The Pan-Canadian Framework

Canada's provincial and territorial legislatures have developed their own educational structures and institutions, creating 13 educational systems with many similarities and some differences. Responsibility for education is usually exercised through one or more departments or ministries responsible for education. Although the federal government makes sizeable investments in post-secondary education through education transfers, individual provinces and territories develop their own goals and strategies reflecting provincial and territorial priorities, and have developed their own accountability frameworks. At the pan-Canadian level, the Council of Minister of Education (CMEC) provides a forum for education ministers to discuss matters of common concern, explore ways to cooperate, share information and coordinate international education activities and representation (CMEC, 2015).

In 2006, the Council of the Federation released a strategy for post-secondary education (Council of the Federation, 2006) that listed improving access to post-secondary studies as the first of its priorities and strategies. The Council proposed strategies to achieve the following goals:

- Provide better access to relevant labour market information to help Canadians make informed career decisions.
- Increase operating funding to enable institutions to continue to be competitive at an international level.
- Substantially increase participation in post-secondary education and skills training programs.
- Develop strategies to encourage greater participation in post-secondary education and skills programs by Aboriginal peoples, persons with disabilities and students from low-income families.
- Encourage the employed and the under-employed, including the working poor, to pursue post-secondary education and skills training.
- Improve student assistance in order to promote higher participation rates in post-secondary education and skills training programs and to provide stronger support for graduate students.
- Increase the number of qualified workers certified annually.
- Develop lifelong learning, literacy and basic skills initiatives for Canadians, including students at risk and the unemployed.
- Provide seamless access to a range of education and training services that foster rapid re-employment.
- Broaden the use of information technology and other accommodations to help educate and train people, including those who live and work in northern and rural areas.
- Encourage the participation of individuals in workplace-based training.

In 2009, provincial and territorial ministers of education (Council of Ministers of Education, Canada) announced a joint framework, *Learn Canada 2020* (CMEC, 2015), to be used to enhance Canada's education systems, learning opportunities and overall education outcomes with a vision of Quality Lifelong Learning Opportunities for All Canadians.

*Learn Canada 2020*'s Post-Secondary Education pillar provides that 'Canada must increase the number of students pursuing postsecondary education by increasing the quality and accessibility of postsecondary education'. The Adult Learning and Skills Development pillar stipulates that 'Canada must develop an accessible, diversified, and integrated system of adult learning and skills development that delivers training when Canadians need it'. Two of the specific objectives are particularly relevant to issues of HE access and success: (1) eliminate the gap in academic achievement and graduation rates between Aboriginal and non-Aboriginal students, and (2) enhance and stabilize the long-term capacity of post-secondary systems to meet the training and learning needs of all Canadians seeking HE learning opportunities (CMEC, 2015).

## Provincial Government Policies and Practices

Between 2004 and 2007, governments of four Canadian provinces – Alberta, British Columbia, Newfoundland and Labrador, and Ontario – undertook wide-ranging reviews of their respective provincial post-secondary education systems (Kirby, 2007):

- Newfoundland and Labrador's *White Paper on Public Post-Secondary Education* (Government of Newfoundland and Labrador, Department of Advanced Education and Skills, 2005)
- Ontario's *Post-Secondary Education Review*, known as the Rae Report (Ministry of Training, Colleges and Universities – Ontario, 2005)
- Alberta's *A Learning Alberta Report* (2006) (Alberta Advanced Education, 2006)
- British Columbia's *Campus 20/20* review (Province of British Columbia, Advanced Education, 2007).

The major themes addressed in the final reports of each of the reviews included affordability, accessibility, accountability, institutional collaboration, diversity, funding and quality.

New Brunswick followed suit with *The Action Plan to Transform Post-Secondary Education in New Brunswick* (Government of New Brunswick, 2008), and by the end of the decade several Canadian provinces and territories had developed specific strategies, action plans and policies designed to broaden access for designated groups and increase student HE success.

In *Increasing Access to HE: A Review of System-Level Policy Initiatives*, Glen Jones and Cynthia Field refer to Dan Lang's comprehensive 2013 (Lang, 2013) analysis of incentive funding mechanisms which showed that eight of the ten Canadian provinces have introduced some form of performance indicators within HE, all of which are directly or indirectly tied to funding. It is not unusual for performance funding to be tied to access, either in terms of participation (incentives to increase overall enrolment), targeted participation (incentives to increase the enrolment of individuals from particular groups) or student success (incentives to increase graduation rates or graduate employment) (Jones and Field, 2013).

Jones and Field also note that, in addition to direct and targeted funding mechanisms, Canada's provincial governments have been combining funding policies with structural reforms such as:

▶ Modifying institutional roles and missions in order to increase access to university degrees (transforming colleges/polytechnics into regional or teaching-intensive universities in Alberta and British Columbia);
▶ Providing community colleges with some restricted ability to offer full degree programs (in British Columbia, Alberta, Manitoba, Ontario, Prince Edward Island and the Yukon Territory);
▶ Differentiating the college sector in binary systems to improve regional access to degree programs (university colleges in British Columbia in the early 1990s, and Institutes of Technology and Advanced Learning in Ontario in 2000);
▶ Improving the ability of students to transfer between institutions in the post-secondary system and increase access and mobility (Councils focusing on transfer issues in Alberta, British Columbia and, most recently, Ontario); and
▶ Expanding distance learning (Thompson River University in British Columbia, Athabasca University in Alberta, Télé Université in Québec, as well as supporting collaborative efforts and consortia within provincial systems) (Jones and Field, 2013).

While provincial government strategies and policies have addressed the goal of widening access fairly broadly, two examples of very targeted efforts are found in the Ontario's government 'first-generation student' policies in the 2003–2008 period and the British Columbia's recent efforts to address the gap in Aboriginal student access and success at the HE level with a $65 million Aboriginal Post-Secondary Education Strategy (Ministry of Advanced

Education British Columbia and the Aboriginal Post-Secondary Education and Training Partners, 2013).

### Institutional Policies and Practices Targeted to Aboriginal Students

A majority of Canadian post-secondary institutions offer special facilities and programs targeted to Aboriginal students. In British Columbia, for example, every public post-secondary institution provides some level of Aboriginal student services. Aboriginal students receive personal and academic support like that offered through the First Nations House of Learning at the University of British Colombia, the University of Victoria's First Peoples House and Simon Fraser University's First Nations Student Centre. Thompson Rivers University, for example, provides an Elder-in-Residence in their Aboriginal Cultural Centre. By way of example, the University of Victoria has a wide range of programs and services for Aboriginal students, including through the LE,NONET network which provides a Bursary Program, Peer Mentoring, Community Internships, Research Apprenticeships, and Staff and Faculty Aboriginal Cultural Training, an Aboriginal Language Revitalization Program, an Office of Indigenous Affairs, First Nations Partnership Programs in Early Childhood and Youth Care, an Indigenous Governance Program, Indigenous Studies Program, Indigenous Initiatives at the School of Social Work, and the Native Students Union.

### Rural Students – E-Learning and Distance Learning

In September 2000, a consortium of seven Canadian universities from four provinces created the Canadian Virtual University (CVU), providing complete programs online, through traditional distance education and classroom learning (Canadian Virtual University, 2015).

▶ **The Case of Ontario: A Model of Inclusive Access**

Of all Canada's provinces and territories, the example of Ontario offers a particularly striking example of the role that government leadership can play in stimulating a broader institutional and community-based response to the challenge of broadening access and increasing student success for underrepresented groups, beginning with interventions early in the post-secondary pathway. Ontario's recent successes are also significant as an example for other jurisdictions given the very high level of diversity in the population, adding another level of complexity to the challenges of preparing students for HE progression and ensuring their success.

In 2003, following a half-decade of controversial reforms, Ontario's new 'education premier' introduced an ambitious strategy to guide the reform of high school education in the province, known as the Student Success/ Learning to 18 (SS/L 18) Strategy. Among its five goals, the Ministry of Education sought to increase the high school graduation rate from 68 to 85 per cent and to support effective transitions from secondary to post-secondary education and training (Ungerleider, 2008).

In response, the Toronto District School Board (TDSB) adopted an urban diversity strategy designed to identify the 20 most under-performing schools and set a target of increasing their performance by 5 per cent per year, to reach 85 per cent by 2013, to match the provincial goal for all students (Toronto District School Board, 2009).

The government also commissioned a major review of post-secondary education guided by four advisory groups, one for each of four key populations under-represented at the post-secondary level: 'first-generation' students, francophones, Aboriginal youth and students from rural areas. In February 2005, *Ontario – A Leader in Learning, Report and Recommendations* (Ministry of Training, Colleges and Universities – Ontario, 2005), outlined five key strategies, and its proponents called on the government to legislate a mission for Ontario as a 'Leader in Learning', founded on access for all qualified students to HE, among other key missions.

The Rae Report, as Ontario's review was known, led to the *Reaching Higher Strategy (2005–2010)*, a $6.2 billion cumulative investment over five years in colleges, universities and training, a 39 per cent increase compared to the 2004–05 funding base. Ontario invested nearly $10 million in projects and bursaries from 2005 to 2007 at colleges, universities and community-based organizations to encourage first-generation students to pursue HE. A further $55 million was invested by 2009–10 to undertake new programs and outreach for under-represented groups such as first-generation students, francophones, Aboriginals and people with disabilities. In all, 18 colleges and universities took advantage of available funding.

Investments were also made to accommodate higher enrolment and improve student success. Improved accountability was sought through the creation of multi-year agreements between the government and institutions that would set out enrolment and quality improvement targets and the establishment of the arm's-length, HE Quality Council of Ontario. The new Council has a broad mandate to advise on improving all aspects of post-secondary education, including quality, access and accountability, the development of targets, the methods and timeframe to achieve them, and performance measures to evaluate the post-secondary education sector. In addition, the 2005 budget provided $358 million in new investment in student financial assistance by 2009–10 (doubling the base funding provided in 2004–05).

Reaching Higher produced notable successes:

- More than 120,000 additional students attended college and university by 2008–09, a 31 per cent increase over 2002–03.
- The degree completion rate increased to 78 per cent from 73 per cent in 2002–03 for university students and to 65 per cent from 57 per cent for college students
- 172,000 students benefited in 2008–09 from enhancements to the Ontario Student Assistance Program introduced in 2004–05
- More than 15,000 new graduate spaces were created by 2011–12, an increase of more than 61 per cent over 2002–03 (Council of Ontario Universities, 2006).

▶ **City-wide Collaboration Strategies**

Supported by TD Bank and the Ontario Government and housed at Toronto City Hall, the Council of Educators of Toronto (CET) brings together many of the colleges and universities that took advantage of the Reaching Higher funding. The Council of Educators of Toronto is a 12-member network comprised of representatives from five colleges, four universities, two school boards and the United Way organisation. CET aims to foster collaboration across access and outreach programs at member organizations to enhance access to post-secondary education.

The United Way of Greater Toronto's Community of Practice on Youth Educational Attainment Partnerships 'provides a forum to support learning, share knowledge about effective practice, explore solutions, and foster innovation with the goal of improving practice and outcomes' (United Way of Greater Toronto, 2015). The mission of United Way of Canada is to improve lives and build community by engaging individuals and mobilizing collective action to address the root causes and symptoms of social problems.

**Community Investments**

The Ontario government's Reaching Higher Strategy gave a boost to a number of existing HEI community outreach initiatives (to under-represented communities), fuelling their expansion, and gave impetus to the creation of several new community-based projects. Although these community-based efforts to widen access exist in other Canadian cities and provinces (Winnipeg's CareerTrek being one notable example), they are particularly concentrated in the Greater Toronto region. Among these are Ryerson University's

*Spanning the Gaps*, George Brown College's Community Partnership Office, Humber College's Community Partnership and the University of Toronto's Law in Action Within Schools (LAWS) programme.

Among its direct investments at the community level, in 2011 the government invested $19 million over four years in Pathways to Education, jointly with a $10 million contribution by the United Way of Greater Toronto, to replicate the Pathways model in the Jamestown and Lawrence Heights districts in Toronto as well as in two other sites in Ontario (Ottawa and Kitchener). This support was a response to Pathways to Education's well-documented success in the Regent Park district of Toronto where the program:

- Reduced dropout rates to 14 per cent from 56 per cent
- Reduced absenteeism in schools by 65 per cent
- Increased high school graduation rates to 75 per cent from 42 per cent: 80 per cent of these students go on to post-secondary education and training – a four-fold increase from the time prior to Pathways operating in the neighbourhood (Pathways to Education, 2015).

The Pathways model is designed to address four barriers typically faced by first-generation students:

- Lack of the community supports needed to graduate from high school
- Insufficient information about the benefits of post-secondary education and training from friends and family
- Lower expectations or confidence about succeeding at college or university
- Limited financial resources

Of those students going on to post-secondary education and training as a result of Pathways in Regent Park, 90 per cent are first-generation students.

### Student Voice

The voice of Ontario's student associations has also been an important factor in shaping Ontario government policy around issues of widening access.

The Ontario Undergraduate Student Alliance (OUSA) Blue Chair campaign (OUSA, 2008–12) was a multi-year, grassroots, student-led campaign that sought to raise awareness around the need to expand access to HE as an equalizer of economic prosperity and social vitality, and ensure student success. During the winter semester, for a week-long period, campuses across

Ontario are packed with empty blue chairs aimed at creating awareness, raising funds and taking action at reducing barriers to post-secondary education. The empty chairs symbolize the lost potential to the province of Ontario when access is restricted. The funds raised at universities across Ontario are donated to early outreach programs across the province. OUSA represents over 140,000 professional and undergraduate, full-time and part-time university students at seven institutions across Ontario. OUSA's vision is for an accessible, affordable, accountable and high-quality post-secondary education in Ontario.

Breaking Barriers: A Strategy for Equal Access to Higher Education was a collaborative advocacy effort directed at the Ontario government by OUSA, the College Student Alliance and the Ontario Student Trustees Association, designed to maintain the government's attention on access as the Reaching Higher Strategy gave way to a focus on attracting more international students (College Student Alliance, 2009).

Founded in 1975, the CSA is a member-driven advocacy and student leadership organization that represents over 70 per cent of all Ontario college students consisting of 17 colleges and 25 student associations with over 135,000 full-time students throughout the province.

The Ontario Student Trustees' Association (OSTA) is the voice for over 2.4 million primary and secondary students in Ontario. OSTA-AECO acts as a consultant on policy for the Ministry of Education, collaborates with stakeholders in the education community and unites all student trustees across the province.

▶ **Conclusions**

In this chapter, a number of facets of the Canadian approach to access to HE work have been discussed. They include the following:

▶ The role of the federally created Canada Millennium Scholarship Foundation from 2000–10 (Canada's major millennium project) in putting a national (and provincial) spotlight on issues related to access and success policies and practices through research and experimentation and in reducing the cost of post-secondary participation through its major bursary and scholarship programs (Canada Millennium Scholarship Foundation, 1998–2010).
▶ The 'access' policies of some provincial governments over the last two decades, that of Ontario in particular, that have sought to influence the post-secondary attainment levels of under-represented populations

through elementary and secondary school reforms, student financial assistance programs and HEI incentive programs as well as community investments (Finnie, Childs and Wismer, 2011; Kirby, 2007).
- The role of activist student movements at both national and provincial levels, including that of the Canadian Alliance of Student Associations (CASA) (Canadian Alliance of Student Organisations, 2013) and the Ontario Undergraduate Student Alliance (OUSA) (The Ontario Undergraduate Student Alliance, 2013).
- The role of HE institutions (HEIs or PSIs) that have seized the opportunity of government incentive programs in some provinces and/or responded to community needs and built capacity in their outreach programs and other student access and success programs and services.
- The ongoing role of key academics and education associations, as well as the Higher Education Quality Council of Ontario (HEQCO) mandated by that province to address issues of accessibility and quality.
- The large number of community-based programs that have provided a range of student supports, including post-secondary awareness and advisory services, mentoring and academic coaching, career development counselling and student financial assistance and helped students in need to address issues such as housing, substance abuse and mental health problems. This includes the emergence of Pathways to Education Canada,[1] from its origins in Toronto's Regent Park district.
- Strong community-based education advocacy organizations that have advocated for school reform policies (e.g. People for Education).
- Federal government education transfers that have kept Canada's per capita education spending at competitive levels.
- A provincial approach to school financing that has had a certain success in equalizing school expenditures across school boards and districts (Tucker, 2011).
- The role of selected foundations[2] and a small number of corporations[3] that have provided financial support and leadership while encouraging greater collaboration and innovation in institutional and community-based approaches.

Despite the comparative richness of Canada's widening access and success policies and initiatives, Canada's capacity to sustain its performance in post-secondary participation is seen to be challenged by a number of trends: low birth rates, an aging workforce, deteriorating infrastructure, government funding constraints and a lack of critical data to assess performance comparatively and make adjustments, among other issues (Canadian Council on Learning, 2006, 2011).

In key areas such as university participation rates and graduate education rates, Canada's education performance is not seen to be keeping pace with innovation leaders in the industrialized world (National Post, 2009). Canada is 'at the crossroads', according to The Council of the Federation. 'Canada has reached a critical juncture. We have an aging workforce. We are not fully capitalizing on the skills and education of new immigrants, Aboriginal people and young people and others. At the same time, new competitors including emerging economies such as India, Brazil and China are making unprecedented investments in the skills of their people' (Council of the Federation, 2006). Although the work of many colleges and universities, community groups and researchers continues to make an important contribution to widening access for individuals and under-represented groups, the loss of a national focus on the issue resulting from the wind-up of the Canada Millennium Scholarship Foundation has led to some fragmentation. The Ontario example continues to stand out for the strength of its efforts in a context of considerable population diversity, making it a model of interest for other jurisdictions exploring more inclusive strategies.

# 2 Marching in the Rain: The TRIO Programme and the Civil Rights Legacy in the United States

Ngondi Kamatuka

## ▶ Introduction

The late 1950s and the early 1960s witnessed a shift of paradigm by educational practitioners and policymakers. The nation started questioning the wisdom of educating a few gifted students at the expense of the majority. Was the nation better off by doing this? Or was the nation denying itself the greater benefits to society by failing to educate a large number of students who would be the engine for a prosperous nation? The realization of this huge untapped human capital began to take shape.

This shift in paradigm became the platform for the discourse on access for the under-represented, low-income and first-generation college students in HE. The nation started to pay attention to those Americans who were denied access to HE. These were, and continue to be, the low-income and first-generation college students. They represent the American national tapestry: They are white, African-American, Latino, Asian, Alaskan, Hawaiian Native and Native American. They are America. Low-income is defined as a family income below 150 per cent of the poverty level ($35,775) for a family of four. 'First-generation college student' refers to a student with neither parent having a baccalaureate degree (US Department of Education, 2014). This chapter explores the products of over 50 years of concerted work in the United States to try to broaden access to HE, outlining the conceptual framework developed through this activity and challenges that remain in this field.

## ▶ The War on Poverty and Access to Higher Education

In the early years, the provision of education in the United States was the exclusive purview of the ecclesiastical establishment. It was mostly imparted through the teaching of catechism classes (Ford, 1962). In fact, the

Constitution of the United States of America has no provision of providing education for the citizens. The Constitution, in its preamble, states, 'We the People of the United States, in Order to form a more perfect Union, establish Justice, insure domestic Tranquility, provide for the common defence, promote the general Welfare, and secure the Blessings of Liberty to ourselves and our Posterity, do ordain and establish this Constitution for the United States of America' (US National Archives and Records Administration, 2014).

The phrase 'general Welfare ... and secure the Blessings of Liberty' has served as the foundation for the involvement of the federal government in the education arena. Extensive government involvement in education has been the responsibility of the states, as enshrined in the state constitutions, even if substantial federal funding of education was effected through grants made possible by the Morrill Land Grant Acts of 1862 and 1890 as well as the Serviceman's Readjustment Act of 1945, also known as the GI Bill (Brubacher and Rudy, 1976; Groutt, 2003).

Racial segregation and inequality came to define the US educational system as it developed through the first half of the twentieth century through the doctrine of 'separate but equal' given legitimacy through the *Plessy v. Ferguson* US Supreme Court decision. This became the conduit for the practice of racial segregation of education in the United States until the 1954 Supreme Court case of *Brown v. Board of Education of Topeka* ruled that racially segregated elementary and secondary schools were inherently unequal (Kahlenberg, 2013).

It was not, however, until the 1960s that policymakers and practitioners finally came to the realization that poverty was the barrier that was preventing a large segment of society from enjoying the fruits of HE for Americans. On 8 January 1964 during his State of the Union Address to Congress and the nation, President Lyndon Baines Johnson declared an 'unconditional war on poverty that we cannot afford to lose'. A Task Force on Poverty prepared legislation to begin the assault on poverty. President Johnson declared that it would 'forever eliminate poverty from the richest nation on earth' (Groutt, 2003: 1).

On 20 August 1964, President Lyndon Baines Johnson signed the Economic Opportunity Act, heralding the TRIO programs. These programs were part of Johnson's War on Poverty, and the nation's response to the access crisis. The Opportunity Act of 1964 established a high school experimental program: the Upward Bound Program. Soon after the passing of the Opportunity Act, the Higher Education Act created the Educational Talent Search Program. Special Services for Disadvantaged Students, later called the Student Support Services Program, was established in 1968, leading to the coinage of the term 'TRIO'. Since then, TRIO programs have changed the lives of millions of low-income and first-generation college students and students with disabilities, by providing access to HE. In 2014, Upward Bound, the first federal TRIO programme designed to prepare low-income and first-generation college students for college, celebrated 50 years of helping high school students go from poverty to middle class through HE (Council for Opportunity in Education, 2014).

The United States Department of Education celebrated Upward Bound under the banner 'TRIO: Celebrating 50 years of Promoting Excellence by Providing Hope and Opportunity for Success' on 21 August 2014. At the celebratory occasion, Arne Duncan, then United States Secretary of Education, acknowledged the important role TRIO has had in levelling the playing field, pronouncing, 'For five decades, young people served by TRIO have seen progress, and programs like TRIO are building a powerful pipeline of more students having access to higher education' (Abdul-Alim, 2014: 2).

The civil rights movement has played a critical role in changing the picture of education in the United Sates. It has helped with the breakdown of the racial access barriers in the school system. 'One of the strengths of the civil-rights movement was that white folks were involved. It wasn't just a African-American thing', and Mitchem (2013) goes on to state that 'so while I'm not marching in the rain today, I like to think what we are doing is a continuation of the spirit and sacrifice of those Americans' (Mitchem, 2013: A10).

## ▶ Barriers to Access and Success in HE

'Today, more than ever, education equals opportunity. In fact, college level learning is now seen as key to individual prosperity' (Lumina Foundation, 2012). The importance of education in twenty-first century America makes it vital to ascertain whether 50 years after Upward Bound was passed into being under-represented groups have access to HE; and are they experiencing success in HE?

Generations of African American parents have told their children that education is the one thing they can never take away from you. There is evidence that graduating from HE proffers advantage across the population, despite what ethnic group you come from. As Haycock states:

> Among those who have finished four years of college, there is no racial gap in economic mobility. Both Whites and African-Americans experience very high rates.
>
> (Haycock, 2013: 81)

However, distinct gaps in participation by different racial and income groups remain. The causes of these gaps in opportunity are usually looked for in the school system, and it certainly provides evidence that could explain the differences. Students from low-income backgrounds are clustered in poor neighbourhood schools as well as small rural schools that are underfunded and poorly equipped. The majority of the teachers in poor inner-city neighbourhood schools are not certified to teach in their fields. In these schools, low-income and first-generation college students are under-represented in rigorous curricula, and they score low on standardized tests. Furthermore, low-income and first-generation college students are less likely to partake in academic and social activities which lead to success in college (Yang and Kezar, 2009).

However, improving the academic rigour of these schools, though crucial on its own, is not enough to affect improvements in HE participation by those from low-income backgrounds. For example, the City of Chicago opened five selective high schools, which offered International Baccalaureate and Advance Placement courses in areas of low income. Research conducted by Nagaoka, Roderick, Coca and Moeller (2008) at these selective schools in Chicago showed that although the students achieve high grade point averages (GPAs) and high scores on the American College Test (ACT), attaining strong qualifications good for attending selective colleges, they still faced difficulties in navigating the complex college application process. These students still attended institutions of higher learning not reflective of their selective *college fit* given their high scores.

It appears that something in addition to academic improvement is needed. Specific attention to HE progression is needed, which has to be built into the culture and structures of the school. Research shows that students who attend schools with strong college-going cultures are more likely to apply to and attend four-year colleges, although a significant predictor of college enrolment is whether teachers report their school as having a strong college climate (Roderick et al., 2010). Low-income and first-generation college students need a total school culture transformation in which they can realize their full, untapped potential. Access for low-income students requires that society hire better-qualified and credentialed teachers to empower them. They need to be exposed to a college-going culture in which they see people who look like them occupying positions of power and influence in the school system. Consequently, in middle school or earlier, low-income and first-generation college students must be exposed to a culture that emphasizes the importance of college attendance. It is too late to do this in high school.

## ▶ College Fit

'College fit' refers to the idea that students attend a college which presents a good choice for them in terms of their academic credentials and from which they have a good chance of earning a college degree.

Low-income and first-generation college students should be empowered in a holistic way to make better-informed decisions about the college of their choice. Research shows that there are many barriers that impede access to HE by low-income and first-generation college students. The first barrier is one of academic under-preparation, marked by low GPA and ACT scores. Other barriers include the complex college and financial aid application process and the lack of college campus visits, including the opportunity to stay on campus during summer programs, in the middle and high school years. The holistic approach of education means that parents, school and programs like TRIO work together in empowering students to acquire the necessary academic skills and mastering the college application process.

The lack of college campus exposure has led to a serious problem of the *college fit* phenomenon, resulting in low-income and first-generation college students attending colleges and universities that are not the right fit for them, which in turn has led to high dropout rates from these colleges as well as a significantly low graduation rates. As Tinto (2013) has argued, access without support is not an opportunity. Low-income and first-generation college students need a credible support system on campus that will make them feel at home. College access and readiness have been hampered by a multitude of serious problems besetting the public education system in the United States, leading to low-income and first-generation being academically underprepared.

In terms of college readiness, it behoves policymakers and practitioners to be explicit about which sets of knowledge and skills they consider necessary ingredients for college access and success. Roderick, Nagaoka and Coca (2009) have identified four essential sets of skills:

1. Content knowledge and basic skills
2. Core academic skills
3. Non-cognitive or behavioural skills
4. College knowledge

Low-income and first-generation college do not engage in rigorous curriculum in middle and high school, partly because the schools they attend do not offer challenging curricula. Students find themselves in their senior year of high school under-prepared for college level work and not having visited a college campus in their entire life. This leads them to make 'safe' choices about which college to attend, often choosing to stay close to home because they are unaware of any other choices. Given the low education level of parents of the neighbourhood schools, parents and students do not engage in family discussions centred on college education.

It seems that the college fit research has by and large focused solely on getting low-income and first-generation college students admitted into highly selective colleges and universities only. The focus should be on all the students for whom access and success are the biggest challenges. Unpublished data by the University of Kansas Center for Educational Opportunity Programs (CEOP) show that the pre-college TRIO programs (Educational Talent Search, Upward Bound and the Upward Bound Math and Science program) have an average high school graduation rate of about 95 per cent and a college placement rate of 90 per cent for the students they serve.

These rates are three times better than those of low-income and first-generation college students who did not participate in these programs, and are in line with the nation-wide TRIO data. TRIO programs and Gaining Early Awareness and Readiness for Undergraduate Programs (GEAR UP) have provided better college fit opportunities to the students they serve by exposing students to a multitude of different colleges and universities through college campus visits. Similarly, the GEAR UP cohort classes of the University of Kansas have the same rates (CEOP, 2014).

National studies have found that TRIO programs are effective at increasing college enrolment and graduation. TRIO and GEAR UP programs must do a better holistic job in providing better college fit to their students. Mathematica Policy Research (2006) conducted a study on the impact of secondary and post-secondary in Texas, Indiana and Florida and found that Educational Talent Search participants were more likely than students of similar background who did not participate in Educational Talent Search to

- apply for financial assistance; and
- enrol in post-secondary education.

In Texas the study found that Educational Talent Search participants were

- 12 per cent more likely to attain a high school diploma;
- 77 per cent more likely to be first time financial aid applicants; and
- 52 per cent more likely to enrol in a Texas public college.

In Indiana, the study found that students were

- 31 per cent more likely to be a first-time financial aid applicant; and
- 8 per cent more likely to enrol in an Indiana public college.

In Florida the study found that students were

- 20 per cent more likely to attain a high school diploma (84% vs. 70%);
- 58 per cent more likely to be first-time applicants for financial aid (52% vs. 33%); and
- 42 per cent more likely to immediately enrol in a Florida public college (51% vs. 36%).

Educational Talent Search is a college access TRIO programme funded by the United States Department of Education and serving low-income youth in the sixth grade through their senior year in high school.

Additional barriers that affect low-income and first-generation college students in gaining access to HE are also manifested through many avenues, as noted below:

- Low parental educational achievement leads to no family engagement in discussions around college issues, as well as parents having misconceptions about college costs of various institutions.
- Students have no role models in the educational arena because of the lack of diversity among teachers and staff.
- Poor neighbourhood schools have unacceptable high rates of dropout rates, which in some cases can be 30 per cent or higher.
- Access to HE is further hampered by the low percentage of low-income and first-generation college students who complete the Free Application for Federal Student Aid (FAFSA). FAFSA determines students' financial need to fund their college education.
- Tuition costs have skyrocketed, making the cost of attending HE within the last ten years, making it impossible for low-income and first-generation college students to enter higher institutions of learning.
- No opportunities to visit college campuses. College culture is unique, and students must acquire the skills set that will enable them to navigate and adapt to the complexities of this culture, from knowing your professor's office hours to classroom decorum.
- Low-income and first-generation college students are lacking the ability to learn the college culture, as they are not given the opportunity to set foot on a college campus.
- In order for the student to find the best college fit, he or she must at least be given the opportunity to visit no less than seven colleges and universities prior to attending college.
- The point of not knowing how the college culture functions is best illustrated by one of the University of Kansas McNair Scholars Program

graduates, who has earned a doctorate degree in reference to her McNair Scholars Program interview. 'I was dressed casually, wearing shorts and an old HALO T-shirt, with my hair braided and tucked into a bandana. It wasn't that I didn't care, it was because I didn't know any different. No one had ever told me how to dress for an interview or how to prepare' (Hinojos, 2014).

▶ The Ronald E. McNair Post-Baccalaureate Achievement Program, which was named after Ronald E. McNair, an African American astronaut who died in the explosion of the *Challenger* Space Shuttle, prepares low-income and first-generation college students for admission into graduate school, to earn the highest academic degree, the doctorate, and join the professoriate ranks.

▶ No involvement in extra-curricular activities by low-income and first-generation college students. Research shows that students who participate in various extracurricular activities, like debate, science and math clubs, and so forth, have high college retention and graduation rates.

## ▶ The Burden of Financing College Education

Although there are a plethora of barriers to college access and success, college affordability presents an insurmountable stumbling block, as student debt levels have risen to high levels (Long, 2013). High tuition rates and related fees have kept the doors of access to HE closed for many low-income and first-generation college students. The cost of attending college has become prohibitively too expensive for many low-income students. Policymakers must address this serious barrier to HE, if the nation is to provide college education to poor students.

The nation has just celebrated 40 years of the Pell Grant Program, which provides need-based financial aid grants to 8.2 million college students from low-income and lower-middle-income families (Mortenson, 2013). The Pell Grant is funded by the United States government and plays a critical role in opening access. It helps the success rate of low-income and first-generation college students on our campuses.

A rapidly growing number of low-income and first-generation college students and other entities have called on policymakers to increase the Pell Grant, currently funded at about $28 billion dollars per year by Congress. To fully fund the growing number of low-income and first-generation college students, Mortenson (2013) advances the point that in order to address this increase in the population needing student financial support, the current maximum Pell Grant support of $5500 should be increased to the level of $12,000 to be at the same level as institutional charges of tuition. This will also be instrumental in meeting President Barack Obama's March 2009 call that the 'United States will regain its position as the nation with the highest percentage of its population holding college degrees and credentials' (The Pell Institute, 2011). Currently, 38 per cent of Americans ages 25–64 hold two- or four-year college degrees. Lumina Foundation 2010 Big Goal calls for 60 per cent of Americans to obtain a college degree by 2025 (Lumina Foundation, 2012).

Another disturbing barrier of access to HE in the United States is the increasing targeting of low-income and first-generation college students by for-profit institutions of higher learning. This practice is a serious affront to the low-income students' ability to earn a college degree. These proprietary institutions use questionable tactics to entice low-income students to their campuses. Those students have little chance of graduating at the for-profit schools. Mitchem (2010) argues that it is an immoral practice. 'Low-income families know very little about the range of postsecondary options and the college admission process.' He further states, 'Students often believe the "salesperson" – individuals serving as "admissions counsellors" at for-profits – who encourage them to take on high-interest loans likely to be defaulted.' Additionally, 'The sophisticated marketing and recruiting techniques of many for-profit institutions take on a predatory nature, similar to what we have seen in the subprime mortgage industry. These high-pressure transactions, in which institutions promise quick degrees and jobs in exchange for high tuition, are deeply dishonourable because there is an inherent inequity in the relationship between the low-income consumer and the industry' (Mitchem, 2010: 1).

▶ **College Graduation**

There is no question that low-income and first-generation college students yearn to earn a college degree and live out the American Dream. Bowen, Chingos and McPherson (2009) believe that public colleges and universities are the logical venues for low-income and first-generation college students to attain their college degrees. Yet Bowen and his fellow researchers (2009) found out that 68 per cent of low-income students graduated from flagship universities in six years.

College graduation is directly connected to how well students are prepared for college work through a rigorous curriculum in middle and high school. A rigorous curriculum also reduces the percentage of low-income and first-generation college students who are in remedial courses in college. This is obviously one of the reasons why low-income and first-generation college students on average take six years to graduate from college. Remedial education is a major hindrance for low-income students doing well in college. Students are sometimes placed in two to three remedial classes at a given time, which costs them time and money in completing their college degree (Swail, 2014).

Time spent in remedial education adversely affects students, because credits earned in remedial courses often are not applied towards meeting degree requirements. Another negative effect is on students' financial aid. Spending a semester in remedial education may result in the student not being able to finish, as financial aid may run out (Long, 2013).

A White House Task Force (2014) found that the major determinant factor of college enrolment and completion is family income. Middle-income level children are half as likely to complete college as wealthier children. They have a 25 per cent completion rate, compared to 53 per cent for children from families in the top fifth income.

## ▶ Best Practice in Extending Access to HE for Low-income Groups

In providing examples of best practices in access to HE and success activities, we draw here on the work of the Center for Educational Opportunity Programs (CEOP) of the Achievement and Assessment Institute at the University of Kansas. Specifically, the best practices of the TRIO, GEAR UP and the Harvest of Hope Leadership Academy programs will be highlighted. Harvest of Hope Leadership Academy, which is not a TRIO programme, provides academic enrichment, leadership development and college preparation for Kansas high school students eligible for Migrant Education Services.

The mission of (CEOP) is empowering historically underrepresented and economically disadvantaged students to advance their achievement in HE. CEOP strives to increase academic success, college access and graduation rates by using research-driven strategies to assist individuals in overcoming financial, academic, social and cultural barriers to HE. CEOP serves 4500 pre-college students, as young as 11 years old in middle school; high school students; college students; adult learners; and students who are veterans. CEOP's programs work with a multitude of target schools in Kansas. CEOP has used a variety of strategies in empowering students to assure access to and success in HE. The strategies are discussed below.

### Strategy 1: Pre-college Programs: Create a Meaningful Partnership between the School Administration, Parents and the CEOP Program

Our first strategy focuses on a buy-in from the parents and school administrators, from the building principal to the superintendent's office, on the benefits students will derive from their participating in TRIO, GEAR UP and Harvest of Hope Leadership Academy. In August, before the start of the school year, CEOP holds a programme retreat to attend to the following items:

- Review the previous year's programme evaluation
- Review student performance data
- Review student enrolment in rigorous curriculum for the up-coming year
- Review the student participation in the Summer Institute held on the campus of the University of Kansas
- Share the student Summer Institute performance and attendance data with the schools and request the schools to provide a 0.5 elective credit to the students who have successfully completed the requirements for the Summer Institute for high school students
- Share the Summer Institute curriculum with parents and schools
- Create a calendar of activities for the upcoming academic year
- Share the calendar of events with students, parents, and school personnel.

### Strategy 2: Engage Students in Rigorous Coursework and Academic Clubs

CEOP focuses on getting students prepared for college enrolment, and this means exposing students early, during middle school, to the university culture, in order to find the best college fit. To provide the opportunity to enrol in rigorous curriculum, CEOP staff provides information to students and parents in the spring when students are enrolling for the next academic year. Research on college fit has focused on high-ability students from low socio-economic status in preparing the high-ability students for admission to selective colleges and universities. What CEOP does, however, is to expose all the students to all types of colleges and universities. TRIO programs provide more than six college campus visits to both two- and four-year public and private institutions for their students. Students are also exposed to a wide range of activities to get them ready for post-secondary education. This means that if the school they attend does not offer a rich rigorous curriculum, it is incumbent upon a CEOP programme to find alternative course offerings during the year and summer. Additionally, students are provided the opportunity to participate in academic clubs. This is critical, as research has shown that students who participate in extra-curricular activities tend to do well in HE.

### Strategy 3: Engage Parents Early and Often on the College Application Process

The student college application process is a daunting task to most parents, but more so to the parents of low-income and first-generation college students. This is compounded by the low academic achievement of the parents. FAFSA requires that parents file their income tax return early and not wait to file by the government-mandated deadline of April 15. Filing by the deadline means that the colleges and university have already awarded the pool of their scholarship funds, which is normally done by February 1. CEOP provides assistance in filing the FAFSA to parents in January. The requirement of CEOP programs *is that all high school seniors, meaning 100 per cent*, complete their FAFSA in January. The aggregate FAFSA completion rate of all CEOP programs is 90 per cent.

### Strategy 4: Provide Mentoring Opportunities

CEOP believes and subscribes to the idea of role modelling and has engaged in this endeavour. It is essential that CEOP employ personnel who have overcome similar barriers to the ones faced by students. Diversity of staff sends a powerful message by which students can say, 'Hey, if she (or he), having come from my neighbourhood, has a college degree, I can do the same.' Mentoring activities must also prepare our students to live and work anywhere in the world. Our diversity must reflect the rainbow nation that is the United States of America.

### Strategy 5: Understand the Needs and Provide Assistance to Adult Learners

CEOP also serves adult learners who for various reasons never completed their high school education or have dropped out of college. CEOP provides information on the process of completing the General Educational Development (GED), a high school equivalency diploma; FAFSA information; college re-entry process; and information on defaulted loan rehabilitation.

### Strategy 6: College Programs: Provide Data Showing How the College Programs for Low-income and First-generation College Students Complement the Overall Mission of the University

CEOP has two federally funded TRIO programs: Student Support Services and the Ronald E. McNair Post-Baccalaureate Achievement Program. These two college success programs provide academic assistance and support to University of Kansas low-income and first-generation college students. They also help students navigate the complexity of the HE system by providing tutoring and undergraduate research opportunities to students. The two offices serve as a home away from home, where students feel a part of a unique, supportive community of learning on the campus of the University of Kansas. The retention and graduation rates of students served by these programs are much higher than those of students with similar backgrounds who are not part of the two programs.

### Strategy 7: Early Student Monitoring and Intervention

CEOP practices early monitoring and appropriate intervention to academically empower students in preparing them for meaningful participation in HE. ACT (2013) data show that students monitored early are more college and career ready than those not monitored early. Early monitoring of students allows CEOP to use real-time data in providing appropriate academic response and support. This is as true at the middle school level as it is at the college level. Engaging students is not an afterthought in CEOP; rather, it is kept front and centre throughout the academic year, summer school and summer camps.

### Strategy 8: Student Leadership Opportunity

Society has the inherent responsibility to prepare leaders for tomorrow to carry and expand the capacity of the nation in all spheres of human interaction. CEOP believes in the principle that students have the capacity to be the agents of change and that poor students are part of this equation. To this end, CEOP provides a multitude of leadership growth opportunities for students to acquire and hone leadership skills and to serve as leaders for their fellow students. These opportunities include travelling to Washington, DC, to speak with policymakers, as well as attending student leadership conferences.

## ▶ Conclusion

There are few countries in the world where disparities in participation in HE by those from different social backgrounds have received such concerted attention as in the United States. This has enabled the development of a range of proven strategies to support HE participation by those from low-income groups. Despite the development of such strategies, bolstered by a highly politicized national body of practitioners who draw from the historical strength of the civil rights movement, deep divisions in participation in HE by income and racial group remain. However, despite the difficulties in extending opportunity in HE in the early twenty-first century, the belief in its importance across the HE sector in the United States remains firm. As Bernadette Gray-Little, chancellor of the University of Kansas, stated in 2014:

> When we talk about educating leaders, we mean more than just preparing students for specific jobs, or even for successful careers ... we are tasked with preparing students for active, engaged lives. We prepare students for lives where they take on challenges as leaders in their communities, their nations, and our world. We prepare them to live meaningful lives where they embrace the fact that we are each part of something bigger than ourselves.
>
> (Gray-Little, 2014)

# 3 Access and Retention in Higher Education in Colombia: The Case of the Children's University EAFIT

Isabel Cristina Montes Gutiérrez and
Ana Cristina Abad

## ▶ Introduction

This chapter offers a detailed analysis of the attempts one university has made to extend access to higher education (HE) through a comprehensive and structured programme of pre-HE support: the Children's University.

### Access to HE in Colombia

In Colombia, education is defined as a process of continual formation provided in approved education centres, with the primary objective of achieving the integral development of students. This education, defined as formal, is offered in both public and private (referred to in Colombia as 'official' and 'unofficial', respectively) facilities and is divided into four levels: preschool, elementary, middle and higher. In addition, it is mandatory that the population participate in formal educational processes between the ages of 5 and 15 years, and it is the duty of the state, society and the family to ensure quality and promote access.

The country has a significant percentage of the population that is of school age (between 5 and 21 years old); from a population of 47,704,427 people, 37 per cent are within this age group. Moreover, this population is, for the most part, homogeneously distributed throughout the 32 departments into which the country is divided and Bogotá, Capital District. With regard to HE, each department has an average of 20 per cent of the school-age population within the relevant age bracket (between 17 and 21 years old) (DANE, 2012).

Given the uniform distribution of the school-age population, opportunities for access to education should be distributed in a uniform manner throughout the country in order to meet the educational needs of the Colombian population. As primary and secondary levels of education enrolment rates in theory exceed 100 per cent (to be precise 100.76%). This is feasible since the numerator includes overage students. A rate close to or above 100 per cent indicates that, in theory, the country has the capacity to serve the entire school-age population, but it does not indicate what proportion of this population has already been registered (MEN, 2012). The national enrolment rate for HE is only 42.4 per cent (SNIES, 2013). This latter rate has increased significantly when compared with rates from almost 30 years ago, which were 6.9 per cent (ICFES, 1985).

Nevertheless, it has not yet provided equitable academic opportunities in relation to geography and the academic, economic and psychological conditions necessary for students to be able to decide to partake in, have access to and remain in HE in order to obtain a professional qualification. Furthermore, without the development of these conditions, barriers continue to exist that limit the efficiency of the HE system to meet the necessities of formation.

Regarding academic opportunities, of the 288 HE Institutions (HEIs) available and the 5834 technical, technological and university programmes they offer, 55 per cent of these are concentrated in Bogotá and the departments of Antioquia and Valle del Cauca (SNIES, 2013). Therefore, geographic location is the first barrier to access because of the move that students who live in regions where the supply of HE is limited or nonexistent must make. Accordingly, regional policies have been created that promote access to education in the places of residence of young people in order to prevent their geographical displacement; however, such policies remain concentrated in only a few departments.

The main indicator of demand for HE is the 551,020 students in the final year of secondary education with the necessary knowledge and heterogeneous skills to enter HE. This figure represents the number of students who took the test Saber 11, a standardized test given to students in Colombia during last year of high school (grade 11). It is the final test of compulsory education and a requirement for admission to the various programmes provided within HE (ICFES, 2012).

Students of a higher socio-economic status who attend private schools perform better in these standardized tests than those of a lower socio-economic status who attend public schools. This inequity in academic preparation generates a greater probability that lower-income students will have access to both public and private HEIs (OECD and The World Bank, 2012: 105). In such a scenario, a significant percentage of Colombian students are faced with two key barriers: a lack of academic preparation and economic capacity. The latter of these presents a vicious circle because it refers back to the lack of preparation that does not provide students with the ability to pay for and thus invest in the acquisition of professional knowledge and skills. This has particular impact on students from lower socio-economic groups and those from the rural regions.

It is the responsibility of schools to improve upon this lack of preparation, but the early results obtained so far are somewhat discouraging. Hence, the Organisation for Economic Co-operation and Development (OECD) and the World Bank (2012) suggest that the length of schooling received be increased to 12 years of education, as is the case in the majority of the world's countries.

To overcome economic barriers, the state finances the provision of education through the supply of resources from the nation and local authorities to public HEIs and SENA. The National Training Service, SENA, is a public institution that falls under the Ministry of Labour of Colombia and provides free training to millions of Colombians who benefit from the technical, technological and complementary programmes on offer.

Furthermore, in light of the fact that 77 per cent of educational provisions within HE are private, the state participates in financing education through The Colombian Institute of Educational Credit and Technical Studies Abroad (ICETEX), which offers access credits in order to prevent students from having their university education interrupted for economic reasons (Caballero and Herrera, 2013: 121). These diverse forms of financing have helped to promote access to HE at all socio-economic levels, yet greater levels of participation continue for those from higher socio-economic backgrounds.

The geographical, academic and economic barriers to HE listed above also create another barrier, which is psychological in form and consists of the perceived lower credibility of various students in terms of their ability to learn. This affects such students in that they do not attempt to enter into a HE programme, desist from trying or, if they are able to access a programme, eventually abandon their studies. This psychological barrier becomes important if one understands that providing 'access to HE' does not end in obtaining the necessary income to attend an educational institution, but also involves the promotion of intrinsic motivation within such students and the provision of the academic and physical conditions necessary for each student to both access and remain in HE.

An analysis of student attrition is one way to assess how efficient the HE system is in terms of students being able to overcome all the relevant barriers to access and successfully complete their educational programmes. In Colombia, the dropout rate in the third semester is 41 per cent on average, that is to say, of 100 students that begin an academic programme, 41 will not complete it (SPADIES, 2014).

Another alternative for reducing barriers to access for HE in Colombia, identified by the OECD and the World Bank (2012), is the improvement of the quality of secondary education through the construction of a 'bridge' between schools and HE, to facilitate greater equity of access and retention. The aim is to improve of the preparation of young people for HE and the lowering of academic and psychological barriers in order to enhance competence and security in terms of learning abilities. In addition, it aims to attenuate the aforementioned economic barrier by providing students with the ability to participate in scholarship programmes and by helping to increase retention in HE.

To improve the relationship that primary and secondary education has with HE, Colombia has created programmes[1] in response to the need, among others, to reduce the gaps that exist between school and university education, and to provide equal opportunities for access to young people, regardless of their socio-economic background. Next, the case study of the Children's University EAFIT, located in the city of Medellín, Colombia, is described in terms of its success in reducing barriers to access to HE for young people.

### ▶ Children's University EAFIT in Medellin, Colombia

Children's Universities are relatively new initiatives that began in Europe in 2003 with the purpose of opening the doors of HEIs to a broader audience, such as children, to enable the communication of scientific ideas from an early age and reduce the gap between school and HE. So far, 356 such Children's Universities have been identified and are located in 40 countries across Europe and worldwide (Götz and Seifert, 2010).

In Latin America, the Children's University EAFIT is the only university of this type registered in the European Children's Universities Network (EUCU.NET).

These initiatives have several characteristics when inserted into the academic world: they are not part of the formal education system and do not follow a formal curricula, meaning that they therefore do not require evaluations of the teaching-learning process; they are constituted within institutions of HE but have a different core audience; their objectives are not framed by formal training, but their purposes are aligned with the core issues that comprise any educational process. In other words, these initiatives are part of a much larger system in which each audience plays a different role, and they

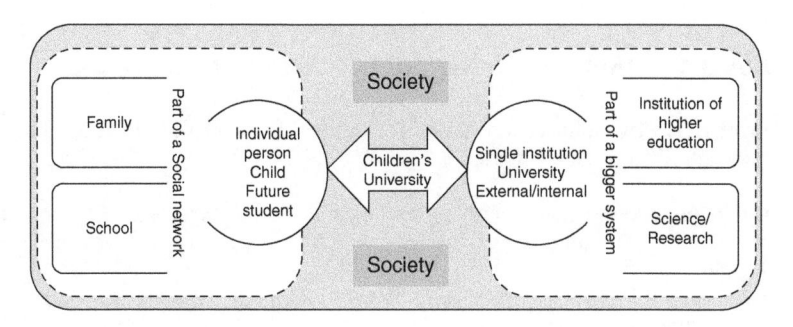

**Figure 3.1** Children's University.
Source: Götz and Seifert (2010: 48).

create a bridge between children and their families, and their schools and the university, as well as vice versa.

As well as motivating children and young people to develop curiosity and critical-thinking skills – the principal sources of science and research – Children's Universities give young people an understanding of their future options, through which access to HE becomes closer and indeed a real possibility (see Figure 3.1).

The Children's University EAFIT has been created within a private university located in Medellin, one of the major cities of Colombia. The initiative began in 2005 and represented a pioneering step in Latin America. The methodology implemented allows children between the ages of 7 and 14 years, from all socio-economic backgrounds present within the city, to participate meaningfully in university life, inviting them to interact with teachers and students in order to approach the research that occurs within the University.

The Children's University EAFIT consists of three stages, each of which is developed annually. The first is called 'encounters with the question' and is aimed at children 8 to 13 years old in order to bring them closer to science and research through questions asked across various topics of interest. The second, 'expeditions in knowledge', is based on a central theme and invites children between 9 and 16 years of age to interact with various investigative perspectives. Finally, 'science projects' is aimed at high-school students (in the 9th to 11th grades) and applies qualitative and quantitative research methodologies in order to develop projects that arise from their own interests in different areas of knowledge. It is important to note that one participant can attend these three stages consecutively, that is, in annual cycles, as follows: First stage (one year), second stage (up to four years) and third stage (just before leaving school) (see annual basic programme information in Box 3.1).

> **Box 3.1 Children's University EAFIT. Basic Annual Data**
>
> **Intensity:** Fifty-eight sessions a year (16 in the first stage, 14 in the second stage and 28 in the third stage).
>
> **Duration:** Six hours per month for the first and second stages and 12 hours per month for the third stage.
>
> **Location:** University campus (auditoriums, workshops, laboratories, classrooms, graduates rooms, etc.).
>
> **Number of children and young people:** Approximately 769 per year for the three stages (200 in the first stage, 540 in the second stage and 29 in the third stage).
>
> **Number of undergraduate and master's students (workshop participants):** 67 undergraduates and seven master's.
>
> **Researchers:** Forty.
>
> **Age of children and young people:** Eight to 16 years old.
>
> **Registration:** Free (for the first stage via schools and in the second stage, independently – each child or young person decides which route to take).

### ▶ The Children's University EAFIT and Access to HE

With nine years of experience of activities and rigorous monitoring of the processes experienced by participants in the Children's University EAFIT, it is possible to assert that such programmes help to reduce barriers to access to HE (versus vocational guidance) and improve motivation towards university studies.

To illustrate this relationship, a particular case study, involving different steps for the collection and analysis of quantitative and qualitative information regarding graduates of the programme, has been conducted. This has been executed in order to establish a panoramic picture of graduates of the Children's University EAFIT in terms of access to HE and also to identify their experiences regarding the processes engaged in and their future projections regarding various aspects of their lives in relation to knowledge. To do this, an analysis of statistics based on a sample of 50 per cent of all graduates (506) of the programme was executed. A survey was then administered for a representative sample of graduates (95% confidence and a margin of error of 5%). Finally, we conducted a focus group with eight alumni children, to expand the information obtained from the statistics and the survey.

## Panorama of the Graduates of the Children's University EAFIT: Statistics

Over 90 per cent of graduates of the Children's University EAFIT progress to HE. This rate is high compared with that of the rest of the country, where 42 of every 100 young people enter at school age. Additionally, this access rate remains high when disaggregated by socio-economic status; apparently, although economic factors present one of the most frequent barriers to access to HE in Colombia, statistics show that this barrier is overcome among graduates of the Children's University EAFIT. In fact, figures show that graduates from official educational institutions exhibit satisfactory access to and retention in HE (91.7% are pursuing an undergraduate degree). The choices of degree programme for graduates from the Children's University EAFIT can be divided into different areas of knowledge that have a similar composition to the areas of study chosen nationally. First, 32.8 per cent of Children's University EAFIT graduates select engineering programmes, compared with 29% in Colombia overall. Second, administrative programmes (19.8%) present a lower percentage when compared to the national level (28.9%). In the area of health programmes, which encompass scientific studies and often prove difficult to access in Colombia, Children's University EAFIT graduates present double the percentage share when compared to the figures for the country as a whole (14.9% and 6.7%, respectively). In terms of access, the last of these figures reflects the positive effects of the processes experienced as part of the programme, through which critical and reflective thinking are promoted, knowledge regarding university programmes is provided and confidence is strengthened in terms of accessing these programmes.

## A Vision of the Past and the Future: A Qualitative Analysis

In the results of the survey, graduates express their memories about the Children's University EAFIT, in particular, the activities realized in the various workshops. In their own words, they perceive the University as a space separate from school in which they learn and establish a relationship with knowledge through playing and enjoyment.

> I remember this experience fondly because there were spaces where one had the opportunity to learn in different ways, in addition to meeting

people from different schools and being in a university environment from an early age.
(Student of international business at the University EAFIT)

Another important factor to note is the role of the workshop leaders, who facilitate the activities within the workshop and do not just focus on a specific field of knowledge, but encourage and develop the collective construction of knowledge through affection and closeness:

Many things, like the friendly treatment of all the workshop leaders and managers, who motivated us to investigate and adopt a love for studying and for possessing knowledge.
(Student of mechanical engineering at the University EAFIT)

The projections of these young people highlight how the Children's University has given them an understanding of their future educational possibilities and options:

I see myself as a great financial engineer working in a very good bank or a financial institution, improving every day in order to gain excellent job opportunities.
(Student of financial engineering at Instituto Tecnológico Metropolitano)

I would like to be happy and develop a career as a social communicator, working with research groups for children and young people within my country.
(Student of social communication at the University EAFIT)

Over 40 per cent of graduates surveyed plan to continue studying (undertake a postgraduate degree or complete studies abroad), thus providing evidence of a relationship with knowledge that extends over time. Another point to note is that all of the graduates have clear their future projections, and none are contemplating the possibility of their studies being interrupted. This raises the chance that they will complete their studies and implement their skills at the employment level (see Table 3.1).

Regarding their future projections in terms of the work that reflects the academic and entrepreneurial visions of the graduates (see Table 3.2), they themselves highlight the following:

Being able to work anywhere in the world, innovating in new constructive ways that facilitate improved ways of living in the increasingly chaotic reality of today.
(Student of architecture at the Universidad Pontificia Bolivariana)

**Table 3.1** Professional Projections for the Future

| Postgraduate Degree | Finish Studies | Finish Studies and Exercise Skills | Complete Studies Abroad | Don't Know/ Don't Have Clear Ideas |
|---|---|---|---|---|
| 37% | 33% | 24% | 6% | 0% |

Source: Universidad de los Niños EAFIT (2014).

**Table 3.2** Student Future Employment Projections

| Graduates | Be Employed by a National Company | Create a Company/ Office | Be a Professor or Researcher | Be Employed by an International Company | Don't Know/ Don't Have Clear Ideas |
|---|---|---|---|---|---|
| | 41% | 29% | 20% | 8% | 2% |

Source: Universidad de los Niños EAFIT (2014).

Being a professor at a university.
(Student of literary studies at the Universidad Pontificia Bolivariana)

I would like to work in market research or any sports marketing company and then, after gathering experience, start my own business.
(Student of marketing at University EAFIT)

In the conversation sustained in the focus group, the participants exalted the symbolic representations that emerged from their experiences of the Children's University EAFIT, namely its relationship with knowledge, investigation and the motivation provided to enter into HE.

Graduates of the programme have a strong relationship with knowledge that in some cases comes from the family but in many others is consolidated by their passing through the Children's University EAFIT. This constitutes a potential determinant for access to and retention in HE:

I've learned that it's okay to love knowledge [...]. In the Children's University EAFIT I found a place where it's okay to ask questions, and where you can talk and ask, 'how do we do this?' or 'why do we do it?' Two things came together for me: what my family taught me and a place like Children's University EAFIT where I could cultivate knowledge. This became a pillar for me because it has defined what I am doing with my life.

(Student of literary studies at the Universidad Pontificia Bolivariana)

Second, the experiences brought about by this type of programme have brought the children closer to university as a space where they are able to, and where they want to, continue their HE studies:

For me, the word 'university' is closely related to large, pretty campuses and professors. It is a space of constant social interaction, and of certain forms of emotions and knowledge. Constant exchange both inside and outside of the classroom, everywhere. In addition, it is enjoyable to know people from other paths. It is this: interaction.

(Student of music at the Children's University EAFIT)

The relationship with the Children's University EAFIT for me, just like university, opened my world because it gave me contact with something much larger and showed me various approaches. It is something that opens doors, it is something new, it's a world you come to, where you explore what you like, meet new people and other cultures and have diverse experiences that help you to grow. The first semester at University has not been so hard for me because I have had contact with universities since I was little, so I know how to manage a larger space.

(Student of business administration at the University EAFIT)

On the other hand, direct contact between graduates of the Children's University EAFIT and day-to-day researchers has allowed the former to change their idea of the scientist as someone far removed from reality. But it has also given graduates the ability to view researchers as references in their own future orientation in terms of their vocation:

In my final year at the Children's University EAFIT I met one of the researchers and I remember the day when we were in the lab with him, I stayed a long time talking and he explained many things to me. After that I realized that I wanted to be an engineer.

(Student of mechanical engineering at University EAFIT)

I very much remember our meetings about the 'question'; in 2007, we were working on the question of how a car works. Noting the work of the engineer of product design, I did not want to go where the cars were made. And I asked several things about product design and fell in love with the programme.

(Student of product design)

Finally, universities help children to develop curiosity and offer them the possibility to take ownership of their learning and understand that while the school and the university are guides in their formation, interest in knowledge actually comes from within themselves. This testimonial provides evidence of this:

It's funny, because one leaves realizing that everything in our studies is very consistent. I think a lot about what I experienced at the Children's University EAFIT and apply it to my studies, because in literary studies such a disposition to questions is very important, and this is why I took the programme. This is something that has taught me a lot – to not swallow answers whole, but instead to wonder and ask: why does this happen here? This methodology has helped me a lot.

(Student of literary studies at the Universidad Pontificia Bolivariana)

## ▶ Challenges

The Children's University EAFIT builds a bridge between the worlds of the school and the university, motivated by interest in knowledge and learning, and ultimately allows participants to overcome barriers to access to HE. These programmes inspire, motivate and enable children and young people, regardless of their socio-economic status, to have the opportunity to actively participate in processes where they are able to recognize the importance of studying and gaining access to HE.

The National Development Plan for Colombia 2010–14 is currently being reviewed (November 2014–18) with a policy of *Solidario*. This has the emphasis on education (health and housing) for all, with the construction and strengthening of education as a tool for transformation. It identifies the explicit requirement of the development of flexible models of educational delivery. Using models similar to the case study from the Children's University EAFIT, there is an opportunity for HE to directly contribute to this agenda through the systematic development of Children's Universities across Colombia. The rural regions would need a new type of provision, for example summer programmes delivered to students in rural areas linked to Universities in urban regions.

The results obtained in this study place in focus the need for the Colombian educational system to include in its projects alternatives that connect different educational levels but which also open spaces for the social appropriation of science as a reality from an early age. This will eventually result in the development of a country like Colombia.

Although such programmes are recent and are not yet supported academically, it is necessary to continue the development of formal research in order to validate the creation of other Children's Universities within the context of Colombia. Therefore, it will then be possible to place this issue on the Colombian political agenda and positively influence the research and education systems of the country.

# 4 Changing the Mindset: How Germany Is Trying to Combine Access and Equity

Julia Mergner, Shweta Mishra and Dominic Orr

## ▶ Background on Access to Higher Education (HE) in Germany

The European HE system has been a target of a number of reform initiatives, mainly attributed to the Bologna Declaration in 1999 and the Lisbon Agenda in 2000. Both of these policy initiatives emphasized the modernization of European HE. While the Bologna declaration stressed structural reforms at the start (HRK, 2014a), the Lisbon Agenda focused on supporting growth and jobs. These issues now coincide in the Bologna and the European Union policy statements (European Commission, 2011), especially following the economic crisis of 2008. Improving the quality of education and widening access to education are seen as central in attaining successful economic and societal outcomes (European Commission, 2010). Simultaneously, creating more inclusive HE according to the so-called social dimension of European HE is also perceived as a high priority (European Commission and Eurydice, 2011). Over the last two decades, HE participation has expanded rapidly in Europe, yet inclusive access to HE remains a major policy challenge. Scholars too have paid increasing attention to the relationship between different education systems and the development of inequalities in access to HE (Mayer, Mueller and Pollack, 2003; Arum, Gamoran and Shavit, 2007; Reimer and Pollak, 2010). They show that the expansion of HE results in improved access for all groups; however, the relative advantage of privileged groups remains, especially with respect to the types of institution attended and fields of study (Arum et al., 2007).

In this context, the German HE system is unique and of special interest due to the existence of the age-old schism between the HE and vocational education and training (VET) (Mayer et al., 2003; Rothe, 2008; Reimer and Pollack, 2010; Orr and Hovdhaugen, 2014). In Germany, tracking into academic and vocational paths through the education system begins early on (Orr and Hovdhaugen, 2014, Orr and Riechers, 2010). Students who qualify to enrol in HE can either study at traditional universities or at the universities of applied sciences (*Fachhochschulen*). These institutions differ on the basis of the types of programmes offered, study times and entry routes (Reimer and Pollak, 2010). Traditional universities are theoretical and research oriented, offering a wide range of subjects. Universities of applied sciences offer vocation-oriented, applied education in particular areas, for example business, engineering and social sciences (HRK, 2014b). About one third of German HE students study in a *Fachochschule* (Statistisches Bundesamt, 2014).

Vocational education and training alternates between two places of learning, the vocational schools (*Berufsschulen*) and the professional settings where trainees gain on-job practical experience and knowledge. The training is usually two to three years long depending upon the occupation and the chosen subject area (Kaulisch and Huisman, 2007). Successful completion of the training entitles the young workers to work in occupations in their respective field of training. After a few years of work experience, they have the opportunity for further training while qualifying as 'master craftsmen', 'technicians' or 'graduate engineers' in their respective fields. This entitles them, for instance, to set up their own business in their area of expertise.

These divisions in the German education system affect pupils' academic performance and therefore their future access to HE, which has been criticized in the context of Germany's PISA results (OECD, 2012). Access to HE is determined by students' success in school leaving examination. The traditional route to HE is through *Abitur*, which is obtained by most holders (three in four) via the academic track school *Gymnasium* (Autorengruppe Bildungsberichterstattung, 2012a: 274). Students with Abitur are eligible to study at all types of tertiary education institutions (Mayer et al. 2003).

Alongside this group of students, there are others who obtain more vocationally oriented qualifications *Fachhochschulreife or Fachgebundene Hochschulreife*. Until recently, holders of these qualifications gained only restricted entry to HE. Students with a *Fachhochschulreife* were eligible to enter only certain types of HE institutions (*Fachhochschulen*, i.e. universities of applied sciences) and students with *Fachgebundene Hochschulreife* were eligible to HE studies only in certain subject areas. These qualifications can be obtained in many ways – most holders obtain it at specialized schools along with vocational training – *Fachoberschulen or Berufsfachschulen* (Kaulisch and Huisman, 2007).

In this highly differentiated system, students' social backgrounds influence their pathways to HE in many ways. First, pupils whose parents have attained HE themselves (i.e. pupils from HE backgrounds) are more likely to succeed in the academic track at school level, and are thus more likely to enter tertiary education via the traditional *Abitur* route. Second, the influence of social origin is also evident in the choice between universities and universities of applied sciences and third, in successfully completing HE degree programmes.

## Under-represented Groups in HE in Germany

### Arbeiterkind, or Children of the 'Working Class'

Germany is characterized by a large number of social inequalities in the access and successful completion of HE (Mayer et al., 2003; Reimer and Pollak, 2010). Traditionally, the impact of sociocultural and economic factors on access to tertiary education has been measured by the educational attainment of students' parents. As highlighted in the latest EUROSTUDENT report, only 2 per cent of all German students come from households with parents who have a low education background (Orr, Gwosc and Netz, 2011). Another study indicates that children of mothers with the highest level of educational attainment have almost three times higher chances of achieving tertiary education compared to children whose mothers had the lowest qualifications (Koucky, Bartusek and Kovarovick, 2010: 45). According to these results, the German HE system with its low social mobility and the considerable overrepresentation of students with high education background can be classified as social exclusive (Orr et al., 2011). It is even concluded that the impact of parental education on HE access has become larger in Germany since 2000 (Koucky et al., 2010).

An alternative indicator of socio-economic background is the occupation of students' parents. Again, several studies were able to prove the social inequalities in access to HE. For example, the recent OECD report highlights an under-representation of students from working-class background in the German tertiary education system. Only 28 per cent of Germans aged 25 to 34 attained tertiary education in 2011, and out of a total student population of 2.5 million in 2000, less than a quarter came from a working-class background (OECD, 2014: 20). Studies have also shown that social class or social origins of students are significantly related to their choice of educational path following secondary school (Duru-Bellat, Kieffer and Reimer, 2008). For example, in Germany students from the upper-service class are more likely to opt for traditional universities while students from the working class tend towards the vocational education and training route (Duru-Bellat et al., 2008).

The strong vocational aspect of the German education system has its advantages and disadvantages. Students with working-class backgrounds often find the vocational education and training route attractive as it provides them quick access to the labour market (Mayer et al., 2003: 35). However, at the same time, it keeps them away from the path of academic learning.

This then produces high levels of class inequality in participation in academic education (Mayer et al., 2003: 35).

*Second-chance Learners*
Another group under-represented in the German HE system includes 'second-chance learners':

> Students leaving school without a formal higher education entrance qualification, completing vocational education and acquiring higher education entrance qualification at (academic track) schools for adults (Abendgymnasium, Kolleg) or students without higher education entrance qualification who enter higher education institutions through special admission procedures.
>
> (Wolter, 2012: 48)

The focus on traditional entry qualification by German HE institutions results in the under-representation of this group of students in the HE system (Wolter, 2012) and also contributes to a low mobility between vocational and academic tracks (European Union, 2013; OECD, 2014). Until recently, second-chance learners were not the main target group of continuing education initiatives, which mainly targeted individuals with HE qualification along with additional work experience (European Union, 2013). In recent years, the Federal Ministry of Education and Research (*Bundesministerium für Bildung und Forschung* [BMBF]) has initiated several programmes to increase the participation of second-chance learners in tertiary education. Although the number of students entering HE via alternative routes has increased, they still constitute a relatively small percentage, especially when compared to other countries, which have had such second-chance routes for many years, for example Sweden and Norway (Orr and Hovdhaugen, 2014). Despite recent reforms, the transition from vocational education and training to HE is rarely made.

## ▶ Policy Programmes and Initiatives for Widening Access to HE

The importance of the social dimension in HE in the Bologna Process has been reaffirmed regularly in the official communiqués, including the most recent communiqué from Bucharest in 2012. In this, the ministers responsible for HE in the countries participating in the Bologna Process agreed

> that widening access to higher education is a precondition for societal progress and economic development and agreed to adopt national measures for widening overall access to quality higher education. The

Ministers emphasised that the student body entering and graduating from higher education institutions should reflect the diversity of Europe's population and agreed to step up their efforts towards underrepresented groups to develop the social dimension of higher education, reduce inequalities and provide adequate student support services, counselling and guidance, flexible learning pathways and alternative access routes, including recognition of prior learning.

(EHEA, 2012: 1)

Germany echoed the initiatives on European level in its Education Summit in October 2008 and later during the Standing Conference of Education and Culture Ministers in March 2009.

## Education Summit

The issue of second-chance entry routes was widely discussed at the Education Summit 2008. Emphasis was placed on opening up new access routes to HE by improving the permeability between vocational and academic education, thereby facilitating second-chance access routes to HE. The representatives of HE institutions as well as the business stakeholders welcomed this proposal. After this Summit, the German Rectors' Conference in cooperation with the German Chamber of Commerce and Industry formulated a joint declaration, in which they demanded valid and transparent entrance qualifications nationwide for people with vocational education and training. Further, they stressed that the study conditions should be modified to suit the needs and requirements of this diverse group of learners. This could be achieved by introducing options for part-time studies, bridging courses, and a family-friendly study structure (HRK and DIHK, 2008).

## Standing Conference of Education and Culture Ministers

Following up on the issue of second-chance access routes to HE, the Standing Conference of Education and Culture Ministers decided on uniform criteria for the transition from vocational education to HE. According to this decision, individuals with an advanced vocational certificate (*Meisterabschluss*) or comparable qualification attain an unconditional general entry qualification to HE. Further, individuals who have completed a two-year vocational education and training and have worked for at least three years in their profession obtain a subject-bound entry qualification to HE (Orr and Hovdhaugen, 2014; KMK, 2009).

In order to integrate the Standing Conference of Education and Culture Minister's decision into the state law, the regulations for HE in different German states have been changed in the last years. In all the states, new regulation for subject-bound entry qualification has been successfully implemented, although the attainment of general entry qualification is regulated differently in each state (Nickel and Duong, 2012: 27; Ulbricht, 2012). Several support programmes funded by the Federal Ministry of Education and Research (BMBF) and the Federal States have also been initiated at the universities and colleges to facilitate the development of second-chance routes to HE and additionally to increase the overall share of students with these new qualifications. These include programmes to encourage people in the labour market to return to HE – 'Advancement through Education' (*Aufstieg durch Bildung: offene Hochschulen*) and 'Crediting of Vocational Competences for Higher Education Study Programmes' (*Anrechnung Beruflicher Kompetenzen auf Hochschulstudiengänge – ANKOM*) as well as the programme 'Study Models of Individual Speeds', an initiative of the Federal State of Baden Württemberg. These programmes target broad groups of learners including employed individuals, part-time students, students with vocational qualifications and individuals with or without formal HE entry qualification.

▶ **Innovation in Practice**

This section describes in detail some of the programmes initiated to increase the share of under-represented groups within German HE institutions. For ease of understanding, these programmes have been grouped together on the basis of agencies responsible for these initiatives. The programme Study Models of Individual Speeds in particular is discussed in detail mainly because of its focus on increasing the flexibility of study programmes and opportunities for individual curriculum planning to meet the needs of specific learners. In addition, two initiatives – 'Rent a Student' and 'Arbeiterkind.de' are described. These two initiatives deserve special attention as they are run by universities, individuals and volunteers and primarily target current and prospective HE students from working-class background. All of these programmes showcase the diversity of agencies/actors involved in widening access to HE in Germany.

*Federal Initiatives – Advancement through Education and ANKOM*

The qualification initiative 'Advancement through Education' encompasses nationwide 26 projects delivered by HE institutions or university networks that have developed study programmes mostly for employed individuals. These study programmes aim to support universities' profiles in the area of lifelong learning in order to assure a pool of skilled professionals in a dynamic economy, improve permeability between vocational and academic education, and ensure a faster knowledge transfer into practice. The study programmes are based on different formats, for instance study courses alongside employment, dual and part-time study courses as well as certificate programmes (BMBF, 2014).

The initiative Crediting of Vocational Competences for Higher Education Study Programmes (ANKOM) was started by the BMBF in 2005 with the objective of increasing the permeability between vocational education and training and HE. The programme entails transferring the learning outcomes of vocational education and training into credits for recognition as part attainment towards a study programme at the HE institutions (BMBF, 2008). This involves first identifying qualifications and competencies as study equivalent to be credited towards bachelors and master's programmes and secondly developing transfer procedures and tools (BMBF, 2008).

These initiatives give evidence of the commitment of the Federal Ministry towards inclusive HE and high-quality academic teaching. The initiatives especially target working adults and strengthen lifelong academic learning. The inclusion of these learners in the HE system also leads to a more heterogeneous student body with varied needs, backgrounds and study requirements, which demands flexible study structures and support mechanisms (Orr, 2012). Consistent with these objectives is the programme Study Models of Individual Speeds that allows for flexible study structures and differentiated study programmes in order to meet the needs of a heterogeneous student body.

### Federal State Initiative – The Example of Baden-Württemberg

Regarded as a direct response to the decision of the Standing Conference of Education and Culture Ministers in 2009, the Ministry for Science, Research and Art Baden-Württemberg announced in the same year its call for proposals named Study Models of Individual Speeds (*Studienmodelle individueller Geschwindigkeit*). The objective of the proposal was to introduce study programmes that shape the first phase of the HE curriculum according to the individual needs and aptitudes of the students. These programmes aim at reducing dropout rates, ensuring success in studies and introducing individual-centred curriculum without compromising the quality of the training.

Funding of €5 million Euros was granted to five universities and six universities of applied sciences over a period of three years to implement these programmes. Every HE institution deals with the diversity of the student population in its own way, taking its own context into account. As a result, the types of interventions developed by the HE institutions under this initiative differ considerably from each other in their objectives and target groups. However, among the different types of study models, the three models of the Esslingen University, the Karlsruhe University of Applied Science and the University of Applied Science Stuttgart are similar in their measures, objectives and target groups. These three study models aim to reduce the HE dropout rates by introducing measures that increase the flexibility of the study programmes. The study models specifically target student groups who are at a particularly high risk of dropping out of the tertiary education, including these:

- New students, who received their entrance qualification at a vocational school or enter tertiary education with a vocational qualification, and those who experience difficulties in the early phase of their studies in adapting to the demands of the university teaching and learning
- New students with insufficient basic knowledge in mathematics and natural science
- New students with a lower scholastic aptitude, in other words, lack of skills related to independent and receptive learning
- Students who spend a greater amount of time per week on work-related activities due to their financial situation, often at the expense of their studies.

Traditionally, these groups of students are under-represented in the German HE system. In comparison to other European countries, the composition of the student population in German universities is relatively homogenous in terms of age and socio-economic background. For instance in Germany there is an overrepresentation of students from a high educational background and only 5 per cent of the students attending bachelor's programmes are 30 years or older (Orr, Gwosc and Netz, 2011). The inclusion of these traditionally under-represented groups in HE may result in a diverse student body but also demands increased flexibility in the curriculum and modes of teaching.

This would not have been such a problem under the old system of HE, where less structured course programmes allowed for greater flexibility, although this was arguably due to a loose study structure rather than purposeful programming consistent with students' needs and aspirations. The introduction of the new bachelor and master structure in the context of the Bologna Reforms has actually reduced the flexibility and increased the intensity of some study programmes. This has been seen as a major problem of the reform, especially when dealing with student populations that differ considerably in their social backgrounds, educational needs and professional experiences (Burckhart, 2014).

In this context, the most significant elements in these study models are the measures to increase flexibility of the study programmes within a defined and coordinated structure, consistent with students' needs and aspirations. The study models offer students who experience difficulties in the first stage of tertiary education an opportunity to divide single study terms to several part-terms. In the additional time thus available, learners are assisted by means of personal consultations, additional lectures and tutorials and skill training for optimized learning behaviour and strategies. The overall goal of these study models is to reduce the dropout rates among students experiencing difficulties in the initial phases of HE because of their previous educational and professional backgrounds. With these measures in place, students at the risk of dropping out can be identified at an early stage and, through individual guidance and counselling, the structure of the course programme can be altered according to their specific requirements. The first results of the evaluation by the DZHW (German Centre for Higher Education Research and Science Studies) indicate that the target groups were adequately reached by the study models. A comparison of the characteristics of participants in the study flexibility programme with the non-participants confirms that students with lower grades or negative self-evaluation of their performance and those at risk of dropping out were more frequently in the model group than in the comparison group. Through their continued participation in the programme, an improvement in individual study situation is expected and a subsequent decrease in performance-based difficulties can be achieved. Such types of measures are significant in encouraging second-chance learners, who differ strongly with regard to their previous education and professional biographies, their social heritage, their study-related conditions, competencies and demands, to enter and successfully graduate out of the HE system.

Another component of the initiative includes the promotion of skills and competencies. The new groups of students, especially second-chance learners who enter tertiary education without formal entrance qualifications, are more likely to lack certain subject specific knowledge and skills, for example mathematics, technology and language skills. While recent reforms have opened up pathways for second-chance learners to enter HE institutions, these learners require support and guidance in successfully transitioning to HE and in acquiring certain academic skills.

One study model that puts special emphasis on the promotion of academic skills is the MINT-Kolleg (mathematics, informatics, natural science, technology), a collaborative project of the University of Stuttgart and the Karlsruhe Institute for Technology (KIT). It is mainly designed for prospective students and new students in the science, technology, engineering and mathematics (STEM) disciplines; however, it also offers special courses for individuals transitioning from school or apprenticeships to universities to advance subject-related requirements and knowledge. There are basic courses in mathematics, information science, physics and chemistry and special preparatory courses for examinations in certain subjects, such as higher mathematics.

Next to deficits in basic knowledge of mathematics, many students lack strategies for an adequate learning behaviour and/or time management. Therefore, some of the study models also include measures that promote learning skills and coping mechanisms to deal with the demands of HE. These measures aim at optimizing learning strategies, time and stress management, and deal with examination-related anxiety.

## University Initiative – Rent-a-student

In addition to the Federal and State initiatives, a number of universities have initiated programmes to support diverse groups of learners throughout the course of their HE. These initiatives primarily target current and prospective HE learners from working-class and non-academic backgrounds. The German HE landscape is changing and is catering to the needs of broad and diverse groups of learners, enabling them to successfully access and complete their HE. In this context, universities are developing programmes and adopting good practices by means of curriculum modification, building teaching and learning competencies, diversity management, counselling and support, peer-to-peer learning and targeted orientation programmes to attract and support diverse learners (HRK, 2014c). One prominent example is the 'Rent-a-Student' initiative at the University of Bremen, which primarily supports first-generation learners through targeted orientation and peer guidance. The initiative Rent-a-Student provides prospective students a chance to experience university life. The prospective HE students accompany current students to their institutions to get an insight into their daily academic routine (PL4SD, 2014). The HE students provide information on courses and address pupils' concerns and questions related to HE system and programmes. This initiative facilitates prospective students in making an informed decision regarding future degrees and study programmes. The initiative is particularly helpful for students from working-class backgrounds and second-chance learners, as it helps them to overcome their inhibitions and anxieties associated with university education. At the same time, it assists young people on the verge of choosing between HE and vocational training in making an informed decision (PL4SD, 2014).

### Individual Initiative – ArbeiterKind.de

To attract new student groups that otherwise would not participate in tertiary education, universities and colleges have intensified their measures for orientation and information. Measures such as online information, open days or orientation weeks are essential for removing the existing barriers and in understanding university life and workloads (Leicht-Scholten, 2013). There is recognition in policy and research that the social and educational heritage of prospective students play an important role in the educational decision-making process. When first-generation students decide to pursue HE, they may lack the necessary information and guidance because of their non-familiarity with the institutions of HE.

Katja Urbatsch was a first-generation student who experienced a lack of support during her studies. Learning from her own experience, she began the initiative ArbeiterKind.de, a support network for pupils and students who are first in their family to aspire for HE. The initiative aims at encouraging pupils from working-class and non-academic backgrounds to opt for tertiary education and supporting them throughout the study phase until successful graduation. To achieve this, a nationwide network of 5000 voluntary mentors who are active in 70 local groups has been developed. These mentors help the students on-site, give answers to their questions and thereby compensate the otherwise lacking parental and peer guidance. Most of these mentors also come from a non-academic background, enabling them to share their experience with the (prospective) students and guide them during their course of study. In addition, the mentors organize information events at schools and HE institutions to attract and support these first-generation learners. The students are made aware of the available scholarship opportunities and are supported and guided in the application process. Further, an Internet portal provides information on study opportunities and requirements and potential sources for obtaining financial support (Urbatsch, 2013).

## ▶ Conclusion

As in other European countries, the German HE system has experienced a strong quantitative growth in student enrolments, although the growth has not been as strong as in other comparative countries. At the same time, the vocational arm of the German education system still remains very strong, and the chances of progressing to higher levels after completing the apprenticeship have been severely limited in the past. Indeed, the proportion of students entering universities via the accreditation of former vocational qualifications continues to be low (about 2%) (HRK, 2014d; Autorengruppe Bildungsberichterstattung, 2012b). Research also suggests that social inequality in access to HE and influence of parental education and social class on HE participation continues to persist.

In agreement with the policy agenda of other European countries towards an inclusive HE, as expressed particularly in the context of the Bologna Process and the communications of the European Union, Germany has committed to opening access to HE for their under-represented student groups. In Germany, administration of the education system, including HE, is the responsibility of the 16 Federal States. The German states have already integrated subject-bound entry qualifications into state laws, as per the decision of the Standing Conference of Education and Culture Ministers of the federal states in 2009. However, at the same time, the regulation on general entry qualification varies in different states. The decentralized state structure in Germany presents challenges in introducing similar measures uniformly across different states.

The German Federal Government and Federal States have promoted several initiatives encouraging universities to develop support structures and programmes to meet the special and diverse (educational) needs of new student groups. One of the most frequently used approaches in this context is the introduction of flexible study structures allowing for a balanced academic and personal life for students with special needs. The development, implementation and organization of flexible study structures entail modifications of the study and examination regulations, special counselling services and flexible time schedules.

All these initiatives provide project-based funding with the aim of kick-starting the development of new ideas and activities in this area. After a pre-determined amount of time, the developed measures should be adopted as normal practice by the HE institutions. However, considering the growing diversity in the composition of the student body as one of the major future challenges, basic funding is often not sufficient to advance study and support structures according to the changed needs and requirements on a sustainable basis. Therefore, the German Rectors' Conference calls for an increased basic funding to support HE institutions in their substantial efforts to improve the field of teaching and learning. Nonetheless, funding mechanisms on a competitive basis are essential in providing additional incentives for the development of support programmes for under-represented groups (HRK, 2013).

A major challenge that still remains is the differences in the mindset of the institutions of HE and vocational and training. The institutions of HE fear that the credit transfer and transition from vocational training may affect the quality of HE (BMBF, 2008).

Finally, regulations for study finances and study grants need to be adapted to the special situation of second-chance learners. Second-chance learners are more likely to be older than 30 years and may have family obligations to fulfil. The present federal student grants (BAföG) are not well suited towards them, as currently the age limit for receiving financial study support is 30 years. Here, a great need for renewal is necessary in order to encourage second-chance learners to enter HE (KMK, 2010).

Germany therefore can be seen as an HE system making efforts to become more inclusive on all system levels. At the same time, the fact that the social selectivity of German HE has existed for so long shows that opening access to under-represented groups also requires a change of mindset to complement the new policies, regulations and initiatives. This change represents the challenge for Germany in the coming years.

# 5 Extending Equity in Higher Education in an Equitable Society: The Finnish Dilemma

Ari Tarkiainen

### ▶ The Finnish Dream

Education systems are a product of the unique character of national decision and policymaking. The national education policy establishes the main goals and priorities pursued by the government in matters of education – at the sector and sub-sector levels – and focuses on specific aspects such as access, quality and teachers, or to a given issue or need. An education policy strategy specifies how the policy goals are to be achieved. An education policy plan defines the targets, activities to be implemented and the timeline, responsibilities and resources needed to realize the policy and strategy (UNESCO, 2013).

Although policymakers may attempt to steer and manipulate the education system, often as an entity in itself, the effectiveness of education is determined by wider social structures. Such structures are preconditions for agency and can be seen as a combination of such factors as social class; castes; ethnic, linguistic and religious division; and socially deprived, marginalized and vulnerable populations. These social groups often display different attitudes and values towards the utility of education, its priorities and the way in which it is delivered. This is often the main dilemma in many countries: the value of education, and in particular the value of higher education (HE), is not always so obvious. Education has had a special role in Finnish culture and history (OECD, 2010). It has been an essential part of the Nordic welfare state model. The value and importance of education is culturally and legally embedded in our society. According to the Constitution, Section 16, every citizen has the basic right to education and culture:

> The public authorities shall, as provided in more detail by an Act, guarantee for everyone equal opportunity to receive other educational services in

accordance with their ability and special needs, as well as the opportunity to develop themselves without being prevented by economic hardship.
(http://web.eduskunta.fi/)

Public authorities and government are obliged to secure equal opportunities for every resident in Finland to benefit from education after compulsory schooling and develop individually irrespective of their financial standing. This right is deeply embedded in the Finnish education policies and its systemic structures. The same opportunities to education should be available to all citizens irrespective of their ethnic origin, age, wealth or where they live. Education policy is built on this lifelong learning principle. Consistent with this commitment education is free at all levels in Finland from pre-primary to HE. Only certain forms of adult education require payment. The Finnish education policy guidelines emphasize four values – equality, efficiency, equity and internationalization. Those guidelines embody the Nordic welfare state model and its implementation in practice. Finland has also attempted to drive forward a broad-based innovation policy paradigm where service innovations, business models, working life innovations and innovations in public services are embedded in public policy. Education is its cornerstone. The education, research and innovation strategy aims to assure sustainable and balanced, social and economic development. This implies that education is also seen as an end in itself.

## ▶ The Finnish Education System

The Finnish education system is composed of three elements:

- ▶ Nine-year basic education (comprehensive school) for the whole age group, preceded by one year of voluntary pre-primary education
- ▶ Upper secondary education, comprising general education and vocational education and training (vocational qualifications and further and specialist qualifications)
- ▶ HE, provided by universities and universities of applied sciences.

Ministry of Education, Finland (2013) http://www.minedu.fi/OPM/Koulutus/koulutusjaerjestelmae/?lang=en.

The Finnish education system places great trust in the proficiency of their school leaders, teachers and educational staff, with no national standardized tests or high-stakes evaluation. Teaching is a highly prestigious profession. Teachers are required to have a master's degree that includes research and practice-based studies. Compared to workers with a tertiary education, their salary is slightly above the OECD average. They have pedagogical autonomy to teach and assess students' learning, which requires capacity and professional development for both. These attributes have been linked with Finland's success in PISA studies (OECD, 2015).

In recent years Finland has implemented many reforms and renewals in its education policy. Early childhood education and care (ECEC) has been the object of different reforms. Administration and steering of ECEC services were transferred from the Ministry of Social Affairs and Health to the Ministry of Education and Culture (2013). A Core Curriculum for Pre-School Education (2000) was established from 2001 and renewed in 2010 with National Curriculum Guidelines on ECEC (2003, renewed in 2005) for the design of local curricula. In addition, legislation on early childhood education and development of uniform pre-primary education instruction are in progress to ensure that all children have equal prerequisites. Finland has also launched some programs which have clear political aim to reduce dropouts and other problems in transition between education levels and entering to work (OECD, 2013). The first of them was The Preparatory Instruction and Guidance for VET (Ammattistartti) programme (initiated in 2006 and permanently adopted in 2010), developed to reduce early school-leaving and prevent school dropout by providing instruction to help students become familiar with educational and vocational opportunities and find a place in upper secondary education and training. This was followed by The Youth Guarantee (2013), which aims to help young people complete post-basic qualifications and find employment. The guarantee provides everyone under 25 years old and recent graduates under 30 years old either a job, a traineeship, a study place, a workshop or a labour market placement within three months of becoming unemployed.

Finland's investment in educational institutions is close to the OECD average. Expenditure on educational institutions at all levels is 6.5 per cent of GDP (the OECD average 6.8%). Between 2005 and 2010, Finland increased spending by 0.5 percentage points (slightly above the OECD average of 0.4 percentage points). Almost all expenditure on educational institutions is from public sources (97.6% compared to the OECD average of 83.6% in 2010). Private funding is marginal at all levels of education (except at the pre-primary level, where it amounts to 9.9% of expenditure), and it represents at most 4.1 per cent of expenditure at the tertiary level (OECD, 2013).

### ▶ The Finnish HE System

Universities receive funding from the state and also do external fundraising. With the Ministry of Education and Culture, the university agrees on operational and qualitative targets which provide the basis for the resources needed. Universities of applied sciences are funded by the government and local authorities and also have external sources of funding.

To ensure everyone has educational opportunities, student financial aid is designed to benefit a large proportion of students. Financial aid includes mainly study grants and housing supplements. Scholarships and/or other grants to households amount to 14.9 per cent of public expenditure for tertiary education, above the OECD average of 11.4 per cent. More than half of national students in first-degree programmes in tertiary-type A education (54%), benefit from scholarships and/or grants (OECD, 2013).

In Finland – as in the other Nordic welfare states – the central political goal has been to provide equal opportunities for students from different backgrounds (socio-economic starting points, gender, place of residence, etc.). All equal opportunity concepts involve determining where to draw the line in the equalization of opportunities and at which point to hold it fair that individuals should make an effort on their own and compete with each other (Roemer, 2000).

In the case of Finnish HE, the government has sought to level out the field first and foremost by means of comprehensive basic education, but just as importantly by increasing study places in HE (new universities and the polytechnics) – with a view to equal opportunity in regional terms – in different parts of the country. Probably the most important measure taken to promote equal opportunity in Finland was the regional expansion of the university sector which allowed some of the rural barriers to educational achievement in the country to be addressed.

The general conclusion to be drawn as regards policies designed to even out social and regional disparities in educational opportunity is that the only effective and thus widely and consistently used measure has been to increase education provision at all levels and throughout the country. However, in spite of the at times aggressive expansion, differences in participation rates have been relatively slow to decrease, which is an indication of the mechanisms of social selection operating within the educational system (MoE, 2013). Women's high participation rates in HE are not an indication of increased equal opportunity as such. In the first place, it can be explained by their large proportion of upper secondary school leavers (matriculated students), which for instance in 2002 was 59 per cent. This number is extraordinarily high compared to other countries, and it illustrates the impact of education policy in Finland. This can be explained partly because of their educational preferences and partly because more female than male (76% vs. 70%, respectively) matriculated students apply for HE. But it is more difficult for women to gain entry to tertiary education. In 2002, 42 per cent of women applicants and 58 per cent of men applicants gained entry and enrolled (MoE, 2013), even though the numbers of female students clearly exceed male students.

There is a distinct lack of data available where participation in HE by other measures of social background – in particular where socio-economic group are concerned (Kooij, 2015). This is a major issue for a country that places such store on education and educational opportunity. What evidence is available here is a little dated. Kivinen, Ahola and Hedman's work looks at the expansion of HE over the 1980s to 1990s. It shows that in 1980, the odds for children of the well-educated participating in HE was 13 times greater than that of children of fathers with only a basic level of education. Up to 1995, the gaps narrowed, but only slightly from 12 in 1985 to 10 in 1995 (Kivinen et al., 2001).

The Finnish university admissions system is unique in Europe. It is highly decentralized in contrast to other Nordic countries, for instance Sweden and Norway, where the system is more centralized and based mainly on grades in school certificates. In Finland admission is based on entrance examinations, which in a majority of cases differ from one university to another. The system in general is considered to be burdensome and expensive. The Ministry of Education (MoE) has permanently pushed universities to collaborate, with relatively little success. One reason for the growth of various forms of entrance examination has been the belief – supported by some research – that school success does not necessarily lead to success in HE. Separate examinations have also served as a part of 'second-chance' policies, especially in those fields where the number of adult applicants is relatively high.

For the Finnish student, financial aid is granted for a predetermined period, depending on the level of education. The amount of aid depends on the student's age, the form of housing, the level of education and means testing. In HE, the means testing usually concerns the student's own income; at other levels the parents' income also influences the amount of aid. The aid is granted by the Social Insurance Institution (KELA) in cooperation with the education institution concerned.

Students in Finland have the right to a study grant, and it is available as soon as they are no longer eligible for child benefits. Its amount depends on your age, housing circumstances, marital status, school and income. They are also entitled to housing, and it can be paid to students living in rented or right-of-occupancy accommodation. No age limits apply. Students who do not qualify for the housing supplement can apply for a general housing allowance.

Students may take with the government guarantee for study loan student can apply for a bank loan. No other security is needed for these loans. The loan is repayable but guaranteed by the government. The maximum amount of state-guaranteed loan is determined annually. The student loan is granted by a bank at its discretion. The interest and other terms are agreed by the bank and the student. The payback time is usually twice the duration of studies.

## ▶ Innovation in Access to HE

A number of specific policies and initiatives have been piloted in Finland which aim to make access to HE more equitable. Two of these initiatives are described here.

## ▶ Promoting, Assessing, Recognizing and Certifying Lifelong Learning

As with several other countries, Finland has introduced attempts to recognize and accredit prior learning. This process enables a student's competence, regardless of the methods of acquiring this competence, to be transferred into his or her studies and degree, if the requirements of the degree and curriculum are met.

The AHOT project, which ran from 2009–13 and was financed by the European Social Fund, aimed to harmonize the existing practices universities and universities of applied sciences. The development work started in 2009 as an experiment, but by the mid-2010s virtually all HE institutions were engaged. Universities and universities of applied sciences have clarified their rules and practices and implemented this process locally.

The challenge, however, has been that the whole system of recognizing and assessing non-formal education and work experience outside HE is very confusing. The AHOT system allows all students equal rights to utilize their earlier learning in different modes. The idea is to help HE institutions to assess, recognize and certify learning in the spirit of lifelong learning (Lafont and Pariat, 2012).

The AHOT system recognizes learning occurs in working life as well as in HE institutions. AHOT is underpinned by developments in counselling and guidance expertise services and reforms in learning and teaching. The range and scope of assessment has increased. Students can prove their learning skills and outcomes in numerous ways like collecting portfolios, writing reflective essays, showing certificates, attending proficiency tests, giving an expert lecture and so on.

This reform has improved greatly students' study trajectories. In terms of HE institutions, this has improved their efficiency and effectiveness. Earlier HE institutions had been very rigid in their lifelong learning practices and often underlined their sovereignty and autonomy. This has implied that the ways of recognition and assessment have varied across the country.

The AHOT system has had many positive outcomes for Finland. It shortens the study process and helps students to understand their capacity and competence; it seems to clarify the study process and decreases overlaps, and it makes the study process more individual.

## Open University Option – Educational and Regional Equity

After the establishment of Open University in the United Kingdom in 1969, Finnish universities also started to build a distance learning model. The Finnish open universities are part of the Finnish adult education system. In the 2010s, there are 15 universities that provide education to promote educational and regional equality. Open universities focus on adult students and pay for their education. The education is based on Finnish universities' undergraduate curricula. Education is open regardless of age or educational background. Students may have different goals such as to improve their general knowledge, to upgrade their basic education or their self-development (Official Statistics Finland, 2015).

Open University education is available in 120 localities throughout Finland, and lectures take place in the evening or weekends together with online learning. Because this kind of education is part-time and general in nature, students are not entitled to any social benefits. Every year over 70,000 people study at Finnish Open Universities (Official Statistics Finland, 2015). Some university departments may offer so-called 'Open University Route', through which they accept a small number of students with excellent grades to continue their university studies. This route is very selective and competitive. In general, one needs to apply for admission through student admission for a regular degree.

One very curious aspect of the Finnish Open University education is the University of the Third Age. This form of education started at the universities of Helsinki and Jyväskylä in 1985. There are nine universities providing this option, and there are 70 localities and 17,000 students (of which 70% are women) at the University of the Third Age. Those universities are open to all, and there no age limits. The activities include lecture series, seminars, courses, IT teaching, online teaching, study groups and travels. Teaching is provided in cooperation with summer universities, adult education centres and other partners.

This diversity in provision does not stop with open or distance learning. Many Finnish HE institutions organize summer schools in various disciplines and forms from May to August. They may consist of intensive courses, selection of individual courses or concentration on one particular scientific discipline. Summer schools are targeted for students and researchers already enrolled in HE.

There is also a national Summer University System in Finland that includes 20 summer universities, and they organize education across the country. Each year nearly 62,000 students, including 1100 foreign students, enrol in courses organized by Summer Universities (Summer Universities in Finland http://www.kesayliopistot.fi/). The association of Summer Universities was founded in 1972. Summer Universities also provide guidance and tutoring services, and have a learning coach network which enables students to participate in HE studies. They also offer many virtual learning and Finnish language courses for foreigners, and they organize support and advice for students having difficulties completing their theses.

Open university–type education is also part of adult education. Adult education in Finland is designed to provide study opportunities for adults. There are 800 educational institutions that arrange future and continuing education non-degree and degree education. Learning usually takes place in working life, and more than 1.7 million citizens participate in adult education each year. The aim is that 60 per cent of the working-age population would participate in adult education each year (Ministry of Education and Culture, Finland, 2012).

## Towards Multicultural Finland and Grappling with Globalization

Finland has always been a culturally very homogenous country. The number of foreign students has been quite low. One explanation for this is Finnish language which is ranked among the most difficult ones globally to master. One of the key issues in terms of integration is the language course but also other cultural and social peculiarities. 'Finland', as well as Finnish, needs much translation to foreigners.

Finland has two official languages: Finnish and Swedish. There are about 300,000 people speaking Swedish at their mother language. There are also other smaller, indigenous cultural minorities in Finland. The first Sami minority consists of 6000 people of which 3000 are speaking their own Sami language (Regional Council of Lapland, 2013). The second cultural minority is Roma minority, which includes 10,000 people and very few of them study in HE institutions (Lähteenmäki-Smith, 2011).

Very much has changed among Roma within the education sector in recent years. While in 2001 one third of Roma students couldn't get their nine-year basic school diploma by 2010 this had changed dramatically and 99 per cent of students were getting their diploma. But very few students take the general upper secondary school option and prefer vocational education instead. Finland is the only country in Europe where the education situation among Roma people has improved (Lähteenmäki-Smith, 2011).

It appears then that the Finnish approach of inclusive education, while a homogenous one, can benefit heterogenous groups. However, how can a country where inclusivity in education is so important to its identity address long-standing inequalities in HE? The major dilemma, where access of HE is concerned, is balancing a universal versus a targeted approach. Social policies are rarely based on purely universal, or purely targeted, approaches. Some measures are universal while others are targeted to groups that may be hard to reach through universal measures. Both types of spending may be justified, depending on each country's situation. A policy framework grounded in universalism in the provision of essential public services but with special measures in implementation can be more effective in reaching certain segments of the population that face greater challenges than others in overcoming poverty and deprivation (United Nations, 2013). Such a methodology may need to be applied to HE in Finland. The question is can this be done, especially as the Finnish HE system also has to cope with the globalization of HE itself.

## ▶ Finland and the Opportunity Wars

Brown, Lauder and Ashton (2011) argue that the traditional link between good education and good job and good life has been cut off. In other words, they claim that the window of opportunity education and in particular HE offers has become opaque in the early twenty-first century. They argue that we have now a 'global auction' for jobs and HE. If we accept this it means that the ethos of education will need to change dramatically.

In terms of HE there are huge challenges governments are facing: what the purpose of HE is in the twenty-first century? How can HE and sustainable economic growth co-exist? To what extent should market forces shape HE and what is the role of the public sector? How should HE be governed? How should tertiary education be arranged in the future and what is the role of HE?

All this implies that governments must rethink what their regulatory regimes will be in the future. Are they national or are they global? Other challenges are the funding procedures of part-time students and new modes of tertiary education. Governments must clarify the connections and relationships between universities, regions and innovation.

Finland has to confront these challenges. It is not clear what kind of impacts the globalization will have. One very disconcerting fact is that Finnish society, while more equal than most others, is still unequal and the distance between the poor and the rich is not decreasing. It is our own choice whether we accept it or not.

# 6 The United Kingdom: The Access-to-Higher-Education Nation?

Graeme Atherton

### ▶ Introduction

The issue of who goes to higher education (HE) is, as in most chapters in this book, of relatively recent concern to most HE institutions and policymakers in the United Kingdom. However, the nature of the concern reflects far more long-standing issues. How inequalities in access to HE are addressed in the United Kingdom in recent years have come even more to reflect these historical differences between the four nations that constitute the union. The policies and practices adopted across the four nations increasingly reflect how the nations themselves are (re)asserting their own individual identities. This chapter explores the evolution of widening access work in the four different nations of the United Kingdom. It looks at how social class pervades access work across the four countries but interacts with particular social and political characteristics so that where access to HE is concerned, it only makes partial sense to talk about the United Kingdom here. It argues that each nation is going in its own way where access to HE is concerned.

### ▶ HE in the United Kingdom

In terms of numbers of learners entering HE, as well as number and range of institutions, England dwarves the other three nations. Table 6.1 shows the number of institutions and learners in the respective nations. It shows how England dwarfs the other nations on each measure.

Table 6.1 shows that in England there are actually over 300 organizations that can provide HE, but only 120 that have the status of institution. It does not include students studying HE in further education institutions. There are approximately 180,000 learners studying in what is described as 'further

**Table 6.1** Total Student Numbers and HE Institutions in the United Kingdom 2013–14

| Country | Undergraduate Students | Postgraduate Students | Institutions |
|---|---|---|---|
| England | 1,456,530 | 445,835 | 120 |
| Scotland | 162,160 | 53,440 | 17 |
| Wales | 100,490 | 28,635 | 8 |
| Northern Ireland | 40,735 | 11,525 | 4 |
| **Total** | | | 149 |

Source: Data taken from www.hesa.ac.uk.

education' (FE) in the United Kingdom in a range of programmes that are separate from those associated with HE.

However, although England may have by far the most students, this does not mean it has the highest percentage of its younger learners progressing to HE. Table 6.1 depicts the number of learners studying in HE, but this is a little different from the tertiary education measure the OECD uses to try to capture the size of the post-secondary education population in a particular country. Figure 6.1 shows that Northern Ireland is by a large margin the best performing of the four UK nations on this measure.

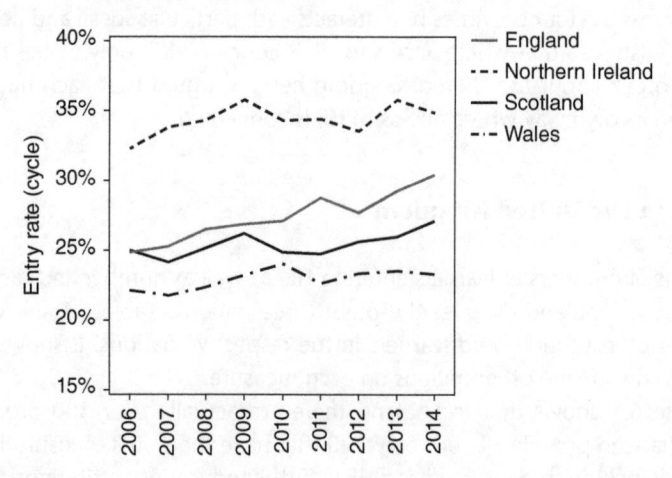

**Figure 6.1** Proportion of 18-year-olds Accepted for Entry to HE by Cycle and Country of Domicile.
Source: UCAS (2014: 12).

Figure 6.1 shows that across the four nations, participation in HE overall has grown over the last 15 years, but that growth has slowed in recent years. Interestingly, growth has slowed across all countries, despite their taking a quite different attitude to how HE should be paid for. In 2012, the English government pushed through a controversial set of reforms that increased the amount that HEIs could charge to enter their institutions to £9000 per year. Virtually all of them chose to do this. The other three nations took very different cues from the English decision, as Table 6.2 shows:

**Table 6.2** HE Financial Support Available in the United Kingdom

| Country | Summary of Costs/Support |
|---|---|
| England | Students from all nations can be charged fees up to £9000. Loans and grants are available for English students dependent on their own or parental income. |
| Scotland | Students from Scotland do not have to pay fees, but universities can charge those from elsewhere in the United Kingdom up to £9000 (although the Welsh Assembly will subsidize costs for Welsh students). |
| Wales | Fees above £3465 are paid by the Welsh assembly for Welsh students, wherever they study in the United Kingdom. But students from England, Scotland and Northern Ireland have to pay the full cost. |
| Northern Ireland | Fees for students from Northern Ireland will remain at about £3500 a year, but students from Scotland, England and Wales will be charged higher fees. |

### *Participation in HE by Social Background*

Figure 6.1 gave an indication of differences in HE participation across the United Kingdom. Differences in HE participation by a measure of socio-economic group and ethnicity are shown in Figure 6.2. The measure of socio-economic group used is geographic. The POLAR (participation of local areas) measure of disadvantage was first produced by HEFCE in the mid-2000s. It classifies applicants on the basis of the university participation rate of their home area. These are small areas, the size of census sub-wards, and are classified into five equally sized groups (quintile groups). The lowest participation quintile (the 20% of areas with the lowest HE participation rates) are taken to be the most disadvantaged where entry to HE is concerned. Figure 6.2 shows how there have been increases in participation rates by younger learners from across all social backgrounds in the early 2010s. As stated in the 2014 publication by the Universities and Colleges Admissions Service (UCAS)

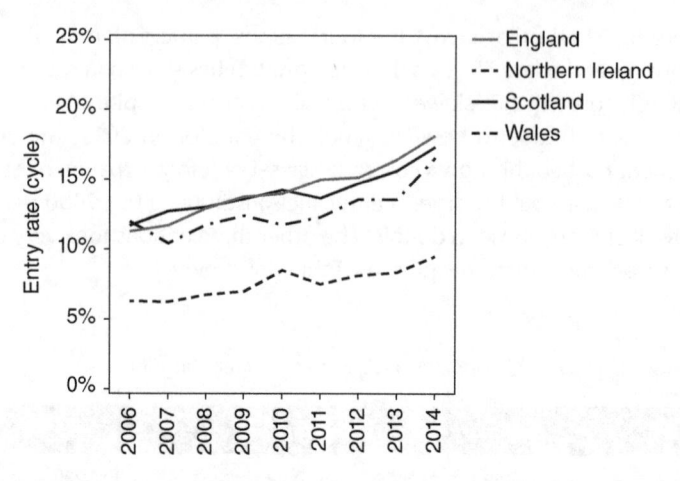

**Figure 6.2** Eighteen-year-old Entry Rates for Disadvantaged Areas (POLAR2 Q1) by Country of Domicile.
Source: UCAS (2014: 74).

from which the figures were taken: 'In all countries, the entry rate for 18 year olds from the most disadvantaged areas increased over the period. Compared with entry rates five years ago, in 2009, 18 year olds from these disadvantaged areas were around 34 per cent (England and Wales), 28 per cent (Northern Ireland) and 36 per cent (Scotland) more likely to be accepted for entry in 2014' (UCAS, 2014: 73).

The data illustrate the differences across the four nations where participation in HE is concerned. Understanding these differences requires a more detailed examination of the policies and practices adopted to address inequalities in access to HE in each nation.

*Northern Ireland*
The principality of Northern Ireland should not be defined by the historic tensions between Protestants and Catholics regarding whether it should be part of the United Kingdom. But neither can anything pertaining to Northern Ireland be understood separately from it. The challenge faced in trying to widen access to HE is unique in the UK context in having to confront a kind of social division based on an interaction between religion and socioeconomic group. Learners from Catholic backgrounds perform better in Northern Ireland. The schooling system is itself segregated to a significant degree, with Catholic pupils tending to go to more high-achieving schools (Fergus, 2014). This feeds through into HE participation with just one in ten working-class Protestant pupils going on to university, compared with one in five Catholics from similar backgrounds (Purvis, 2011).

Differences by religion interact with socio-economic inequality. The result is that although, as shown above, by the geographic POLAR measure Northern Ireland may lead the UK, white Protestant boys in receipt of free school lunches (young people from low-income families in the United Kingdom are in receipt of such a benefit) have the lowest levels of HE participation of any social group in the United Kingdom (Nolan, 2014).

The years since the mid-1990s have seen a political stability between the two groups that contrasts greatly with the troubles of the 1970s and 1980s. The foundation for this stability was the devolution of political power, including responsibility for HE, to Northern Ireland in 1998. This has enabled Northern Ireland to take its own approach to access to HE, and it has in recent years attempted to prioritize access through Access to Success, it's new regional strategy for widening participation, published in 2012. Rather than being a strategy led and shaped by one government department, as it is in England, the aim was to work with a range of stakeholders throughout. As the Deputy Secretary for Employment and Learning stated in 2010:

> My Department is now leading in the development and delivery of a regional integrated strategy for widening participation. It had received commitments from the Department of Enterprise, Trade and Investment, the Department of Education, the Department of Health Social Services and Public Safety and the Department for Social Development to work with it and other key stakeholders in the Universities, the University Colleges, Schools, Further Education colleges and Students Unions in the development and implementation of a fully integrated regional strategy for widening participation.
>
> (Hamilton, 2010)

This approach by the government and the work of the different universities show how widening community access can be extended beyond those just in education. The strategy lays out a national plan for widening access to HE, including a range of measures that commit to advancing the use of contextual data, rigorous evaluation, a coherent access programme and a recognition of the importance of attainment.

> To achieve a high level of integration the new widening participation outreach programmes will be overtly 'badged' with the generic widening participation branding developed in the single awareness raising programme. Programmes may cover any of the identified widening participation cohorts of disadvantage or disability and will incorporate significant attainment raising elements.
>
> (DELNI, 2012: 27)

There are excellent examples of innovative practice from the two universities in Northern Ireland. The Step Up programme from the University of Ulster is particularly interesting. It is based around the delivery of a full Applied Science A Level qualification to 16- to 18-year-old students. There are two key features to this project: first, the focus on curriculum delivery and attainment, as opposed to the broader, less intensive access work more common in England. The second is the range of partners involved in the delivery of the qualification. Besides universities and participating schools, it involves companies, government organizations and local hospitals.

Taking a lead from the work of the Office for Fair Access (OFFA) in England, as described below, Northern Ireland has also constructed its own Access Agreements. Introduced in 2006, their objective was that 'any institution that decided to raise its full-time undergraduate tuition fees above the standard level was required to have an Access Agreement in place which would outline its provision of student support, including bursaries and outreach activities' (DELNI, 2010b).

## Scotland

The position of Scotland with regard to tuition fees usually marks them out as distinctive in the United Kingdom. In 2001, the decision was taken to abolish fees and introduce a 'graduate endowment'. Graduates paid a maximum of £2289, with the money raised being given to poorer students in the form of bursaries. This was abolished in 2008, leaving them as the only nation in the United Kingdom where it is free for all students to go to HE. One would expect this disparity not only to lead to an exodus of learners from England to Scotland (it does not because they have to pay the same fees as in England), but also a clamour to enter HE. There has not been such a clamour. As Figure 6.1 shows, entry to HE has not increased in percentage terms by very much in recent years. This shows clearly that student finance regimes do not alone define who enters HE. Scotland has a significant number of areas where incomes are low; a rural element to its population where HE lacks visibility; and an economic profile that still remains skewed toward industrial sectors, where HE qualifications have not in the past been required to progress. These factors feed through to relative underachievement in schooling for many young people, as would be expected. Scotland does have a much stronger tradition of post-secondary education at sub-degrees of what the OECD may describe as Tertiary B level than England, for example (McGoldrick, 2005). The reason for this greater role for FE in HE provision is historical and relates to the way in which Scotland dealt with the expansion in HE participation across the whole of the United Kingdom in the early 1990s,[1] and also the longer tradition of local authority involvement in vocational education (McGoldrick, 2005).

Of those studying for HE level qualifications in Scotland, nearly 20 per cent are based at FE colleges, and these students are more likely to be from lower socio-economic groups (SFC, 2015). Progression into the FE sector in Scotland provides a route into HE that is again distinctive in the UK context.

The lack of tuition fees in Scotland, in comparison to the inflated costs in England, has understandably been something that Scottish politicians have been keen to use to make political capital. As Alex Salmon, ex-leader of the Scottish National Party (SNP), stated in 2014:

> The single biggest achievement by this Government has been the abolition of tuition fees. This one action has restored Scotland's long tradition of education being based on ability to learn – not the ability to pay.
> (Johnson, 2014)

Access has therefore been prominent on the policy agenda, and it becomes intertwined with a bigger narrative surrounding Scotland's place or (as many would prefer it, lack of a place within the United Kingdom. To a considerable extent as well, the rhetoric regarding the importance of access to HE in Scotland can be supported by the broader policies implemented here. Since the 1990s, Scotland has been enjoying funded collaborative initiatives to bring together schools, colleges and HEIs. The Scottish government, like that in England, invested heavily in widening access partnership based work in the 2000s. The widening access regional forums (WARFs) were set up in 1999–2000 and funded by the Scottish HE funding council. There were four WARFs covering the whole of Scotland, and they were partnerships of universities, colleges, local authorities, Skills Development Scotland and other relevant stakeholders. The WARFs were led and funded through HEIs and received approximately £3 million of funding per year (SFC, 2009). The WARFs developed widening access tools in the 2000s, delivered in sequential, planned ways (SFC, 2009; LEAPS, 2011). They not only worked with schools but also engaged with adults and community organizations (SFC, 2009). Scotland restructured this investment in 2011, ending its WARF programme, but since the 1990s, it has continued to have government-funded access partnerships. The Schools for Higher Education Programme focuses on named schools with low progression to HE, and pupils aged 14–18 who may not achieve their HE potential (SFC, 2011).

*Access in Scotland in the 2010s*
Neither has the government been content to see a commitment to free tuition as the extent of its efforts where access is concerned. In 2012, it introduced 'outcome agreements' to try to structure the relationship between the Scottish government's HE Funding Agency and individual HE institutions

(HEIs). These outcome agreements cover not just access to HE but also the student experience, knowledge exchange, employability and reducing carbon emissions. They are designed to be based around the different nature of Scotland's 19 HEIs (Universities Scotland, 2014).

In addition to the outcome agreements, Scotland went a step further than the other home nations in 2013 by 'ring-fencing' places in nine of their HEIs specifically for young people from the most deprived 40 per cent of neighbourhoods. The Scottish government invested £10 million in these 2000 extra places (SFC, 2015). The aim was to try to create a scenario where universities felt able to admit extra students and not lose out financially.

The commitment to access to HE shown by the Scottish government has led to progress. Like all the four nations, Scotland has its own set of targets where access is concerned. *Learning for All*, an annual publication produced by the Scottish government, contains data on HE progression by a range of groups. These include progression rates among those who live in the 20–40 per cent most deprived areas in Scotland, the profile of those learners progressing pupils from low-participation schools, students who enter university direct from FE and those who have benefited from the ring-fenced places described above. The 2015 report shows progress in all these areas – and in particular the impact of the ring-fenced places on the make-up of students at the universities who have enjoyed such places.

What the report does not highlight is the differences in participation by institutional type and social background. As in England, there are some clear divisions in Scotland in terms of participation between research-intensive (branded 'the ancients') and non-research-intensive institutions (Weedon, 2014).

## Wales

As with Scotland and Northern Ireland, Wales also has a mix of state-supported pro-active investment in university activities with schools and other organizations to encourage the broadening of participation in HE, along with compliance agreements that form the basis of the Scottish approach. Wales also echoes Scotland in having its own unique geographical way of identifying those from lower socio-economic backgrounds and targeting investment to them. Communities First areas are the 100 most deprived geographical areas in Wales. There are also targets for the numbers of students that the Welsh government would like to see taking some of their courses through the medium of the Welsh language and from Communities First areas (HEFCW, 2011).

Wales has its own partnership-based, state-funded programme to widen access to HE. The Reaching Wider programme, established in 2002, aims to increase HE participation from groups and communities in Wales by raising aspirations and creating new study opportunities and learning pathways to HE. It engages with four main groups of people of all ages who are currently under-represented in HE:

- People living in Communities First areas
- People who wish to study in the medium of Welsh
- Disabled students
- Those from black and ethnic minority communities

Four regional Reaching Wider Partnerships have been established to co-ordinate activities in North Wales, West and Mid Wales, South West Wales and South East Wales, and ensure local skills are used to provide relevant learning opportunities for local people.

The Reaching Wider partnerships received nearly £2 million in 2014. The challenges that Reaching Wider faces include engaging non–HEI stakeholders as equal partners, aligning the work to broader HE strategies and HEIs own access work, identifying and targeting the right learners and producing a convincing narrative around impact (HEFCW, 2011). A review of widening access and Reaching Higher Strategies in Wales in 2012, however, presents the access work in Wales in a favourable light, arguing that significant progress is being made there to connect the work of HEIs strategically with that of the state-funded Reaching Wider Partnerships.

> The review welcomed the strong commitment to widening access demonstrated in the strategies by the HE sector in Wales. The Welsh Government and HEFCW have continued to regard widening access (WA) as a priority and the strategies showed that the institutions and Partnerships were enhancing their approaches to contribute to a regional framework to further this agenda. There were seven examples of excellent practice which were effective and innovative contributing to high quality WA work in Wales. In some areas, such as Partnerships and work with looked-after young people, Wales is ahead of the other nations in the UK and is leading the way with these developments.
> (Hill and Hatt, 2012: 3)

Rather than Access Agreements like those in Northern Ireland or England, or outcome agreements like those in Scotland, in Wales HEIs have to agree 'fee plans' with the Higher Education Funding Council for Wales (HEFCW). These are annually submitted documents 'detailing the investment they will make in support of equality of opportunity and the promotion of HE' (HEFCW, 2015: 1).

## England

The contemporary history of access to HE in England dates from the late 1990s. However, the roots of the policies and practice pursued since this time can be traced further back. The review of HE instigated by a Conservative government in the early 1960s introduced the idea that HE should be available to all of those who were able to benefit from it (Committee on Higher Education, 1963). The review came after the system started to expand with the introduction of 'polytechnics', which were designed to be institutions of higher vocational learning akin to similar institutions.

The expansion of the system was steady, but not spectacular, up to the 1990s. Overall participation in HE increased from 3.4 per cent in 1950 to 8.4 per cent in 1970, 19.3 per cent in 1990 and 33 per cent in 2000 (National Committee of Inquiry into Higher Education Dearing Report, 1997). In terms of access and equity, neither was this a preoccupation of policymakers over this period. Where it did become an issue was in relation to the participation of adult learners. The 1970s saw the advent of specific courses for older students with no or few school-level qualifications which provided a direct entry route into HE (albeit in the majority of cases, into only certain subject disciplines). These courses were the product of activists drawing on a long tradition of working-class-led education, positioning access in political narrative surrounding the disempowerment of the working class in the midst of the deindustrialization of the 1970s and 1980s. In contrast to the widening access work that followed in the 2000s, the 'access movement' was far more bottom-up based around action at local and community levels (Benn and Burton, 1995).

## ▶ Aimhigher and the Widening Participation Years

The binary system of HE in England effectively ended in the early 1990s as polytechnics and other non-university-titled HE institutions were able to apply for university status. Without exception, polytechnics saw this as an opportunity to cement their academic credibility and one not to be missed. It was in many ways a logical progression. Unlike in much of mainland Europe, the polytechnics had not defined themselves in any way as providers of vocational education. There had been a process of 'academic drift' since the 1960s as the polytechnics started to offer courses much closer to what universities provided (Pratt, 1997).

Following the creation of the much more unitary university system, enrolments increased dramatically. This increase was also fuelled by changes in the examination system in English schools, which pushed up qualification rates sharply at the end of compulsory schooling. This expanded the pool of qualified potential HE entrants. The final ingredient was a UK economy finding a new identity after the traumas of the late 1970s and 1980s. Many of the old 'good' jobs for school leavers, in administration work and manufacturing, were gone. Going to university suddenly became the default option for many more young people than ever before.

It was not until the late 1990s and election of a new Labour government, however, that this increase in access fed through to a concern for equity issues. Shortly after this government came to power in 1997, another major review of HE was released, authored by the academic Ron Dearing (National Committee of Inquiry into Higher Education [Dearing Report, 1997]). It recommended for the expansion of sub-degree courses, and degree-level courses at university, arguing that there was a case for HE expansion based on demand from employers for applicants with higher qualifications. Although the so-called Dearing Review may have highlighted the importance of greater access, more important was the way in which further extending both access and equity fitted with Labour's broader vision for education in the twenty-first century, and indeed social democracy. Labour's ambition at this time was to couch its principles in terms which resonated with the challenges of the era. Where this fits with access to HE is best encapsulated in what sociologist Anthony Giddens describes as the 'redistribution of possibilities' (1998: 101). The focus became less on the direct distribution of resources to those in lower-income groups and more on how they could be supported to take their position in the knowledge economy of the twenty-first century. Such beliefs gave an ideological foundation to the commitment made by the Labour government in 2001 that 'by the end of the decade, 50% of young people should have the opportunity to benefit from higher education by the time they reach 30 years of age' (Court, 2001).

The major vehicle by which the increase in participation from groups under-represented in HE was to be achieved was through the Aimhigher programme. Aimhigher brought together schools and FE and HE institutions in 42 regional partnerships across England. Over £500 million was invested in Aimhigher from 2004 to 2011. Aimhigher focused on supporting wider participation in all HEIs and all forms of HE study, with a concentration on learners from lower socio-economic groups. It did, however, also fund work for those with disabilities, those from specific ethnic groups and those young people who were in the care of local authorities. It also concentrated the vast majority of its efforts on young entrants. The objectives of Aimhigher were to raise the aspirations of learners and improve the information, advice and guidance they received regarding HE, and to support schools and FE colleges to improve attainment (Atherton, 2012).

## ▶ After Aimhigher

The increase in the maximum tuition fee chargeable by a HEI to £9000 in 2012 also ushered in a new era for access to HE in England with the much-heightened importance placed on access agreements and the greater prominence given to the Office for Fair Access (OFFA). When fees were first introduced in 2003, Access Agreements and the Office for Fair Access (OFFA) were also born. However, it was not until 2012 that these agreements gathered real importance. Reproduced below is the view of the government at the time regarding the role of OFFA, its Director and also Access Agreements.

> The remit of the Director of Fair Access is to promote and safeguard fair access to higher education. The principal mechanism for achieving this will be requiring institutions that wish to charge more than the basic level of graduate contributions to agree new Access Agreements with you, setting out how they will promote access by underrepresented groups and the progress they intend to make. The level of ambition set out by the Access Agreement should be proportionate to how much more than the basic level the institution intends to charge. While recognising that it is for each institution to determine its own admission arrangements, the Government believes that it would be appropriate for every Access Agreement to include a quantified assessment of the improvement the institution intends to make against appropriate benchmarks. The larger the gap between current performance and benchmarks for a given institution, the more ambitious its targets should be.
>
> (BIS, 2011)

OFFA was to be given the power to impose sanctions on institutions which do not take adequate measures to safeguard equity in access. It is argued that this new regime has led to increased investment overall in access to HE work. Figure 6.3 shows how investment has increased since the early 2010s.

Most of this investment, however, is in the form of financial support and is in place mainly to ameliorate the high levels of tuition fees. Nor has there been any evidence yet of the sanctions that OFFA, in theory, could implement (Attwood, 2011).

Access Agreements themselves, though, have secured a commitment to widening access work from institutions themselves, which could be perceived as more significant than under the state-funded regime of the 2000s. This commitment, however, is constructed through the lens of institutional strategic interest. How HEIs choose to fulfil their Access Agreement therefore differs significantly by size, location and institutional type.

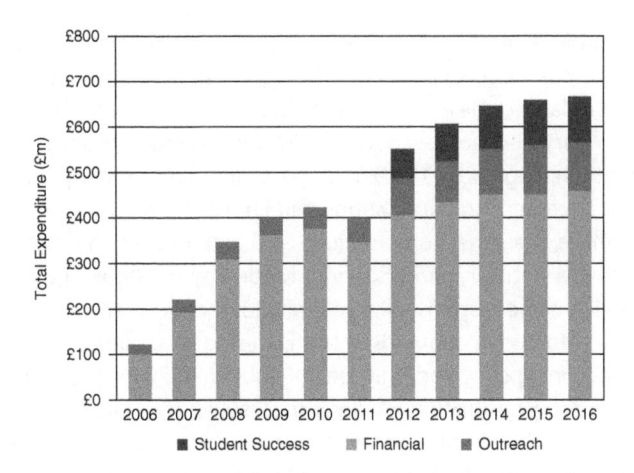

**Figure 6.3** Expenditure on Office for Fair Access–related Activities 2006–07 to 2016–17.
Source: HEFCE/OFFA (2013).

The investment in access by the state did not end with Aimhigher, however. As well as the Aimhigher investment, there was an even bigger amount allocated to HEIs on a pro rata basis related to the number of students attending the institution. The student opportunity allocation began in 1999. It is worth over £300 million per year to the sector (HEFCE, 2015). The majority of that allocation is steered toward supporting the success of the learners from widening access backgrounds when they enter HE, as opposed to helping more such learners in.

## After Labour

There is a case to be made that since 2000 no country in the world has benefited from as much investment per capita in widening access to HE work. The reasons for this are entirely a reflection of the politics of the times (and to an extent the past). Labour's legacy where access was concerned was to move up the policy agenda so that their successors felt obliged to put in place a system to deal with inequalities in HE participation that could be argued politically to be as, if not more, robust than what it replaced. But challenges remain. They fall into three main areas in the mid-2010s.

## Engagement of Schools

There is no specific ring-fenced funding to enable schools to engage staff with a specific remit for supporting progression into HE for those from lower socio-economic groups, as was the case under Aimhigher. Nor during the 2010s, so far, has it been a priority of the Department of Education, who fund schools in England (unlike in the other three nations, where the responsibility for secondary and post-secondary education is separated across different departments in England). The 2010s have also seen a sharp reduction in investment in careers guidance support in England (Watts, 2013).

Again unlike the other three nations and many other countries, England does not have a statutory careers service funded by the state. The provision of careers advice is the responsibility of individual schools. This responsibility is very weakly enforced in comparison to the raising of attainment, which dominates educational policy and practice in England. In 2015, the consequences of placing the responsibility for widening access entirely with HEIs in terms of patchy and variable school engagement was somewhat belatedly recognized by policymakers, and £20 million was invested in a new National Networks of Collaborative Outreach (NNCO) programme to provide online single points of contact (SPoC) at the local level (Morgan, 2015). These SPoCs would mainly constitute websites, where HEIs would place information regarding the outreach work they were providing for schools and colleges.

▶ *The progression of older and part-time students*

Although there has been measurable progress in improvements in participation among younger learners from lower socio-economic groups since the increase in fees in 2012, there have been very worrying falls in participation among older learners. There have been attempts to account for this decline, but they remain partial in their ability to explain it. Undoubtedly the increase in cost has been a major factor, but a system that is still culturally and structurally constructed around a narrow model of full-time study for young people as being what HE participation means may be equally to blame (Universities UK, 2013).

▶ *Supporting success and progression*

In the early 2010s, the combination of steady progress in the widening of access in England, the large increase in fees and increasing concerns regarding graduate unemployment/under-employment has led to a shift in priorities where this agenda is concerned. Access still matters, but attention is turning more and more to progression and success for learners from groups under-represented in HE. The HEFCE released research in 2013 which seemed to capture the problem. HEFCE's analysis appeared to show that even after controlling for prior educational attainment and institution attended, students

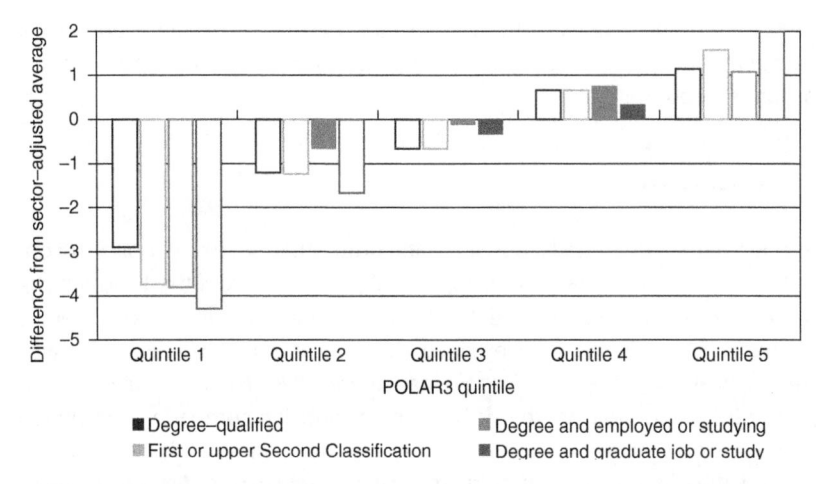

**Figure 6.4** Percentage Point Difference of the Outcome from the Sector-adjusted Average, Split by POLAR3 Quintile.
Source: HEFCE/OFFA (2013).

from lower socio-economic groups, those with disabilities and black students were less likely to achieve their possible potential either when in HE or post HE. Figure 6.4 illustrates the 'potential gap' by POLAR quintile for those from lower socio-economic groups. Those in the lowest participation neighbourhoods are significantly more likely to under-achieve.

The approach taken to success and progression challenge has relied in the main on improvements in learning and teaching (Thomas, 2012). Other approaches, in particular the more specific targeting of learners from certain social backgrounds, appear to be difficult to countenance in the English context, unlike in the United States.

Access without success is of limited value. Indeed, in the English context it may be quite damaging given the debt it is necessary to accumulate. The danger here is that the progress being made in gradually increasing the number of learners from access background entering HE is either assumed to be something that can continue without investment, and/or the view is taken that enough progress has been made. The concept that best describes the need to focus on not just access but also success is the student life cycle (BIS, 2014). First developed in the early 2000s, it refers to the journey taken by students from pre- to post-HE. It suggests that conceiving of the HE 'student experience' as something that occurs only from the point of admission to graduation is to take a narrow viewpoint. But what is important here is that the already febrile institutional and cultural support for access, in comparison to that of other nations in the United Kingdom, is not made even weaker by attempts to focus on the success of students from widening access backgrounds through HE.

## ▶ Conclusions

In their 2011 article, Gallacher and Raffe argue that where HE policy is concerned, despite the changes in responsibility for HE across the United Kingdom since the late 1990s, initiated by the demand for devolution, there is as much convergence as divergence. Looking at access to HE specifically, there has also been a mix of convergence and divergence. However, when placed in the context of what is happening globally, comparing the United Kingdom to other countries in this book, it is the commonalities in approach in the United Kingdom that start to appear more striking. Moreover, these commonalities are in the main distinctive from any of the countries examined in this book. These commonalities can be summarized below:

### Depth of Commitment to 'Outreach Work'

With the exception of the United States, the United Kingdom has probably the most developed body of practice and largest community of practitioners working on collaborative activities between schools/colleges and HEIs which support HE progression for those from under-represented groups in the world.

### Richness of Data

The United Kingdom also is one of the richest environments in the world where data on who participates in HE are concerned. There are well-developed systems of data collection and analysis that include all four countries. Each nation also has its own idiosyncratic way of prioritizing who participates. There is, however, a common reliance on geographical measures – a trait criticized by some for its inaccuracies (Osborne and Shuttleworth, 2004).

### Prevalence of Compliance Agreements

Where the United Kingdom is particularly unique is in its use of compliance, target-based HE participation agreements between government and HEIs. Although all the agreements differ slightly, they cover many of the same issues (student financial support and outreach work). They are also designed to be sensitive to individual difference.

## The Dominance of Social Class

The final area of commonality concerns the importance placed on socio-economic background or proxy measures of it in defining whom access to HE should be widened for. Although each nation may have its own version of how socio-economic background should play into access to HE, relative to the majority of countries examined in this book there is a heavy reliance on this 'legitimized category' for access to HE.

However, although the commonalities above are important, they do not mean that the differences between the nations do not matter. The United Kingdom in the mid-2010s is undergoing a profound period of introspection where the 'state of the union' is concerned. The narrow rejection of independence by the Scottish people in the 2014 referendum only precipitated a landslide victory for the nationalist party in Scotland at the 2015 UK general election.

Although access to HE could not be described as an issue that features significantly in the most prominent debates surrounding the future of the United Kingdom, the policies adopted in the area across the different nations undoubtedly reflect the contrasting sociopolitical nature of each one of them. In Scotland in particular, free tuition for all students has been taken as emblematic of the greater commitment to social justice and equity in comparison to their English neighbours. The Welsh and Irish approaches each reflect, especially in whom they target where access and equity are concerned, the particular contours of inequality in these nations. It could be argued that for Scotland, Wales and Northern Ireland, access has taken on a particular importance in the post-devolution context as a way of signifying their distinctiveness from England. Enabling those from the most economically disadvantaged communities (the emphasis on community being important and placing access as a collective endeavour) is a relatively high-profile way in the UK context of stating your social equity credentials, especially in the 2010s when these have been questioned so much in England.

Regardless of the extent of convergence and divergence, though, across the four nations of the United Kingdom, access to HE in both policy and practice terms appears to be an issue that will remain a prominent one for the foreseeable future. The alternatives to HE progression in all four of the nations are relatively weak – especially when compared to many countries in Western Europe. The English experience since 2011 has shown the resilience of HE participation even when price increases dramatically. Hence, it is hard to see HE participation declining in importance or number in the United Kingdom. At the same time, the nations outside of England are keen to profile their social-democratic credentials, and after the 2015 election, an increasingly Conservative England does not wish to reject altogether an attachment to social equity.

# 7 Access to Post-secondary Education in Malaysia: Realities and Aspirations

Glenda Crosling, Mien Wee Cheng and Ruma Lopes

## ▶ Introduction

Malaysia gained independence from Britain in 1959 and has made huge strides over the past few decades in increasing the participation of its population in post-secondary education. From a benchmark in 1970, when close to 50 per cent of the population lived in poverty (Symaco, 2010: 267), the participation rate has continued to increase significantly; the gross enrolment higher education (HE) ratio was 38 per cent in 2009, having risen from 32 per cent in 1985 and from 2 per cent in 1965 (Tham, 2011). The 2009 level is approaching the Malaysian government's goal, set in 2010 and to be achieved by 2020, whereby 40 per cent of the relevant population group will be enrolled in post-secondary education (Tham, 2011). In Malaysia, post-secondary education normally refers to post–grade 11 programmes.

A country of about 28 million people, Malaysia is situated in the South East Asian region and consists of Peninsula Malaysia, and Sabah and Sarawak, which are located on the neighbouring island of Borneo. A newly industrialized market economy, Malaysia has one of the best economic records in Asia and in 2011 was the third largest economy of the ASEAN countries. It can be said that Malaysia's infrastructure is among the most developed in Asia. Furthermore, Malaysia's high post-secondary education participation rate has been achieved in what has been described as 'one of the most multi-ethnic and multi-religious countries in Southeast Asia' (Brown, 2005: 3), comprised of the major ethnic groups of the Bumiputera, that is, the Malay ethnic group (about 67% of the population); the Chinese (approximately 25% of the population); the Indians (about 7% of the population; and the Indigenous groups (about 0.7% of the population), such as the Kadazans and Ibans in Sabah and Sarawak (Mukherjee, 2010).

The situation in regard to access to post-secondary education in Malaysia is complex. Concurrently, it is apparent that the policies over time have been successful, as demonstrated by the participation figures cited above. In effect, the policy of affirmative action for one particular ethnic group, the Bumiputera, and their participation largely through the public universities, has undoubtedly been successful. At the same time, the participation rate of non-Bumiputeras (mainly the Chinese and the Indians) has increased markedly over this time, but at an economic cost in that these students and their families had to fund their participation in the private HE system or go overseas to study. But raw figures related to access cannot be considered in isolation from the notion of success, and as we put forward in this chapter, the outcomes for these students alongside the rates of access from the different policy stages also need to be considered.

## ▶ Access to Post-secondary Education in Malaysia

Despite the advantages of its position globally and its economic potential, Malaysia is located in a region where the need to widen participation in post-secondary education is a nation-building reality. The efforts taken in Malaysia to increase access to post-secondary education are evidence of the government's recognition of the importance for the country's economic development of a post-secondary-educated populace, reflecting the well-accepted view that an educated workforce provides 'a sustainable human resource base upon which to build a country's development' (Asian Development Bank, 2012: vi; Symaco, 2010: 267; Crosling, Nair and Vaithilingam, 2014). According to the Malaysian Ministry of Education (MoE), 2012 total enrolments in all public and private HE institutions (HEIs) in the country totalled 412,891 students, an increase of 11 per cent from the previous year's total of 366,079 students (see Table 7.1).

However, data on the breakdown in student enrolments by race (ethnicity) in these public and private HEIs is extremely limited.

The participation rate of the various ethnic groups in Malaysia in the public and private systems has been variable and responsive to the governmental policies in place at various stages. For instance, in 2002, the proportional participation of the ethnic groups in Malaysian national universities indicated the success of the first-stage policy of affirmative action for the Bumiputera group. Bumiputera enrolment was 68.7 per cent; Chinese, 26.4 per cent; Indians, 4.7 per cent (Rao, 2009). At the same time, the enrolment of people in the public universities from the other ethnic groups has increased, but not to the same degree as the Bumiputeras. It has been the private HEIs

**Table 7.1** Student Enrolments in HE Institutions in Malaysia (2008–12)

| Year<br>Institution Type | 2008 | 2009 | 2010 | 2011 | 2012 |
|---|---|---|---|---|---|
| Public HEIs | 133,100 | 153,470 | 167,159 | 188,766 | 180,558 |
| % Increase |  | 13 | 8 | 11 | –5 |
| Private HEIs | 185,846 | 168,677 | 160,484 | 125,845 | 157,899 |
| % Increase |  | –10 | –5 | –28 | 20 |
| Polytechnics | 40,574 | 38,503 | 41,332 | 39,578 | 38,172 |
| % Increase |  | –5 | 7 | –4 | –4 |
| Community Colleges | 9,664 | 9,145 | 10,689 | 0 | 24,236 |
| % Increase |  | –6 | 14 | 0 | 0 |
| KTAR (a non profit quasi-private HE institution) | 13,192 | 11,541 | 11,622 | 11,890 | 12,026 |
| % Increase |  | –14 | 1 | 2 | 1 |
| Total | 382,376 | 381,336 | 391,286 | 366,079 | 412,891 |
| % Increase (from previous year) |  | 0 | 3 | –7 | 11 |

Source: Ministry of Education, Malaysia, HE Indicator (2011–12: 13).

that have provided access for the other ethnicities of the Chinese and Indians, largely in Malaysia.

In discussing further the notion of participation and measures of it, Tham (2011: 7) points out that the term 'access' is subject to a range of definitions, often varying from country to country and depending on the social situation and agendas (Tham, 2011: 7). Importantly for Malaysia, however, we concur with Tham (2011) that the definition should, alongside the overall participation rate, consider 'the different pathways [to post-secondary education] provided by the variety of programmes available in the country' (Tham, 2011: 8). The linking of participation rate and pathways in the definition of access is valid in Malaysia, where private provision in post-secondary education has widened access pathways, and has also 'been proactively supported by the government as a means of increasing access' (Tham, 2011: 8).

Closely allied with the notion of access is that of success; the entrance of students to post-secondary education is of limited value if the students are not able to achieve successful outcomes. In today's world, in line with Hudzik (2011), an authority on twenty-first-century graduate attributes, educational outcomes should include the capacity for graduates to participate in the internationalized as well as the localized world. Indeed, the Malaysian government's more recent policies for the enhancement of the national HE system for quality human capital development (NHESP, 2011) and the Economic Transformation Policy (PEMANDU, 2010) emphasize Malaysia's advances in widening access and enhancing the quality of HE, together with internationalization strategies for global integration (Wan, 2008). In this chapter, we thus consider pathways in the concept of access and also include outcomes for students. We define optimum outcomes to include graduates being equipped to function in the globalized world of the twenty-first century.

Malaysian government policies to widen post-secondary participation since independence have indeed facilitated many citizens from the different ethnic groups to achieve post-secondary education qualifications via a range of pathways. The figures in Table 7.1 show the increase in the overall participation rate in Malaysian HE at 11 per cent in the period 2008–12. As also seen in Table 7.1, the participation rate in the public HEIs increased from 2008 to 2011, indicating that a greater percentage of those eligible for the national system are being educated. However, as also indicated above, the Bumiputera people have had the highest access because of the ethnic quota system. Although the participation rates in the private HEIs have shown instability, with the global financial crisis and the period required for recovery as plausible explanations for the decline in numbers of students in 2009 to 2011, the significant increase of 20 per cent in 2012 in the private system indicates a growing economic optimism and that significant numbers of citizens and international students are seeking the private pathway to post-secondary qualifications.

From an educational perspective, those benefiting from the first post-independence initiative, which increased public university places via the race-based quota system (mainly Bumiputera students [Lee, 1999; Tan, 2002], experienced an education focused on the local setting, studying in Bahasa Malaysia as the language of instruction. The mainly non-Bumiputera students that benefited from the next two stages of government initiatives were self- rather than state-funded, and studied in private HEIs in the English language. Because of the linkages of private HEI educational programmes with those of foreign countries, participating students demonstrate a significant element of what we consider constitutes access *and* success in Malaysia.

## ▶ Phases of Access to Post-secondary Education in Post-independence Malaysia

Prior to independence in Malaysia and for more than 150 years under the British rule, limited opportunities existed for formal and higher education, with only one public university in 1962, the University of Malaya. Since then, post-secondary education in Malaysia has passed through three major phases, each benefiting particular ethnic groups in regard to access.

The first of these, the *post-independence and nation-building* stage, opened up enrolments in the national HE system on a quota basis (Symaco, 2011) through the government's 1970 New Economic Policy, which in this nation-building stage acknowledged HE as a mechanism to promote national unity in the light of the country's three major ethnic groups, and provided the human capital needed to advance the country economically (Symaca, 2010: 267). Nation building was facilitated by the Bahasa Malaysia language replacing English as the medium of instruction, and the Malaysian society being restructured by a quota system of 55:45 in favour of the Bumiputera people in national universities. This quota remained in place until 2002, when the policy of meritocracy was introduced.

The quota system disadvantaged large numbers of Malaysians who could not attend the national universities, so they went overseas to study in the English language, and at considerable financial cost (Cheng, 1997; Tan, 2002). For example, in 1985 only 15,000 Malaysian students were studying in local HEIs, compared with 68,000 studying overseas through their private funds, especially in the United Kingdom, the United States and Australia (Tan, 2002: 8). Furthermore, in 1992, the MoE reported that only a third of the qualified candidates could gain access into local government-sponsored HEIs (Cheng, 1997). In this situation, which led to frustrations in the community, as Tham (p. 3) explains, Malaysia adopted an approach that is similar to other developing countries: turning to private HEIs to meet the increasing demand, as they cannot afford to fund it from public money.

The inability of some citizens to access public HE paved the way for the second stage of post-secondary education access in the 1980s and 1990s: the *liberalization of HE*. In response to the lack of availability of national university positions, the government allowed private providers to offer post-secondary education to Malaysian students, and also to students from other countries. As a consequence, the private tertiary education system expanded dramatically, driven by the limited number of places at public universities, the overall population's increasing education rates and the increasing cost of overseas education (Brown, 2005: 7). The introduction of private providers was 'proactively supported by the government as a means of increasing access' (Tham, 2011: 3), so that in a country of only 27 million people at that point in time, the large supply of private providers has dramatically increased access for Malaysians, and for international students through cross-border flows (Tham, 2011: 4).

Amid this trend, the Private High Educational Institutions Act (PHEIA) of 1996 was the 'watershed' legislation that liberalized HE in Malaysia (Fernandez-Chung, 2006; Morshidi, 2009; Tan, 2002) and allowed Malaysian private HE institutions to offer the entire curricula of foreign universities locally. This legislation opened the way for more transnational students to participate and for foreign curricula to be delivered in the English language in Malaysia, with a major purpose being the desire to recall Malaysian students studying overseas to complete their studies locally. Malaysian students in such programmes were therefore subject to curricula that reflected more than the local Malaysian context, which had been the case in the former nation-building stage.

In the context of the initiatives outlined above, the third stage of the internationalization of HE emerged, with the aim to produce knowledge workers for the innovation-based economy desired by the government. The Ministry of High Education's (MoHE) National High Education Strategic Plan 2020 included in its seven thrusts: (i) widening access to HE so that 33 per cent of the workforce is educated to tertiary levels by 2020 (Tham, 2011: 6); and (ii) intensifying internationalization of HE by encouraging greater collaborative networking with foreign HEIs, increasing international student enrolments and attracting more foreign academic expertise. Internationalization is a key thrust in the NHESP to elevate Malaysian HEIs to become institutions of world repute and to develop Malaysia as an international education hub by 2020 (NHESP, 2011: 43). The objective of thrust (i) listed above 'includes ensuring access for students from diverse backgrounds through the provision of various programmes of financial assistance' (Tham, 2011: 6) and through the provision of 'alternative pathways and admission approaches' (Tham, 2011: 6). Selected private HEIs were granted degree-awarding powers, opening access to all qualified students if they could pay the fees. However, Malaysians in diploma and degree-level programmes in private provision can obtain study loans via the government-managed PTPTN scheme and/or make withdrawals from their parents' superannuation or Employee Provident Fund (EPF).

The government's 2010 Economic Transformation Programme (ETP) (PEMANDU, 2010) stresses the importance of quality HE for economic growth and for the private HE sector to be the country's engine of growth. The focus in both the NHESP and ETP is on attracting international student enrolments, rather than capacity building at all education levels for local students. According to UNESCO's Global Education Digest 2010, in 2009, approximately 70 per cent of international students were studying in private HEIs; hence, for Malaysia, ranked 11th in the world for international student enrolments, the private sector is poised to play a key role in widening access and meeting local and international demands for HE places.

With the advent of the liberalization and internationalization stages, the private providers have become major players in the sector, such that of the total enrolments in HE in 2009, private HEIs accounted for about half (Tham, 2011: 8). Demonstrating the diversity in the private system, in 2010 in Malaysia, there were five types of private HE institutions, including private universities, university colleges, foreign branch campuses and colleges (Tham, 2011: 4). From a mere seven public universities in the late 1970s, there are now within the purview of the Malaysian Ministry of Education some 530 private HEIs. Of these, there are nine international branch campuses, 59 universities, 32 university colleges and 430 colleges, with the number of students enrolled in the private HEIs reported at 500,000 (MoE, 2014), which is a threefold increase over the past two years, based on the number reported for 2012, as shown in Table 7.1.

## ▶ Innovative Access Pathways in Private Post-secondary Education in Malaysia

The post-secondary education setting in Malaysia, following the first-stage initiatives, created a group of citizens that was not segregated due to socio-economic position, but due to its ethnicity and consequent inability to access public HE because of the shortfall in available places. The radical approach of allowing private educational institutions to offer education options alongside the public system that was granted by the Ministry of HE in the second stage provided access opportunities for the Chinese, Indian and other groups, and resulted in an enormous shift in the country, where innovative arrangements with international universities were driven by the enterprising private sector. These arrangements provided opportunities for Malaysian students to experience what may be seen as internationalized HE programmes in the English language in their own country, with the option to spend time in the country of the home university if they wished to do so. More specifically, some of these arrangements are as follows:

1. **University Preparatory Programmes**
    a. International pre-university programmes that ease transition into overseas programmes

b. Home-grown (indigenous) university foundation studies curricula offered by local HEIs
c. Corporate sponsored programmes through CSR to provide high educational opportunities for less privileged students.
2. **Undergraduate Collaborative Programmes with Foreign Universities**
   a. Twinning arrangements with foreign universities, where the curricula of foreign (home countries) universities are delivered partly or fully by HEIs in Malaysia (host country), for example the United Kingdom and Australia
   b. Degree transfer programmes with American universities
   c. Programmes by branch campuses of foreign universities in Malaysia
   d. In-service professional development programmes

### ▶ International Pre-university Programmes

At the stage of liberalization, the Ministry of HE allowed pre-university programmes to be franchised so as to ease demand that could not be met for entry into STPM (public school grade 12 equivalent qualification) in public schools. A number of private HEIs took up this challenge to establish what was deemed an alternative route for local citizens in that they can complete a foreign pre-university qualification (e.g. Cambridge A-level, Canadian matriculation and Australian matriculation) and subsequently a foreign degree qualification (e.g. twinning degree) without having to go overseas at all (Cheng, 1997; Tan, 2002). This was a strategic move because it alleviated the anxiety of a discontented segment of the population, based on their inability to gain places in the public STPM programme despite having the means and ability to do so.

Some of the Malaysian entrepreneurs who set up private HEIs in Malaysia had studied overseas in UK and Australian universities, and those who had close ties with the MoE were able to bring to Malaysia these university qualifying programmes. As such, the pre-university, grade 12 or matriculation programmes of countries like Australia and Canada became attractive and affordable alternatives in Malaysia. For example, it is estimated that in 2013 there are close to 3000 students in Malaysia studying in the Western Australian Year 12, South Australian Year 12 and New South Wales Higher Certificate of Education programmes. Similarly, a few private colleges in Malaysia, like Sunway College and Taylor's College, applied to the Malaysian government to offer the grade 12 programme of the Ontario Ministry of Education in Canada which leads to the conferment of the Ontario Secondary School

Diploma (OSSD), under conditions that there is an on-site Canadian principal and the curriculum is delivered by teachers certified by the Ontario College of Teachers (OCT).

All these international provisions offer interesting learning experiences and international exposure to a group of Malaysian students who, a few decades ago, could not obtain a place in a public institution. Currently, they can choose to self-fund study in a private HE institution for an international pre-university or matriculation qualification. Through such programmes, the education systems and curricula of other countries have been introduced and transplanted into the Malaysian education space and serve as prolific means for many more local and foreign students to attain internationally recognized qualifications, thus leading to greater internationalization of HE.

### ▶ Local Foundation Programmes

In the last decade, the Malaysian Qualifications Agency (MQA) recognized a new typology in pre-university or matriculation curricula, called the university foundation programmes, and these opened up a range of options that had cost-saving advantages as well as the guarantee of entry into a specific university and/or discipline of study upon successful completion of the programme. The first foundation programme to be accredited by the MQA was the Monash University Foundation Year (MUFY) in 1999. In 2005, approval was given to Sunway University College to offer its own foundation programme. Designed and displaying the attributes of the Australian Monash University foundation curriculum in delivery, the Sunway and Monash foundation programmes prepare students at the pre-university level for the expectations of the universities concerned. Today, many private branch campus universities in Malaysia, like Nottingham University Malaysia and Swinburne University Sarawak, also offer their own foundation programmes as direct entry pathways for students to progress into undergraduate studies at the respective universities.

### *1 c Corporate-sponsored (CSR) Programmes*

Efforts to improve access to HE in Malaysia include public funding, for example via the government's Public Services Department, and corporate sponsorship programmes, especially financial assistance and scholarships to deserving and qualified students, with examples including scholarships by the Central Bank (*Bank Negara*) and PETRONAS. As mentioned earlier, to support achievement of Vision 2020 goals, more funding has been made available for students through public loan schemes (e.g. PTPTN). Bumiputera students have greater opportunities for financial support as they can tap into dedicated funding by organizations like MARA and Peneraju which are not available to non-Bumiputera students. These scholarships for less privileged students provide HE opportunities to more students and are distributed across public and private universities. There has been substantial support from charity organizations and foundations, although official data on the extent these foundations have benefited the needy in terms of increasing their access to HEIs is not available.

## 2 a Twinning Programmes

Developing from a handful of students in the 1960s and 1970s who were unable to enter local public institutions but with the economic means to travel abroad for study in the United Kingdom, the United States, Australia and Europe, twinning arrangements have allowed a significant number of students to enter the HE systems of other countries while staying in their own country for part of the duration of study or for the entire programme. Such programmes reduce the outflow of local currency to foreign countries and inadvertently, curb the loss of human capital. The global economic downturn in the mid-1990s allowed many more local entrepreneurs to offer a wider range of international degrees in a range of disciplines, resulting in specialized qualifications through alternative pathways for students.

The twinning programmes with British and Australian universities in Malaysia allowed students to pursue curricula that are identical to those offered at home campuses overseas. For example, Sunway College, which is one of the pioneers in twinning programmes in the 1980s, had negotiated with foreign universities like Lester University in the United Kingdom to offer their law and engineering degrees as twinning programmes. The students completed the first academic year at Sunway College and the subsequent two years at Lester University, gaining the academic scroll from Lester University. This led Sunway College to establish other twinning programmes with Curtin University, University of Western Australia, Flinders University and University of Melbourne in Australia, and with the University of Waikato in New Zealand. Twinning programmes are popular alternatives and they have allowed thousands of Malaysian students in private HEIs, who were not able to enrol into public universities due to limited access, to 'have the best of both worlds' without going overseas. Many private HEIs collaborated with foreign universities, and through twinning or credit transfer (advanced standing) arrangements, allowed students to transfer from a Malaysian HEIs to the home campus of a foreign university for completion of their studies. Sunway College, for example, offers the '3+0' twinning programme in business education with Victoria University, Australia, and students can complete their studies locally or transfer to the home campus to do so. Hence, the transnational twinning degrees which entered the Malaysian HE landscape to meet the insatiable demand for HE by non-Bumiputera students have become popular and more affordable options for international education for these students.

## 2 b American Degree Transfer Programme

The Malaysian private education system diversified its transnational HE (TNHE) reach with credit transfer arrangements with American universities whereby students can also complete part of their overseas education locally. Sunway College established the Western Michigan University (WMU), United States, in 1987 when it also had affiliations with British, Australian, and New Zealand universities. With the diverse transnational HE (TNHE) options, students can choose to pursue HE from different countries. The American credit transfer programme allows students who have SPM qualifications (Malaysian equivalent of grade 11 studies) to complete locally 60 credits out of the 120 credits required of an American liberal arts undergraduate qualification. The remaining academic credits being completed at an American university like WMU meant considerable cost savings. This model is also practised by other private HEIs like Taylor's College, INTI College, and other profit–oriented institutions set up by individual proprietors, private companies, public listed companies, and consortia of companies (Lee, 1999; 2001).

## 2 c Branch Campuses in Malaysia

The Malaysian government's Private HE Institutions Act (PHEIA) 1996, which liberalized the HE sector, also allowed the setting up of branch campuses of foreign universities. Private HEIs like Sunway College participated in such initiatives with Monash University, Australia, establishing the first overseas branch campus in Malaysia in 1998. Since then, branch campuses of Australian universities like Curtin University of Technology (in 1999) and Swinburne University of Technology (in 2004), and of UK universities like University of Nottingham (in 2000) and Newcastle University of Medicine (in 2009), have been set up in Malaysia. These foreign branch campuses offer greater options for international education to local students (mainly non-Bumiputera), as well as attract international student enrolments. The Malaysian government's Vision 2020 goal of achieving a developed economy by increasing access to HE also involves envisioning Malaysia as an education hub (Tham, 2011).

Another interesting TNHE development in Malaysia involves the upgrading to university colleges to full-fledged colleges by the Ministry of HE with the condition that the newly upgraded universities deliver their own homegrown diplomas and degrees instead of those of their foreign partners. Examples of private colleges upgraded to universities include Sunway College to Sunway University (in 2007) and Taylor's College to Taylor's University (in 2006). The newly upgraded universities are not allowed to conduct twinning programmes, but they maintain affiliation with their foreign partner universities through dual and joint degree programmes. Sunway University offers dual degrees in business, psychology and information technology with Lancaster University, UK, and Taylor's University offers similar dual degrees with University of West London, UK. The dual degree is another innovative approach where the value proposition lies in students attaining two degrees, one local and the other foreign, without going overseas and the local qualification being validated as equal in standard to the foreign one. These newly upgraded private universities are then able to state that their academic standards are endorsed internationally.

What began as simple approaches to provide alternative education opportunities to Malaysians who could not access HE in public universities due to the quota system practised in Malaysia and to reduce the outflow of currency for students studying in foreign universities have become transnational education models that are being adopted by other countries in South-east Asia.

### 2 d In-service Professional Development Programmes

In cases where working adults have missed the opportunity of public HE when they were young and had entered the workforce, they have been able to tap into the corporate-sponsored programmes conducted with foreign universities through 'top-up' or 'work-based learning' pathways. An example of the former is the Bachelor of Arts in International Business by Lincoln University, UK, which Motorola Malaysia sponsored in the 1990s for its employees, and the Master of Arts in Sales Management via work-based learning studies with Middlesex University, UK, to which Citibank in Malaysia sponsored its sales staff in the mid-2000s (Cheng, 2005).

### ▶ Outcomes of the Developmental Phases in Malaysian Post-secondary Education

A large percentage of the Bumiputera population in Malaysia accessed public universities through the quota system. Although the Chinese, Indian and other groups were disadvantaged and had to enter private universities or study overseas at considerable cost, they could benefit from the innovative pathways arising from private provision that emerged in the liberalization and internationalization stages of Malaysian HE. Many Malaysian students of Chinese, Indian and other backgrounds have thus experienced post-secondary education that was not available to them in the public universities. Furthermore, their education has had an international flavour. The linkages and partnerships of private providers with foreign universities as outlined above have impacted on the curriculum and the study experience of these students, exposing them to the world of their foreign partner university. Although there are many interpretations of what an internationalized curriculum involves (Leask, 2014), there is general agreement that it is connected with globalization, and that a major objective is to prepare all graduates to live and work in a global society (Leask, 2014). For many Malaysian students in private universities, this aspiration has indeed been the reality.

The first major advantage arising for such students has been their exposure to the English language as the medium of instruction, which is the global *lingua franca*. Graduates of these programmes are advantaged in the globalized world, where a good command of English provides them with greater opportunity for employment in, for instance, organizations that have international interactions and organizations located in overseas countries. It also increases their chances of successfully taking up further study abroad. The functioning of education programmes through English as the medium of instruction means that the participating students have suitable levels of English before admittance to their studies, and with further immersion in English as they study, their English proficiency increases. This impacts not only on the mechanics of their language proficiency but also on their flexibility in its use, so that they are able to adjust their English language use for particular situations. For instance, in studying in English, students are confronted with English in textbooks, in the classroom, and in the different disciplines in which they study. Implicitly as they engage increasingly with academic, professional and the standard form of English, their ability to consider the appropriateness of forms of English is enhanced so that they are positioned to appreciate, for instance, when the local Malaysian version of English is appropriate, and when a different form of English is required, as well as, for instance, the contextualized use of formal and informal language. Such an attribute positions them well for the successful intercultural interaction that is required in the globalized world.

Alongside increased proficiency in English, students exposed to foreign education systems have experienced, to varying degrees, transformation in their perspective, from a localized to a broadened view. Through the innovative arrangements of, for example, twinning, franchise or foreign branch campuses, the education programmes embed assumptions about institutions in the world of the foreign university, their ways of thinking and modes of operation. When considered in the context of the Malaysian community, such programmes have by their very nature a global or international outlook. At the same time, they are adapted to and accommodating of the domestic environment (Karram, 2014; Edwards, Crosling and Lim, 2014) and so reflect dual foci, exposing students to the global reality of differing systems and preparing them to live in a global society. Given the evolution of government policies in Malaysia and the recent expectations via the NHESP 2007 and ETP 2010 for Malaysia to merge into the global world, it appears that the educational programmes of other countries that were made available to Malaysian students have provided benefits that were perhaps less obvious at the time of their inception.

The educational programmes of private HEIs exposed students to the curriculum, student assessment processes, quality assurance standards and to teaching supervised from the home campus, shaped by home campus perspectives (Coleman, 2003). Moreover, the inclusion in the curriculum, and in the textbooks set by the home campus of foreign examples for the concepts and principles of study, subtly encouraged Malaysian students to compare and contrast with the Malaysian setting, assisting them to develop broad and perhaps more flexible perspectives of the content of their studies (Crosling, Edwards and Schroder, 2008).

Many of the students studying in private institutions travelled to study part of their programmes in the countries of the home campuses for short periods or longer, complying with conditions suitable for students to develop internationalized perspectives (Edwards et al., 2003). It is logical to expect that the outlooks of such students would be expanded as they grappled with the practicalities of living in a different country. At the deepest level, this experience facilitates the development of relativist perspectives, leading to a tolerance for diversity in viewpoints and experiences, and this is a capacity that underpins individuals' ability to collaborate and work effectively across cultural settings and with personnel from differing cultural and national settings (Crosling and Martin, 2004).

## ▶ Conclusion

As measured by the overall participation rate and the range of pathways provided, there can be no doubt that participation in post-secondary education has been widened considerably in Malaysia over the period since independence. The first group to benefit were the Bumiputeras, through the affirmative action quota system for the public universities. Private provision has contributed strongly to access for the Chinese, Indians and others who were disadvantaged by the affirmative action policy. For instance, in taking Sunway University as a benchmark: around one third of the approximately 4000 enrolled students are from overseas, leaving an overwhelming majority being Malaysian citizens that have taken up this pathway. Extrapolated nationally, these figures indicate that a large number of Malaysians are taking advantage of post-secondary education opportunities.

Additionally, as we have explained in this chapter, the quality of the access to post-secondary education in Malaysia is entangled with the notion of success, that is, of the outcomes of the educational experience for the participating students. In Malaysia, the government's directions for the development provide guidelines as to desired outcomes. As spelt out in the ETP (PEMANDU, 2010), the aim for Malaysia is that it integrates into the globalized world. Therefore, the outcome of internationalized perspectives and abilities as discussed in this chapter is very much in line with Malaysian government objectives and can only be seen as a successful venture from the viewpoint of students who have participated in private HEIs in Malaysia.

Notwithstanding this, it is important that not only private HEIs with their foreign linkages but all HEIs in Malaysia provide for the student outcome of globalized perspectives, in line with the objectives of the ETP.

Although these initiatives in one form or another at various stages have provided for access for the major ethnic groups in Malaysia of the Bumiputera, Chinese and Indians, access has been costly in financial terms for the latter groups, and it does raise the question of equity alongside access. Highly significant and in line with the access and equity provision of the NHESP and the principle of CSR funding, the strategy must be extended to the Indigenous people, the Orang Asli, who are yet to be represented substantially in post-secondary education. Data relating to the Orang Asli people's access to HE are often lumped together with the Bumiputera Malays, and so it is not easy to fully describe the levels of access or marginalization affecting these Indigenous peoples in the implementation of these policies over the time since independence. In the spirit of true access and equity, the extent to which this group have or have not enjoyed access is unknown, and contrapuntal actions need to be investigated in future research.

# 8 Expanding Higher Education in India: The Challenge for Equity

Manasi Thapliyal Navani

## ▶ Introduction

India has a vast higher education (HE) system, in terms of both students and institutions, and there are ambitions to greatly expand it further. However, it is one riven by inequality which reflects a society that, although it has aspirations to become one of the leading economic nations of the twenty-first century, is also grappling with social structures with their origins in feudal eras.

## ▶ Access to HE in India

India is one of the largest HE systems across the world, second only to China in terms of absolute numbers, with over 25 million student enrolments (including open and distance learning), a GER of around 19 per cent (for age group of 18–23) and an anticipated increase in capacity of 10 million seats by 2020 (Planning Commission, 2012). The Indian HE system comprises (as of 2011) 645 degree-awarding institutions (DAIs), 33,023 colleges affiliated to 174 universities, 43 central universities, 289 state universities, 94 state private universities and over 12,000 diploma-granting institutions. Although India has such a large system, only a fraction of students who enrol in grade 1 are able to complete their schooling and participate in any kind of tertiary or post-secondary HE. The institutional framework of HE system consists of universities established by an act of Parliament (Central Universities) or at the provincial level, the State Legislature (State Universities); Deemed Universities, Institutes of National Importance, institutions established by a State Legislative Act, colleges affiliated to a university, and professional and technical institutions, among others.

There has been a significant growth in the presence of private actors in more recent years. The public expenditure in HE has remained close to 1 per cent of the country's gross domestic product (GDP) over the years, which has been quite low in proportion to the burgeoning requirements of this sector.

However, the number of private HEIs has increased by more than 60 per cent during the five-year period between 2007 and 2012. Private institutions now account for nearly three fourths of the total enrolments in the sector; and given the current policy thrusts that are pushing for a greater role for the private sector in HE, this share is likely to increase in the coming years. Most of the private universities and over 60 per cent of private colleges offer almost exclusively engineering, management, law and teacher education programmes, and so effectively cater to a very select population and ignore the broad-based liberal arts and science education.

India's gross enrolment ratio (GER) in HE is far below the world average. There is also a tremendous disparity and unevenness in the geographical and demographic distribution of HE institutions across the country, the balance tipping significantly in favour of urban compared to rural. Within this matrix of a differential and inegalitarian spread of institutions, India's HE system also mirrors the fault lines of India's unequal development narrative, where access to resources and institutions by people is tightly correlated to one's social class, caste, religion, gender, disability and linguistic profile. Access to post-secondary education is thus negotiated and determined along the intersectionality of these categories and profiles. Equity has therefore been a major concern in planning for access to HE in the country.

### ▶ Who Participates in HE in India

The Government of India's Planning Commission brings out once in every five years a plan document that charts the national plan for development. The 11th such plan document for the period 2007–12, in its section on the social sectors, reiterated the long-identified need to address the gaping skews in the distribution of opportunities to HE in the country, noting the high disparities and the distant goal of inclusive education. Over 370 districts among the 584 in the country with GERs less than the national average were identified as needing enrolment drives and rapid expansion of HE institutions (UGC, 2008). Of the total districts identified above, about 3 per cent had GER less than 3 per cent; 21 per cent had a GER which varied between 3 per cent and 6 per cent; and another 38 per cent had a GER between 6 per cent and 9 per cent. The remaining 37 per cent had GER between 9 per cent and 12 per cent (UGC, 2008).

By religion, in both rural and urban India, the worst-off group has been found to be Muslims (Sundaram, 2007). In the country as a whole, the share of Hindus is 81.7 per cent; of the Muslims, 12.9 per cent; the Christians, 2.2 per cent; and the Sikhs, 1.9 per cent; with the residual category of 'Others'

**Table 8.1** GER among Religious Groups

|       | Hindu (%) | Muslim (%) | Christian (%) | Sikh (%) | Jain (%) | Buddhist (%) |
|-------|-----------|------------|---------------|----------|----------|--------------|
| Rural | 14.7      | 6.8        | 24.3          | 18.8     | 38.5     | 11.7         |
| Urban | 34.9      | 19.2       | 44.2          | 37.3     | 56.2     | 25.9         |

Source: NSSO 66th Round 2009–10, as cited in MHRD, 2013.

accounting for the balance, 1.3 per cent. With a share of over 80 per cent in the total population, the performance of the Hindus, as a group, is barely above the average for the total population (Sundaram, 2007). This division between religious groups is shown in Table 8.1 above.

## The Role of Caste

The government identifies the main disadvantaged groups eligible for state support as those who have been historically marginalized like the scheduled castes (SC), scheduled tribes (STs), and the other backward classes (OBCs). A focus on these disadvantaged groups in society (SCs, STs, OBCs and minorities) holds the key to increasing the GER (as acknowledged in the Government of India's 11th Plan Document). The nature of inter-caste disparities in HE participation is shown in Table 8.2 below.

The scheduled castes (SCs) and scheduled tribes (STs) are two groups of historically disadvantaged people recognized in the Constitution of India. The former had to endure the worst of the systematic discrimination of the Hindu Varna System, where identified as a distinct social group they obtained unequal rights and the identity of 'untouchables', ascribed at birth. The scheduled tribes or the tribals were identified with a distinct culture, language and social organization, and their exclusion is attributed to geographical isolation and neglect. As per the Government of India Census 2011, SC population is around 16.6 per cent of the total population, and the ST population is 8.6 per cent of the total population of the country.

In the Indian Constitution, OBCs are described as 'socially and educationally backward classes', and the Government of India is enjoined to ensure their social and educational development. The reservation of seats in educational institutions mirrors this share, respectively, with SC quota being 15 per cent and ST quota being 7.5 per cent of the total positions. The OBC reservations amount to 27 per cent of the total seats, making a net reservation of almost 50 per cent of the seats in any institution.

**Table 8.2** GER (18–23) and Inter-caste Disparities

| SC (%) | ST (%) | OBC (%) | Others (%) |
|---|---|---|---|
| 12.2 | 9.7 | 18.7 | 28 |

Source: NSSO 66th Round 2009–10, as cited in MHRD, (2013).

The representation of scheduled castes (SCs) and scheduled tribes (STs) in enrolments in the Indian HE have remained significantly lower than the national average.

The inter-caste or inter-religious or gender divides become even sharper as one examines disparities contingent on physical location. The overall GER in urban areas (32.5%) is more than double that of the GER in rural areas (13.9%) (MHRD, 2013). This is reflective of the skew in the distribution of HEIs, particularly a far greater number of universities in urban locations than rural, as well as the emerging concentration of private HEIs, both universities and colleges, in urban areas which aim to attract the more affluent young urban population.

The problem of access to HE in the country is twofold. It is critically tied to the goal of rapid expansion, which should simultaneously be inclusive and redress the existing imbalances. There are structural and financial implications at the level of organizational set-up of HE in the country as is shown in Table 8.3 below, as well as the practices at institutional level. Over the last two decades, inequalities in access and differential access to institutions have been of immediate concern to the Indian polity, but there has been a shifting emphasis in the state's conviction regarding its role in pursuing the expansion of HE. In this context, the next section presents the State's focus on access through its policy of affirmative action and then traces the pulls that emanate from the limits of institutional capacity to meet the access challenges.

**Table 8.3** Location-wise Distribution of Institutions

|  | Stand-Alone Institutions (%) | College (%) | University (%) |
|---|---|---|---|
| **Rural** | 56 | 48 | 36 |
| **Urban** | 44 | 52 | 64 |

Source: MHRD (2013).

## State, Access and Affirmative Action

The major tool for redressing the skews in participation and to ensure that access to education for economically and historically socially underprivileged students is enhanced has been the policy of positive discrimination through affirmative action in admissions to institutions of higher learning. Until the last decade, the State was the primary provider for HE in the country. State's intervention in addressing inequalities was manifest through positive discrimination or affirmative action for disadvantaged groups to increase their participation in all the public education institutions. India's affirmative action programme in HE, the largest and oldest such initiative in world history, has been built around caste as the chief justificatory criterion, and quotas as the delivery mechanism (Deshpande, 2013). The constitutional basis for reservations in jobs and educational institutions is Article 15(4) of the Constitution, which enables the state to make 'any special provisions for the advancement of any socially and economically backward classes of citizens, or for the scheduled castes and scheduled tribes'. Reservation quotas instituted as constitutional safeguards for increasing the representation of socially excluded communities have been expanded in recent years by including economic status, along with caste and tribal identity, as a marker of disadvantage (Deshpande, 2013). Through the 93rd Amendment Act of 2005 to the Constitution of India, reservations have been extended to the other backward classes (OBCs) in the public-funded higher education institutions since 2006.

The National Policy on Education 1986 also focused specifically in context of HE on access, reiterating that greater access requires an enhancement of the institutional capacity of the HE sector to provide opportunities to all those who deserve and desire HE and equity involves fair access of the poor and the socially disadvantaged groups to HE. The Action Plan of 1992, framed to implement the 1986 National Policy on Education, included schemes and programs that were directed towards the expansion of intake capacity in general, and with respect to the disadvantaged groups such as the poor, SCs, STs, minorities, girls, physically challenged persons and those in the educationally backward regions, in particular.

It is found that despite enough emphasis in policy, there is a persistence of critical gaps in participation across gender and rural–urban divide for minorities and even for the scheduled tribes and scheduled castes despite a history of reservations. This needs to also be seen in the light of politics of under-representation of various groups of population in the education system as a whole and the quality of school education across the country. The problem, as Sundaram (2007) points out, is found to be more acute when one notes the gap between the share of disadvantaged groups in population (in the relevant age group) and their share in the population eligible for enrolments for HE, a gap that is quite significant for Muslims in both rural and urban India and for OBCs in urban India.

Reservations for different social groups were an attempt to address the policy objective of promoting access to HE among the historically marginalized and under-represented groups. This premise, that through the policy of reservation/affirmative action, participation rates of the marginalized communities in HE would rise, may in absolute numbers have been effective over the years, but for the most part this discourse has not ventured into the social context of the institutions where affirmative action as an instrument is often the last word on equity, with no continuity with the question of the nature of participation. What often does not get documented in the literature on HE in the country is the microcosm of the institutions and their struggles to cater to student diversity almost as representative of the great Indian divide.

There are ongoing debates on the nature of reservations and their desirability in the context of identifying multiple, cross-cutting and graded inequalities and marginalization in society—as they operate across caste, gender, urban/rural, and class configurations and dynamics that play across HE in the country. At one end, the expanding middle class (having a significant proportion of upper castes), aspiring to lay claim to educational institutions on the basis of 'merit', has stood firmly in opposition to the recent expansion of the reservation quotas. At the other end, analysts (like Basant and Sen, 2010; Sundaram, 2007) have questioned the fundamental categories along which the State is identifying the segments of population most in need of reservations and affirmative action, questioning if this tool is really reaching out to the most marginalized in the country.

The meritocratic argument against reservation perforce is voiced by various civil society groups resenting state intervention in HE by way of positive discrimination in ensuring access to 'limited' educational resources. Deshpande and Yadav (2006) have refuted the claims of the upper-caste civil society groups that oppose reservations on the principle that 'merit' gets discounted for in the process. They argue

> it is their confidence in having monopolised the educational system and its prerequisites that sustains the upper caste demand to consider only merit and not caste. If educational opportunities were truly equalised, the upper castes' share in professional education would be roughly in proportion to their population share, that is, between one fourth and one third. This would not only be roughly one third of their present strength in HE; it would also be much less than the 50 per cent share they are assured of even after implementation of OBC reservations.

Deshpande and Yadav (2006) also point towards the absurdity of the construction of the notion of 'merit' in it. 'Merit', as its construction unfolds in the Indian HE institutional contexts, namely in the form of second-decimal cut-off points in the scores obtained in the school-leaving examinations or highly selective competitive entrance examinations to professional courses, they argue, has nothing to do with any genuine differences in ability, thus showing the fallacy of the argument that affirmative action subverts principle of merit.

On the other hand, there are systemic arguments like the one made by Basant and Sen (2010) for the need to arrive at an appropriate measure of 'deficits' in participation in HE that is representative of socio-economic status, religious affiliation and demographic characteristics. In the context of entrenched inequalities that India as a society and polity faces, it is also true that reservations are essential, but they are only a part and one form of affirmative action and inequality needs to be seen in a broader framework, as the National Knowledge Commission (NKC) set up by the government has also noted. NKC (2009: 65) acknowledged, 'Disparities in educational attainments are related to caste and social groups, but are also strongly related to other indicators such as income, gender, region and place of residence. Therefore, we need to develop a meaningful and comprehensive framework that would account for the multi-dimensionality of differences that still persist.'

In terms of policy initiatives, there have been other concrete steps taken at the level of the University Grants Commission (UGC), like, for instance, the creation of Equal Opportunity Cells across central- and state-funded universities and colleges. Equal opportunity cells (EOCs) have been entrusted with the tasks of creating an enabling environment for learning and adjusting to university/college environment for the underprivileged students, identified primarily as the SC/ST, the OBC and minorities and the physically disabled. Apart from this, merit scholarships instituted for disadvantaged/minority students and special schemes of funding have been created for the provision of remedial teaching in university and colleges to support progression of disadvantaged sections in HE. The functioning of EOCs varies from being just a grievance redressal administrative unit to, in some cases, being a space co-owned by proactive teacher and student groups. The focus taken up is often the one for which there is a champion in the university, which could be a student group or faculty in charge. Detailed documentation of what and how student support offered through these units impacts university/college experiences of students coming from disadvantaged contexts is often missing and not pursued within institutions. But an indicator of lack of active student support in institutions is the increase over the years in the number of cases where students have legally challenged institutions on practices of discrimination.

The efficacy of both the equal opportunity cells as well as remedial teaching centres across institutions varies as we move from elite, top-tier institutions to the barely functional affiliated provincial colleges.

## ▶ Equitable Expansion: Between Social Justice and Market Forces

The issues that plague the quality of the school system are also evident in the differential spread of institutions, not just quantitatively but in terms of quality across the country. In this context, one wonders how and if affirmative action or implementation of a quota system or setting up of opportunity cells is enough to redress the inequity in access to HE in the country. What do students coming from disadvantaged contexts achieve in institutions of higher learning, a disadvantage that is not merely material, but embedded in the training they receive to adapt to culture of post-secondary education?

Among those who are able to survive the testing waters of K–12 education and can possibly bear the opportunity cost to stay in any kind of post-secondary education, the access question acquires the dimension of what does the enrolment translate into in terms of effective participation and even success in HE. In fact, the report of the Committee to Advise on Renovation and Rejuvenation of Higher Education (Government of India, 2010: 17) points out what the Indian HE system is not able to deliver: 'Many students passing out from institutions of HE do so without obtaining the kind of skills they really need to work in a real-world environment. Among the drawbacks many students face are lack of ability to analyze or solve problems, relate problems to different contexts, communicate clearly and have an integrated understanding of different branches of knowledge'. These observations have formed the bedrock of changes and reforms being pursued in the country, but in the generic critique they also make obsolete the peculiarities of institutional failure to reverse the social and economic disadvantages that students bring with them.

What can institutions of higher learning do to translate a policy provision into an effective instrument for social and personal transformation of historical and material disadvantage? A lot can be achieved, many argue, if an institution has the motivation and the capacity to not just comply with the regulations of the State by admitting students under various categories but do something to supplement their learning environment in the university/college and transform their educational and later employment opportunities. Most institutions, however, who think critically about students' experiences as a priority struggle in this endeavour.

But what is important to note here is the concentration of unrest over opportunities in higher education to a very select set of professional institutes like the IITs, IIMs, IISERs, medical colleges and a few central universities recognized as the top-tier institutions. As reflected in the 12th Plan document brought out by the Planning Commission (2012), disparity in the scales is self-evident from the skew in public spending. On one hand, there are a set of institutions (the Central educational institutions – IIT, NIT, IIIT, IIM, IISER, CU) that account for no more than 2.5 per cent of total enrolments in the country and have, on average, a student per capita expenditure of Rs. 1.25 lakhs (125,000 Indian rupees). On the other hand, the student per capita expenditure across different states/provinces, which are funded by provincial governments, varies from Rs. 426 in the state of Jharkhand, Rs. 522 in Uttar Pradesh, to 14,646 for Goa and an average across states of just over Rs. 7500. These state/provincial government–funded institutions account for nearly 40 per cent of the total enrolments and are responsible for the bulk of undergraduate studies in broad-based liberal arts, science and commerce education. This differential in financial resources available to institutions manifests itself in the erosion of basic parameters of quality; in terms of availability of qualified faculty members (in fact, any faculty at all, as most state universities and colleges run sub-optimally, without any recruitment of academic staff); virtually non-existent and impoverished library and other learning resources; and stagnant academic environment. Most affiliated colleges have had to sustain themselves for dearth of funds by running self-financing courses which are out of reach of economically disadvantaged students. There is very little that affirmative action alone could achieve for Indian youth if the general educational context is embedded in a quagmire marked by elitism and insufficient opportunities.

The State's response to this crisis of equitable expansion has come in terms of increased financial outlays for HE in the country. Excellence, expansion and equity have been the central tenets espoused in the HE policy, as evident in the former and current Five-year Plan documents. Steps have been initiated since the 11th Five-year Plan that mark a paradigm shift in planning for HE in India. Even as the State struggles to achieve universalization of secondary education through a full-scale implementation of its flagship universalization of secondary education programme, the RMSA (*Rashtriya Madhyamik Shiksha Abhiyan*), it has launched its first National Higher Education Mission called the *Rashtriya Uchhatar Shiksha Abhiyan*, or RUSA, to achieve equitable expansion and access to HE.

RUSA is a centrally sponsored scheme, with participation of both the central and the state governments. As per UGC (2013), 306 state universities and about 8500 colleges are to be covered under RUSA. The scheme aims, among other objectives, to correct regional imbalances in access to HE and facilitate access to high-quality institutions in urban and rural areas by setting up institutions in un-served and underserved areas; and improve equity in HE in providing adequate opportunities to socially and educationally backward classes, women and differently abled persons.

It is hoped that RUSA would help in redressing the imbalance that exists between the state and the central governments' funded institutions and make the Central government a critical stakeholder in the higher education sector. The RUSA mission statement recognizes that '[g]iven the complexities of managing access and equity issues within and amongst states as well as the large number of institutions that already come under the state university system, there is a crying need for holistic planning in higher education focusing on the state as the basic unit. This planning should be done by an autonomous body, which can raise and allocate funds from the state as well as central government and explore options of revenue generation through research, consulting, private and industry partnerships' (MHRD, 2013, p. XVII). It therefore calls for the formation of State Higher Education Councils within each state to coordinate, plan and look after the funds received from both the central and the state governments. These councils are expected to come up with a perspective plan for the states, articulating the needs and areas of intervention required for realization of the mission's objectives.

The focus on increasing access is not only through creation of new universities but as the 12th Five-year Plan emphasizes, preferably though consolidation of existing institutions, like turning a cluster of colleges into a new university and opening new model colleges in the educationally backward districts. The emphasis in the RUSA on organizationally altering the planning landscape of HEIs in the provinces emanates from the conviction that allocating greater amount of funds to the State Universities, although it is the immediate need, is not sufficient by itself and requires awareness that the capacity of the State Universities to absorb funds is low. Hence, it is argued that in addition to providing a larger quantum of funds, reforms need to be pursued in the entire state sector. The emphasis in RUSA (MHRD, 2013: 48) is on removing the hurdles in fund absorption, such as restrictive bureaucratic processes, slow decision-making and archaic administrative systems, some of the recognized maladies of HE governance in the country.

### ▶ Challenges

It is expected that the reforms initiated under RUSA will build a self-sustaining momentum that will push for greater accountability and autonomy of state institutions and bring through much-needed reforms in the pattern of public funding for state institutions. Despite these initiatives, motivation of the State to expand the HE sector and remain its primary supporter and funder continues to remain the central challenge. With the universalization of elementary education in the country, it is hoped that the percentage of HE aspirants who are going to be first-generation learners coming from disadvantaged contexts is going to increase exponentially. The majority of the next 10 million students that the 12th Five-year plan hopes to enrol in HE are hardly going to be from the expanding but still small middle class that prides itself in the cultural capital that defines its success in institutions of learning. In this context the persistent reiteration by the State in espousing private investment and interest in HE, be it through the National Knowledge Commission or the RUSA sounds alarming.

In the 12th plan outlay for RUSA, the Centre-State funding has been kept in the ratio of 90:10 for special category States (North-eastern states, Sikkim, Jammu and Kashmir, Himachal Pradesh and Uttarakhand) and it is 65:35 for other States and Union Territories. Moreover, it is expected that 50 per cent of the state share could be mobilized through private participation/PPP. The continued focus even within RUSA on the nature of private funding and PPP models that the provincial governments are to generate raises questions on the possibilities this limits for equitable expansion. There has been a de facto privatization in engineering, medicine and management education, and around 58 per cent of total enrolments are in the private colleges/universities controlled and regulated by the State governments. Would participation rates for disadvantaged groups, backward classes, women and minority groups, among others, improve under the National Higher Education Mission or is it one more opportunity for pushing private sector firmly into the domain of HE?

Assessment of other recent policy initiatives does not paint an optimistic picture. Various commentators argue that although the 11th Five-year Plan and subsequently the ongoing 12th Five-year Plan have marked a watershed in the history of Indian planning in terms of increased outlays to education and especially to HE, very little measurable change, by way of reducing inequalities between groups, is discernible. Only modest variation seems to have occurred, and there is considerable tokenism in the nature of the schemes available that explicitly address equity issues (Deshpande, 2013; John, 2012).

Other commentators like Tilak (2012) argue that the major transition in HE policy of the Indian state since the late 1990s have been in favour of privatization through Public Private Partnership and effectively the creation of a 'market' in HE by any means, often at the cost of inclusive growth. Tilak (2012: 40) points out that ever since the liberalization of economy and the emphasis on privatization, inequalities have increased, and the absolute numbers of those attaining HE in the bottom income groups have fallen. This makes the pursuit of the dream of equitable and inclusive growth in HE participation a tall order.

Chattopadhyay (2009) and Tilak (2007) have shown how the market logic can seriously compromises value and quality of HE and weaken the State's ability to build an inclusive society. It is critical to note this as the current policy environment, while pushing the State into a pro-active role in managing the affairs of HE, simultaneously seems to be moving towards a largely pro-private and market oriented mode for expansion of HE much evident in RUSA's canvassing for 50 per cent of state share to be mobilized through private participation/PPP.

Be it the National Knowledge Commission or the National Higher Education Mission, both reiterate the need to stimulate private investment as a means of extending educational opportunities. The underlying assumption that increases in the number of private (and foreign) institutions will increase substantially the educational opportunities in HE is not based on any empirical evidence and the rhetoric of equity with the upsurge of privatization is circumspect (Tilak, 2007).

The irony of the current phase of expansion is that although it talks about equity and expansion and governance reforms and simultaneously pursues privatization, it ignores the fact that there is very little institutional learning to draw on in terms of good practices where affirmative action, student support in the institution and an inclusive learning environment come together. It will take not only State commitment and political will but tremendous institutional introspection on learning, merit and capacity to engage with diversity and pedagogical challenges in its classrooms.

# 9 National Access Policies for Higher Education in China: Creating Equal Opportunities in Education

Baocun Liu and Yang Su

## ▶ Introduction

'Knowledge changes your destiny, and learning leads to your future success.' This is a proverb that everyone knows and practices in China. With a long history of Confucian culture, China is a country that values education. It is China's national policy to prioritize the development of education, and in the era of mass higher education (HE), it becomes the wish of every young man and woman to receive HE. Since the early twenty-first century, China has had the biggest HE system in the world, with more than 34.6 million of students in 2788 colleges and universities in 2013 (MoE, 2014). As a centralized country, China implements a unified examination and enrolment policy in all of its 34 provincial-level administrative units except Hong Kong, Macao and Taiwan, which have their own policies because of historical reasons. But at different levels of HE, the examination and enrolment policies are also different. In keeping with the other case study countries in this book, this chapter mainly discusses the examination and enrolment policies of undergraduate and short-cycle programmes, focusing on national policies to promote the participation in HE of the 'disadvantaged' or 'under-represented' groups.

## ▶ HE Entry in China

Policies related to access to HE in China focus mainly on the examination policy and enrolment policy. In China, colleges and universities recruit students based on their academic achievement in Gaokao, the National College Entrance Examination. Therefore, the examination policy is the core of the access policy and the basis of enrolment policy.

## ▶ Gaokao and Proposition

Gaokao is an academic examination held annually in China. It is a prerequisite for students' entrance into almost all HE institutions at the undergraduate level and two-year certificate programme level. Though its effectiveness has been disputed, Gaokao is still the most important examination used by colleges and universities to measure students' scholastic ability. Each year Gaokao is organized and its time set uniformly by the state. Before 2003, the dates for each year's Gaokao were on 6, 7 and 8 July. But in order to reduce the impact that extreme heat and natural disasters in the summer may have on examinees, the Ministry of Education (MoE) adjusted the dates to the same dates in June, one month earlier from the dates of 2003.

The Gaokao consists of components set by both the state and by individual provinces. However, not all provinces are authorized to set their own components and have to have their provincial element actually set by the state. Before provincial proposition was introduced, examinees across the nation all used national examination papers. This caused some concern as it was argued that the uneven educational level of different provinces and regions was not fully being taken into account. Provincial proposition was intended to let each province or region formulate the most suitable test for its students. Shanghai was the first municipality in China to self-design Gaokao papers in 1985. This pilot experiment was regarded as an important milestone in the process of Gaokao reform. Increasingly, provinces and municipalities started to conduct the same practices. In 2004, 11 provinces started to adopt the mechanism of provincial proposition and by 2012, there were 17 provinces (including municipalities) that customized their own exams.

In terms of the contents of Gaokao, most of the provinces now advocate the '3 + X' model. There are three mandatory subjects – Chinese, mathematics and foreign language (usually English, but this may be substituted by Japanese, Russian, French, German or Spanish), and X refers to a kind of integrated comprehensive test. Such a test is either a science integrated test (usually covering physics, chemistry and biology) or a humanities integrated test (usually covering history, geography and politics). This X means more than putting three subjects in one paper; it actually emphasizes the interdisciplinary features of those three subjects. This model was first put into use in Guangdong Province in 1999 and then extended across China.

### *Admission Sequence*

There are five different routes into HE after the Gaokao, and as illustrated below, they are ranked in order of prestige. The different routes are as follows:

▶ Early admission undergraduate programmes
Early admission undergraduate programmes usually cover several categories of programs: military sciences and other programs enrolling prospective national defence students; public security, political science and law; maritime programmes; teacher education programmes; physical education and sport programmes; programmes in the arts.

▶ First-class undergraduate programmes
First-class undergraduate programmes are usually programmes in the higher-ranked universities at the national or provincial level.

▶ Second-class undergraduate programmes
Second-class undergraduate programmes are usually ordinary programmes in the higher-ranked universities or relatively strong programmes in the new undergraduate colleges.

▶ Third-class undergraduate programmes
Third-class undergraduate programmes are usually programmes of the new undergraduate colleges.

▶ Two-year certificate programmes
Two-year certificate programmes usually refer to the certificate programmes offered by the two-year vocational and technical institutions, similar to those in community colleges and polytechnic schools in other parts of the world.

The ranking of institutions is fundamental to understating HE admission in China. Outlined below is an example of how this ranking affects the progress of an individual student. Let's assume a student named Vic applies to five categories of programmes in HE institutions, A, B, C, D and E, respectively. A belongs to early admission undergraduate programmes; B belongs to first-class undergraduate programmes; C belongs to second-class undergraduate programmes; D belongs to third-class undergraduate programmes; and E belongs to two-year certificate programmes. Because A belongs to early admission undergraduate programmes, it first decides whether it wants to admit Vic. If yes, Vic's personal files and documents will be handed into A by the enrolment office, which means Vic must go to A to pursue his undergraduate study and the rest of the universities – B, C, D or E – will not see his personal information. But if A refuses to admit Vic, then B will decide whether it wants Vic to be admitted. If yes, then Vic can go to institution B to study, and only to institution B. Otherwise, C will see if Vic can be admitted. If yes, Vic will study at C. If not, D will see if Vic can be admitted. If yes, Vic will study at D. If not, E will determine the fate of Vic as to whether he can get a chance to study in an HE institution. Here A, B, C, D and E do not refer to one programme, but to a category of programmes. For each category, the applicant usually can apply to four to six universities and about six majors in each university. The enrolment decision will be made in sequence of universities and majors in each category of programmes.

## Universities' Enrolment Quota in Each Province

Enrolment for each HE institution is decided by individual institutions based on their capacity and resources, with the approval of the local education authorities and MoE. The quota for each province is informed by history. In the early 1950s, the colleges and universities decided the quota according to their own assessment of the level of development of basic education and school performance of the province. Since then, the colleges and universities have been implementing a policy informed by these considerations, but also taking into account a range of other factors. These include the number of candidates from senior high schools, the number of graduates of the university, overall national enrolment plan, faculties in different programmes and the requirements of the provisional government. According to HE law, enrolment autonomy is one of the important rights of colleges and universities. Every year, colleges and universities plan their quota and report to the different departments of HE, planning and student affairs in the MoE. The MoE will basically agree with them as long as the gap between their expectations and that of the colleges and universities is not big. Most higher-ranked universities want to enrol more students from regions with high-quality secondary education, yet they must give their quota to the provinces with weak secondary education, especially the underdeveloped mid-western provinces, to guarantee opportunities for students in those regions.

Since the late 1990s, China began to co-support some national universities. Such national universities usually recruit more students, though from their own local province rather than others. For example, Tsinghua University and Peking University recruit quite a large percentage of students from Beijing because these universities are located in Beijing. Fudan University recruits large parts of students from Shanghai, and Xi'an Jiaotong University recruits most of its students from Xi'an. This phenomenon is called 'priority for the local'. But this also means that the provinces with more national universities have more opportunities than other ones.

## ▶ The 'Disadvantaged' or 'Under-represented' Groups in HE in China

### *A Huge Country Full of Diversity and the 'Disadvantaged' Groups in Society*

As one of the largest countries in the world, the geographical environment of China varies from east to west as well as from north to south. You can find all the five basic terrain types on land in China: magnificent plateaus, undulating hills, the vast plains, low hills and basins of different size surrounded by hills. Mountainous area accounts for two thirds of the total area of the country. The terrain in China has the features of a ladder-like distribution, with a high west and low east. The first (highest) step of the ladder is the Qinghai Tibet Plateau, with an average altitude of 4000 meters. The northern and eastern edge of the Kunlun Mountains, the Qilian Mountains and the Transverse Mountains, is the dividing line between the first and the second step. The second step of the terrain is distributed on large basins and plateaus, with an average altitude of 1000–2000 meters. The Greater Khingan Range, Taihang Mountains, Wushan Mountains and Xuefeng Mountain in its east is the dividing line between the second step and the third step. On the third level of the ladder are vast plains with hills and low mountains, mostly 500 meters above sea level. The geographical environment has a great influence on weather, economy, population distribution and so forth. Since the reform and 'opening up' of the country in 1978, China's economy has been growing rapidly. Participation in HE has increased relatively rapidly, from 3.5 per cent in 1991 to over 34 per cent in 2013 (Mu, 2014).

But the economic development in China is not balanced. The east coast regions are developed and growing in contrast to the underdeveloped midwest regions. Even in the same geographical ladder or same province, economic development is unbalanced. Some provinces or areas are developed, whereas others are poor. The unbalanced economic development structures opportunities to participate in HE. There are a range of 'under-represented groups' in Chinese HE, including ethnic minority groups, rural students, migrant students, students from lower socio-economic groups and students with disabilities.

### *Migrant Students*

The difference between urban and rural has been enshrined in Chinese law since the 1950s, when China enacted the first regulation of household registration. The People's Republic of China Household Registration Ordinance in 1958 symbolized the formal establishment of the household registration system in China. This regulation fixed in law the difference between urban and rural by building the restricted migration system into law. It is stipulated that citizens can only migrate from rural to urban when they get proof of employment, a college enrolment certificate or a city household registration certificate.

The barriers between urban and rural areas are gradually coming down. Millions of rural migrant workers have flooded into cities since the late 1970s and into education. In 2011, there were 12.6 million migrant students in compulsory education, accounting for 8.4 per cent of all students (MoE, 2012a). However, many of these students will have difficulty entering HE institutions because of their household registration. Due to the residence registration system, the children of the rural migrant workers in cities are deprived of their rights to take part in the National College Entrance Examination in the cities in which they live, and are forced to go back to the rural area to take such examinations. Sometimes when the migrant students go back to the rural areas, they are refused permission to take the National College Entrance Examination, because they are not registered in the schools there. There is a rising number of migrant students living with migrant workers and studying in the senior high schools in cities. However, their school registration conflicts with household registration under the current system of college entrance examination and enrolment.

### Minority Ethnic Students

China has the largest population in the world. It also has 56 ethnic groups. The Han population accounts for 90 per cent of the total population, which is more than 1.3 billion, while the ethnic minority is about 10 per cent (Branigan, 2010).

Though ethnic minorities are distributed throughout the country, most ethnic minorities live in the underdeveloped mid-western regions, border and mountain areas. There are fewer colleges and universities and weaker basic education here than other parts of China. Because of historical and geographical reasons, most of the Chinese ethnic minority population have been denied the opportunities available to many in the majority population. In 2013, just over 7 per cent of undergraduates came from ethnic minority backgrounds (Mu, 2014).

### Students with Disabilities

According to the sixth national census of the total population and two national sample surveys on the disabled in China, at the end of the year 2010, China's total number of persons with disabilities was about 85,020,000 people.

This is a population larger than the total population of most countries. It includes 12,630,000 people with visual disability, 20,540,000 people with hearing disability, 1,300,000 people with speech disability, 24,720,000 people with physical disabilities, 5,680,000 people with intellectual disabilities, 6,290,000 people with mental disability and 13,860,000 people with multiple disabilities (CDPA, 2012). Similar to other countries, disabled people experience multiple disadvantages, including in the area of education.

### Rural Students

There is a huge gap in the enrolment rates in HE institutions between urban and rural students. The enrolment rate for rural students in 2002 was 2.37 per cent, contrasting with 19.89 per cent for urban students. Moreover, in the decade from 1990 to 1999, the enrolment rate in rural areas increased by 4.33 per cent, whereas the figure soared by 147.13 per cent in urban areas (Gou, 2005). Students in rural areas have been experiencing clear disadvantage in competing with their urban counterparts. The urban–rural disparity is a major aspect of the access to HE picture in China.

### Students from Lower Socio-economic Groups

There is an uneven distribution of students by socio-economic background in the HE system. In the higher-ranked national universities, students from families with more cultural, economic and social capital are squeezing out students from needy families, although the latter ones tend to concentrate in provincial or local institutions with lesser resources and of lower quality. Gaps also exist with regard to the distribution of students by majors and the number of students who pursue graduate studies. Students from the more advantaged socio-economic status families are more likely to study those popular majors that are in high demand and charge higher tuition. They are also more likely to pursue graduate studies.

## ▶ Policies and Practices to Support Progress to HE for Disadvantaged Groups

It is one of the goals of the Chinese government to build a harmonious socialist society. Such a society should be characterized with democracy and governance based on law, fairness and justice, honesty and friendship, vitality, stability and order, harmony between human being and nature. To build a harmonious socialist society, especially to realize fairness and justice, education is considered of paramount importance. In the field of education, China has not only passed different laws to guarantee equal opportunities for education to all the citizens by law, but also taken concrete measures to implement this legal regulation into practice.

## ▶ The Legal Basis of Access Policy of HE

The Compulsory Education Law in 1986 (the first law in the field of education after 1949) stipulates that the state shall implement a system of nine-year compulsory education which is free from tuition fees. Whoever has the nationality of the People's Republic of China while of school age, regardless of their gender, nationality, race, family property status, religion, etc., in accordance with the law shall have the right to receive compulsory education equally. The governments at various levels and departments concerned shall perform the duties stipulated in this law, to guarantee school-age children and adolescents' rights to receive compulsory education while parents or other statutory guardians of the school-age children and adolescents shall ensure that they receive and complete compulsory education in time.

The Education Law in 1995 stipulates that citizens of the People's Republic of China shall have the right and obligation to receive education, and all citizens, regardless of their ethnic group, race, sex, occupation, property status or religious belief, shall enjoy equal opportunities for education according to law. According to the law, the State, in light of the characteristics and needs of the different minority ethnic groups, provides assistance to the development of education in regions inhabited by minority ethnic groups, and supports those in outlying and poverty-stricken areas. It also supports and develops education for the disabled.

## ▶ Measures to Enlarge the Participation of the Disadvantaged Groups in HE

In many cases, the above 'disadvantaged' or 'under-represented' groups overlap. Their classification is only for research and policymaking. In order to change the inferior position of the disadvantaged groups, the Chinese government and universities have undertaken a series of measures.

### *Widening Opportunities for Mid-western Applicants*

In 2004, the government decided to start The Project for Minority's High-level Administrative Talents. This project was implemented from 2006, cultivating highly educated professional talents of ethnic minorities. The project focused on recruiting students from the western provinces. Students would still take part in the annual National College Entrance Examination; however, the scores required for HE enrolment would be lowered.

In 2008, the MoE implemented The Cooperative Programme of Supporting the Enrolment in Mid-western Regions. The 11 provinces with the most abundant education resources, such as Tianjin, Shanghai and Shandong and so on, would recruit students from five mid-western provinces with lower enrolment rates and lack of educational resources, including the Inner Mongolia Autonomous Region, Anhui, Henan, Guizhou as well as Gansu. This programme aims to provide more opportunities for students from mid-western regions and narrow regional gaps. From 2008 to 2012, the number of students enrolled by this programme increased from 35,000 to 170,000. The number of provinces receiving support came to eight, with Shanxi, Guangxi and Yunnan provinces joining them. Compared with 2007, the number of students enrolled in mid-western regions increased to 520,000 in 2011, and the promotion rate was more than 60 per cent (MoE, 2012b).

In July 2010, *The National Outline of the Long and Mid-term Plan For Education Development and Reform 2010–20* was issued by the CPC Central Committee and the State Council. It pointed out that China should increase support for HE in the Midwest, and implement a special plan for HE in the Midwest. The increased enrolment quota should go to Midwestern regions short of HE resources, expanding the enrolment scale of the eastern institutions in the Mid-west. The outline also wants to strengthen the partnership system between HE institutions in the east and western regions

Later in 2011, the MoE put forward *The Revitalization Plan of Higher Education in Mid-western Regions (2012–2020)*. The plan aims to address the imbalance in HE resources by building a number of new universities in Mid-western regions and elevating the quality of HE in the Mid-western regions to reduce the educational gaps between the east and the west. On 20 February 2013, this plan was formally published by the MoE, the National Development and Reform Commission and Ministry of Finance.

### Widening Opportunities for Students from Ethnic Minority Groups

In areas where the majority of the population comes from minority ethnic groups, bilingual (Chinese and ethnic minority language) teaching is used in schools. This leaves students from minority groups particularly disadvantaged when facing the Gaokao.

To address this issue *The Regulation of Preparatory Course and Classes of Minority Groups and Minority Classes for Regular HE Institutions* was launched in 2002. The preparatory courses are a system which aims to lay a strong foundation for ethnic minority students before they start their degree programmes.

The ethnic minority students who are recruited by this programme will study a preparatory course for 1–2 years, mainly focusing on the study of Chinese, mathematics, English and other related courses. As for minority classes, they are teaching classes specially established for ethnic minority students in the big cities in the east. They are delivered in secondary schools, higher institution institutions and Party schools/Youth League schools.

The minority classes in secondary schools help the minority students to strengthen their competitiveness in the national college entrance examination. In 1980, the MoE published *The Notice of Holding Minority Classes in National Key Universities*, deciding to run minority classes in national key universities. Later on, the national universities and local universities also ran minority classes. Besides that, 13 colleges and universities of ethnic minorities were established, mainly recruiting ethnic minority students.

The Chinese government implemented other policies to support the participation in HE of those from ethnic minority groups, in addition to this supplementary tuition. In 2010, *The Regulation of Enrolment for Regular HE Institutions* was published. There are three clauses relevant to minority groups. Firstly, in national autonomous regions, when applying for Chinese-taught programmes, the graduates of the native language–taught schools can answer the test in their native language except in the Chinese language test in Gaokao. What's more, the autonomous regions can also choose a native language test instead of Chinese language. Second, for ethnic students from border, mountainous, pasturing areas and minority population dominated areas, the admissions committees at the provincial level are entitled to decrease the admission scores appropriately. Thirdly, the ethnic students dispersing in the Han nationality regions will get the priority in admission when they are under the equal condition with students of the Han nationality.

Finally, students from ethnic minority groups are eligible to gain ten bonus points in the Gaokao. For example, when an ethnic minority student gets 500 marks in the national college entrance examination, his or her final score is actually increased to 510 marks when he or she applies for colleges and universities. The enrolment quota for each university also give priority to the ethnic minority population dominated areas. The minimum score of the applicants from these areas are much lower than other provinces. The system ensures that ethnic minority applicants compete with other applicants from their own provinces rather than those from the developed provinces.

### *Widening Opportunities for Rural Students*

In 2010, the rural population accounted for 50.32 per cent of the total population (National Bureau of Statistics, 2011). There is not enough official data to know the exact percentage of rural students in colleges and universities. However, some investigations show rural students accounted for around 25.88 per cent during 2007–11 in the leading universities in China (Chen, 2012). In the top universities as Peking University, the percentage of rural students was much lower (Liu et al., 2009). How to recruit more rural students to the leading universities has become one of the main tasks for the government.

In April 2015, the MoE issued *The Notice for Key Universities to Recruit Rural Students in 2015* to increase the enrolment rate of rural students in key universities. According to this document, the government will continue to implement the special project of recruiting students from poor rural areas, that is, 50,000 rural students will be admitted by the national universities and local universities belonging to Project 211. The enrolment areas involve 832 poverty-stricken counties as well as provinces with lower enrolment rate, such as Hebei, Shanxi, Anhui, Henan, Guangdong, Yunnan, Gansu and so on. The government will continue to implement the special project of exclusively recruiting rural students. The scale of enrolment will be no less than 2 per cent of the total. This project is mainly for excellent rural students from remote, poor or ethnic minority counties, towns and townships. Finally, the government will continue to implement a special project to encourage local key universities to recruit rural students (MoE, 2015a).

Soon after *The Notice for Key Universities to Recruit Rural Students in 2015*, four key universities, including Peking University, Tsinghua University, Beijing Normal University and Beihang University, announced their enrolment schemes for rural students. As the most famous and outstanding universities in China (especially Peking University and Tsinghua University, which are always in first and second place in Chinese university rankings), their policies displayed a commitment to recruiting rural students.

The enrolment scheme of Peking University for rural students is known as the Dream-building Project. The applicants must pass a written examination, an interview as well as a physical test, and the admission committee finally decides who to enrol based on examination results. The Dream-building Project consists of 27 subjects from 25 departments, involving a majority of all the disciplines. Through the scheme, students can have their enrolment requirements reduced to the 'first-class undergraduate programmes' score, which is much lower than the normal requirement (Peking University, 2015).

The enrolment scheme for rural students of Tsinghua University is called the Self-improvement Project. The range of enrolment will be decided by each province, autonomous region and municipality, mainly for excellent rural students from remote, poor or ethnic minority county, towns and townships areas. The enrolment number will account for 5 per cent of total undergraduate enrolment. The Self-improvement Project consists of 26 majors in seven categories of disciplines, and students can apply for three majors at most. Tsinghua University will reduce the number of points required for entry from 30 to 60, according to the students' marks, and students who get outstanding scores in a physical test will get an extra 5 points reduction in requirement (Tsinghua University, 2015).

Beijing Normal University will recruit what is described as 'free' normal students from rural applicants. The target is 50 students per year, and the applicants who want to join the scheme need to apply by themselves. There are 11 majors for free normal students, including Chinese language and literature, history, and English language and literature. Subsequent to a satisfactory review of their application documents, applicants will attend the ability test and an interview. Based on the ability test and interview result, the selected students on the humanities track and sciences track can get 40 or 60 dropping points (but the scores cannot be inferior to 'first-class undergraduate programmes' score), respectively.

The rural enrolment project of Beihang University is based on recommendations from senior secondary schools. The enrolment ratio of rural students will be no less than 2 per cent of the total undergraduate enrolment. The scores of rural students who are selected to this project can be 30 points lower than local entry scores (Beihang University, 2015).

### Widening Opportunities for Migrant Students

In August 2012, the State Council introduced *Opinions on Children of Migrant Workers Attending the National College Entrance Examination after Compulsory Education* from the MoE, the National Development and Reform Commission, the Ministry of Public Security and the Ministry of Human Resources and Social Security. The *Opinions* call on the provincial governments to recognize the importance of preparing the national college entrance examination for migrant students and to lay down the specific policies for the college entrance examination for migrant students, according to local conditions. All the provinces, autonomous regions and municipalities are required to issue their own entrance examination regulations for migrant students by the end of 2012. By the spring of 2013, with the exception of Tibet and Qinghai in the mainland of China, the other 29 provinces, autonomous regions and municipalities had all published their own college entrance examination regulations for migrant students.

Most of the reform plans published by the provinces, autonomous regions and municipalities have made immediate provision for uniform standards whereby migrant students, who live with migrant workers, can qualify for access to take the college entrance examination in the area where their parents work. The factors that are taken into account when considering whether a migrant student qualifies to take part in the examination where they now live can be classified into three categories: the time limit for school registration for migrant students in cities where they are receiving education, the time for which the parents have legally lived and worked in their new location, and the time for which they have contributed to social insurance in their new employment. Though with some limitations, it is a great progress that most of the migrant students can participate the college entrance examination where they live now.

## Widening Opportunities for Students from Lower Socio-economic Groups

Students from lower socio-economic groups can be found in any part of China, even in some coastal cities in the most developed provinces. It is the policy of the governments and universities that no students should lose their opportunities to go to college or leave their studies prematurely because of poverty. Besides regular scholarships, financial support specially designed for students from lower socio-economic groups includes the National Endeavour Fellowship, national grants and student loans as well as work-study programmes.

The National Endeavour Fellowship is mainly for students from lower socio-economic groups. It aims to award hard-working students from lower socio-economic groups, but with excellence in character and academic achievement in undergraduate institutions, vocational and technical colleges as well as secondary vocational schools. In order to help more students from poor families to finish their studies, the Chinese government established the National Endeavour Fellowship in 2007, subsidized by central and local governments. In September 2007, 1.4 billion yuan was used to finance assistance to students from poor families, and this was the first round of funds. The average scholarship recipient can get 5000 yuan per year.

In order to help students from lower socio-economic groups to finish their studies smoothly, the government established a national grant programme. National grants are used to finance students from lower socio-economic groups at full-time undergraduate and short-cycle institutions. The programme is subsidized by central and local governments. The funds for national universities are provided by the central government, and the funds for local universities are shared by central and regional governments proportionally. National Grants are usually used to help the students from lower socio-economic groups to solve the problem of their living costs. The range of grants average from 1500 to 4000 yuan per year, and the average scholarship recipient can get 3000 yuan per year. The level of grant for students from national universities is determined by the central government, and regional governments make the specific grants standard for local universities. Students can also borrow up to 8000 yuan per year.

At the university level, a range of scholarships is available. There are also some universities that establish some funds to provide financial support for students from lower socio-economic backgrounds. Besides that, many universities also establish work-study programmes to provide teaching assistant, research assistant and administrative assistant positions for such students.

### Widening Opportunities for Students with Disabilities

*The National Outline of the Long and Mid-term Plan for Education Development and Reform 2010–2020* advocates special education as the way to support disabled people. It required government at all levels to speed up the development of special education and put special education into the local economic and social development planning and agenda. The government encourages all cities and counties with more than 300,000 people to set up at least one special education school. At the same time, the government encouraged and supported various schools to accept disabled students, and accelerate the development of HE for the disabled.

According to *The Regulation on the Administration of Participation of the Students with Disabilities in the National College Entrance Examination,* in 2015, college entrance examination departments at all levels should provide equal opportunities and support for students with disabilities, for example to provide Braille examination papers and larger size examination papers; exempt hearing-impaired students from foreign language listening test and so on (MoE, 2015b).

## ▶ New Challenges and Directions in Access to HE in China

Gaokao, the national college entrance examination, has been the hot topic of discussion for decades. Many suggest China should abolish it and use new standards to recruit students, whereas many others strongly support Gaokao.

### The National Survey on Gaokao

In 2007, the National Education Examinations Authority and China Youth Daily jointly conducted a survey in memory of the 30th anniversary of Gaokao. The survey aimed to collect public opinions on Gaokao over the past 30 years, and it collected data from 38,087 ordinary people nationwide and 551 school teachers from six provinces via the Internet, phone calls, newspapers and other means (Zhao, 2007) The results showed support from the public of Gaokao as the most important and fairest measure for colleges and universities to recruit students from high school graduates. The results showed that

- 73.3 per cent of interviewees said that the current Gaokao system is generally fair.
- 77.5 per cent of interviewees thought that there are flaws in the system, but there is no better system than Gaokao in terms of ensuring fairness so far.
- 89.6% of interviews admit that Gaokao once changed their destiny, of whom 69.1 per cent were from rural areas and 30.9 per cent were from urban areas. (Zhao, 2007).

On the one hand, the public hold a generally positive attitude toward Gaokao's role in ensuring fairness; on the other hand, however, people also show concerns about the quality of education under the current enrolment system education at present, and 55.9 per cent of teachers were also 'dissatisfied' (Zhao, 2007).

These figures reflect common concern about Gaokao's fairness. Though it poses unexpected challenges to students from rural areas, the minority groups, rural migrant workers in cities and needy families, the abolition of the Gaokao is unlikely, and it is the government who must try its best to meet the challenges in order to really improve the quality of education.

### New Directions in Access Policy on HE

On 3 September 2014, the State Council released *Implementation Suggestions for Deepening the Reform of Examination and Enrolment System*. This document emphasized the reforms both in the national college entrance examination and enrolment policies.

The new policy approach aims to increase the enrolment rate in Midwestern regions as well as populous provinces. The government will continue to implement the Cooperative Plan of Enrolment in Mid-western Regions, a project started in 2008 by the MoE, asking 14 provinces with abundant HE resources to allocate a certain proportion of their total enrolment for eight midwestern regions which are faced with great enrolment pressure and lack of HE resources. The policy requires universities of eastern regions to arrange special enrolment quota for the applicants in the midwest. Compared with the average enrolment rate all over the country, the target is that the gap between the provinces with lowest enrolment rate and the average should be reduced from 6 per cent in 2013 to no more than 4 per cent by 2017 (TSC, 2014).

It is also one of the priorities of the new policy framework to increase the number of rural students in key universities. The MoE will continue to aim to increase the number of rural students in key universities. National universities and key local universities should arrange a certain proportion of enrolment for excellent applicants from remote, poor or ethnic regions. The aim is that rural students from these areas admitted into key universities will increase by 2017.

The new policy framework does not ignore the need of migrant students. The aim is to reduce and standardize the bonus points for the Gaokao. Bonus points will be significantly reduced and strictly controlled. From 2015 onwards, bonus points for applicants with specialty in sports and arts will be cancelled. Bonus points for ethnic minority applicants from poverty-stricken border areas will still be effective, but should be improved and standardized.

From this comprehensive access to HE policy framework, we can see that China will give more priority to equity and transparency than before. This is a very important signal in the area of access to HE in China.

## *A Long Way to Go for Equal Opportunities for the Disadvantaged Groups in HE*

Increasing opportunities for the disadvantaged groups in HE is not just an issue of education, it is closely related to economic, cultural and social development with economic development being particularly important. The disadvantaged situation where access to HE is concerned for the groups described above is rooted in the unbalanced development of economy. If China wants to provide equal opportunities for the disadvantaged groups in HE, China should devote itself to narrowing the gap between the underdeveloped and developed regions in economy.

From the goals of the current government, it is obvious China wants to build a more inclusive and harmonious society. Equity is one of the priorities of the current government policy. In the field of HE, the government is trying to provide more resources and opportunities to the disadvantaged groups. In the near future, China will continue and strengthen such a policy trend.

China has made great efforts to widen the participation for disadvantaged groups in HE and has made significant progress in this regard. But there is still a long way to go to realize equal opportunities in HE. Inequality in participation in HE is caused by many historical and realistic reasons; it is not easy to change them overnight.

# 10 Access to Higher Education in South Africa: Addressing the Myths

Ncedikaya Magopeni and Lullu Tshiwula

## ▶ Background

In this context, the term 'access' is defined as extending opportunities for those who were previously excluded from higher education (HE). However, increasing access does not ultimately make the system 'fair'. The access debate thus shows two faces: invitation and exclusion. It also raises the question of cost, debates about which are not new to HE. These questions remain a challenge for both developed and developing countries.

Governments globally have developed different strategies to ensure that keen and capable but financially disadvantaged students are not hindered from enjoying HE. In this, South Africa is no exception. However, access is not an end in itself, and a distinction should be made between formal and epistemological access.

Formal access concerns registration, including fulfilling entry requirements, determining student fees and accessing financial resources. Once this has been completed, the student will need to be engaged in the academic programme for which he or she has registered. This initiation into the discourses and practices of the discipline is termed 'epistemological access'. A useful concept to describe the essential nature of access, it was coined by Rollnick (2010), citing Morrow's (1994) work on epistemological access, which described the relationship of such access to the culture of an institution.

The issue of access to HE differs from country to country, depending on each country's unique history. The brief in this chapter is to explore the South African understanding of access. It begins with the country's history of legalized apartheid, as this has a bearing on the present problem of access to HE (Rollnick, 2010: 21–22).

Today, the South African Constitution recognizes blacks in general, but includes Africans, Coloured and Indians as specific groups. These divisions were one of the legacies of the apartheid era. Historically, the black group was denied socio-economic rights, so various legal and policy instruments have been devised since the advent of democracy to redress these practices.

Many discriminatory policies were put in place during apartheid. However, those discussed in this text were selected specifically because of their negative impact on the access to HE for under-represented groups.

## Population Registration Act 1950

This Act categorized the South African population on the basis of colour, depending on whether one was White, Indian, Coloured or African. Here, we will use 'African' as the preferred term, as opposed to the variety of names African people were then given, including 'Bantu' and 'Plural' as well as 'Blacks'. It was on this basis of colour differentiation that the kind of schooling a person would receive and where it took place were determined.

## Group Areas Act No. 41 1950

Depending on your colour, this Act determined where you would reside. In general, the lighter your skin, the better the area in which you lived. The Act was enforced by moving black communities to designated areas, which were always away from the central business districts. Africans were further segregated on the basis of language, in a country which, after the adoption of the new Constitution, recognized 11 official languages, nine of which were African languages.

## Natives Act, Act No. 67 of 1952

Based on the different languages, the government established homelands for Africans in rural areas. This Act stipulated that Africans had to carry a separate reference book, as opposed to the unitary identity document carried by all South Africans. This made it an offence to be in a non-designated area.

## Bantu Education Act, Act No. 47 of 1953

Provision of education was separated along racial lines, resulting in four separate and distinct departments. White schooling was free and compulsory up to grade 8. Africans, Indians and Coloureds, however, had to pay for their education, with the result that only a handful of families could afford schooling. This is probably one of the reasons why the illiteracy rate for under-represented groups was 46 per cent, especially for Africans, who were at the lowest funding rate from government. This is the context within which the issue of access to HE today should be viewed and understood (Magopeni and Tshiwula, 2010).

## Extension of Universities Act, Act No. 45 1959

This Act established non-white colleges deep in rural areas. Their position on the margins of the economy ensured their own and their students' exclusion from financial and other networks. The Act made it a criminal offence for a non-white person to register at an open university without permission from the minister of Bantu Education. Among the oldest of these former colleges is the University of Fort Hare, in Alice, which boasts famous alumni such as Nelson Mandela.

All HE institutions were structured along racial lines in terms of both admission and tuition. Enrolment and staffing patterns largely adhered to the policy of separate development, with the exception of black institutions, which tended to have black students and predominantly white staff, particularly in senior positions (Kennedy-Dubourdieu, 2006; Soudien, 2007). In addition, some 'white institutions' such as the University of Cape Town, were reserved mainly for English-speakers. Others, such as the University of Stellenbosch and the University of the Orange Free State, catered mainly to Afrikaans-speaking students. Campus locations, environments, cultures and funding sources were similarly differentiated. Today, access continues to have a lot to do with an existing pipeline that comes through from high school and, given the present conditions, lends itself to some difficulties.

### ▶ The Supply Chain from Secondary Schooling

Access to HE should be open to those who have successfully completed secondary school or its equivalent, or who present valid entry qualifications. As far as possible, they should be accepted at any age and without discrimination. At present in South Africa, the school system is failing the country, and African students are the worst hit by this failure. This is worsened by a student-to-educator ratio that often increases, without being matched by a corresponding financial investment.

This situation affects the performance of many students, who drop out of the system in large numbers, thus negating the principle of access. Equity and access are important because HE confers significant benefits on the individual in terms of personal development, career possibilities, social status and lifetime earnings. In the broader context, improving the participation of disadvantaged individuals and groups in HE is essential for building a cohesive and more economically successful society of the kind to which South Africa aspires.

The result is that South Africa has had to assist its formerly excluded communities by direct intervention. The position the country finds itself in is not unique in Africa. It is similar to that of other post-independence colonial countries which have undergone political and social change. Evidence from many countries shows that students of colour are not gaining access, especially to science and engineering courses, at university, nor are they succeeding even when they do so. The need for access programmes is therefore acute, if alignment with the developed policy is to be ensured. HE institutions need to work to create a seamless system, starting with early childhood and primary education and continuing through life.

This institutional framework should include active partnerships with parents, schools, students, socio-economic groups and communities. Not only should secondary education prepare candidates for HE, but it should also develop the capacity to learn on a broad basis and open the way to an active life by providing training for a wide range of jobs. A number of models are on offer to address those gaps in the system which prevent some students from qualifying for access to HE, especially in the sciences. To meet the needs of these students, universities have designed post-school interventions, taking care that the students should not perceive the bridging or foundation course as patronizing or believe that 'real' work is not being done. In terms of length, both bridging and foundation modules can vary from as little as a week to one academic year.

## ▶ Models of Post-school Interventions

The most important aim of science foundation programmes is to ensure flexible entry and active redress with regard to tertiary-level science-based courses.

These models are represented schematically below in Table 10.1.

**Table 10.1** Science Foundation Programme Models in South Africa

| Type of Model | Year 0 | Year 1 | Year 2 | Year 3 |
|---|---|---|---|---|
| Normal course and extra tutorial/enrichment model | Non-existent | Normal degree structure | | |
| 1 + 3 | | Foundation year | Normal degree structure | |
| 2 + 2 | | Two-year access programme | | Senior years of main degree |
| Complete restructuring | | Year 1 | Year 2 | Year 3 | Year 4 |

Source: Rollnick (2010: 14).

## ▶ Government Interventions

After 1994, many changes were ushered into HE in South Africa. Through mergers and incorporations, these resulted in 23 public universities. They were made up of 11 'traditional' universities, six universities of technology (formerly known as technikons) and six comprehensive universities. The latter are defined as those which combine traditional universities and universities of technology. There are also two institutes of HE in two provinces which serve as administrative hubs, coordinating HE provision in partnership with the universities. The government has also built two new comprehensive universities which will open their doors in 2014. The HE hubs will be gradually phased out while ensuring that HE provision is not compromised (DHET, 2013: 27, 31).

## ▶ Policies and Practices Supporting Progression to HE

In 2001, then–Minister of HE and Training Kader Asmal acknowledged that, despite achievements such as increasing enrolment rates for Africans, the HE sector had not met its transformational goals. Although progress had been made, he saw the sector as still grappling with apartheid's past legacies. The current minister took the decision to call for an HE Summit for 22–23 April 2010. In it, he echoed Kader Asmal, also referring to unachieved goals, mentioning low participation rates, high dropout rates, low throughput rates, insufficient number of postgraduates, a perceived lack of fit between HE graduates and the world of work, as well as the failure of the sector to replace its ageing academic workforce.

The summit's overall objectives were as follows:

1. Revisit the notion of transformation holistically, focusing on access, equity and quality in respect of the core functions of HE.
2. Examine the role of HE in national development.
3. Identify key objectives for HE.
4. Discuss the need, feasibility and possible modalities for more systematic and structured communication between the sector and the minister.

This engagement was followed by the introduction of a new green paper, overhauling the previous white paper adopted in 2010, when the basic and HE departments were still combined. The green paper was circulated for public comment, and the comments were integrated into the document. In 2013, a white paper for post-school education and training was released.

This aimed to analyse the post-school education and training system, defining objectives and priorities for the various systems, including for HE, and setting out a vision for the integration of education and training. It was aligned with other national policy initiatives, among them the National Development Plan, the New Growth Path, the Industrial Policy Action Plan and the Draft Human Resource Development Strategy for South Africa. The white paper set forth both the government's vision and the principles governing this vision, as well as future policies consistent with Vision 2030 of the National Development Plan, to be developed and implemented. It included a framework defining the Department of Higher Education and Training's (DHET) prioritized focus (DHET, 2013: vii).

The government's goal is for a public university enrolment of 1.6 million by 2030. Participation rates increase from the current rate of 17.3 per cent to 25 per cent. This will mean the capping of fees to maintain affordability for individual students, and will involve funders and the National Student Financial Aid Scheme (NSFAS). Created through an Act of Parliament in 1991, the NSFAS provides a sustainable system for loans and bursaries to increase university access for poor students and to address equity. The NSFAS funds reached R6 billion in 2011 and continue to grow.

Higher Education South Africa (HESA) is the body of South Africa's university leadership, represented by 23 vice chancellors from public universities. The organization's press statement of 28 January 2010 committed it to facilitating increased access to HE. This would be effected by ensuring that university fees remained affordable. For example, 2010 tuition fees, as a percentage across the sector, reflected those of 2009 and were kept within the range of 9–15 per cent, in line with inflationary pressures. HESA is also finalizing guidelines helping individual institutions to arrive at affordable tuition fees. This process will unfold in tandem with maintaining institutional quality teaching and learning, research facilities and student support. HESA is further committed to ensuring that no deserving student will be denied an educational opportunity, expediting the NSFAS upfront payments for the first fee instalment. It has established an early warning system for student performance, with appropriate interventions, and effective collection of student debt, which in 2010 was R2.8 billion. Special attention is being given to broadening access and improving the success of students from Quintile 1 schools, located in poor communities in the rural areas. HE South Africa and the Ministry of HE are thus aligned to achieving national goals.

The national government envisions a central application system (CAS) to support informed access to universities, proposing a single application fee for a variety of institutions, as compared to the present system of paying of an application fee to individual universities. The universities would still make their own admission decisions but would be required to address throughput rates; in 2011, these were low, at 74 per cent, compared to the required 80 per cent.

In particular, the universities are tasked with expanding access and educating black professionals and graduates in scarce skills. To provide poor students with such skills, the Department of Higher Education and Training (DHET) will engage and sign performance agreements with universities, allocate ring-fenced funds, introduce full-cost bursaries through NSFAS and prioritize the updated scarce skills lists needed for South Africa's economic development. This intervention will be accompanied by academic support and a comprehensive student mentoring system.

Access for the targeted under-represented groups is especially important for those living outside high-technology areas. Universities today are moving towards online applications and phasing out physical documents, as are some urban schools. This has implications for rural students. They have to travel long distances to access a computer with Internet, which also comes at a high financial cost.

### ▶ Myths about Access to HE

The ongoing debates around access to HE lend themselves to a number of myths. These are found globally, but in this text are seen through the authors' South African lenses (DHET, 2013: 7–8, 30–33, 36; and HESA, 2010).

Several such myths are current in South Africa. One of these is the notion that if access for under-represented groups is free or at a low cost, this may lead to higher participation rates. In fact, it could result in a further stratification of HE, with access to 'privileged' universities and sought-after programmes being skewed in favour of higher social classes. In Australia, this approach has left the university population largely the same.

Secondly, it is assumed that addressing under-preparedness in high school will result in a better access system in HE. In South Africa, there is much lamenting on secondary school barriers to access, but less so on redressing total schooling. Most young people's futures are decided long before they arrive in grade 12. However, the onus is not necessarily on the universities to resolve this problem, but rather on government establishing a system of phasing addressing all levels of education.

The third myth assumes that widening participation will lower retention and completion rates. This suggests that opening access to under-represented groups will lead to more dropouts and failures. This thinking could well persist until better measures for outputs are found. The final myth assumes that selection of students on the basis of academic merit will meet the HE goal of increasing participation rates for 20- to 24-year-olds. However, it does not spell out how this goal will be achieved. Universities are left to work out its implementation while dealing with the ministry's capping of student numbers (Bitzer, 2010: 301–2, 304).

## Access Progress

In order to meet the country's constitutional imperatives, virtually all of South Africa's higher-education institutions are grappling with the issue of access. Table 10.2 below shows participation rates by race for the period 2005–11. From this it can be deduced that, although these figures point to real improvements, the goal of equal opportunity in terms of access and achieving success is, from a number of critical perspectives, a long way off. The growth is not sufficient to meet the human resource needs for South Africa, as is reflected in the continued shortages of high-level skills.

The HE participation rate used in Table 10.2 is the gross enrolment ratio (GER), defined by UNESCO (2010) as the total enrolment of all ages, expressed as a percentage of the 20- to 24-year-old age group in the population. It gives a measure of access to HE and is critical to understanding and assessing the performance of HE. The participation rate in South Africa increased from 15 per cent in 2000 to 18 per cent in 2010. The steady growth since 2005 is in line with the 20 per cent target set by the National Plan for HE over a 10- to 15-year period, which is likely to be met by 2015–16. The indicated rate is higher than the 6 per cent recorded for sub-Saharan Africa, but still lower than Latin America's 34 per cent or Central Asia's 31 per cent. Although the number of Africans has increased substantially, it is still smaller than the proportion of Africans in the 52.98 million population, with Africans at 79.8 per cent compared to Coloureds at 9 per cent, Indians at 2.5 per cent and whites at 8.7 per cent. It seems that the rate for Africans and Coloureds continues to

**Table 10.2** Gross HE Participation Rates by Race (2005–11)

| Ethnic Background/ Gross Enrolment Ratio | 2005 (%) | 2006 (%) | 2007 (%) | 2008 (%) | 2009 (%) | 2010 (%) | 2011 (%) |
| --- | --- | --- | --- | --- | --- | --- | --- |
| African | 10 | 11 | 12 | 13 | 13 | 14 | 14 |
| Coloured | 12 | 12 | 12 | 13 | 14 | 15 | 14 |
| Indian | 44 | 44 | 43 | 45 | 45 | 46 | 47 |
| White | 51 | 53 | 54 | 58 | 58 | 57 | 57 |

show racial inequalities. The participation rate for white and Indian students, on the other hand, is comparable with the figures for developed countries (CHE, 2013: 41; DoE, 2001: 21–22; DHET, 2013: 28; Lehohla, 2013: 302).

South Africa's past continues to hinder the access and participation of certain students in the higher-education sector. The language of instruction is a key factor in this. South Africa has 11 official languages, of which 9 are African languages. Given that many of the universities were single-language institutions before 1994, the issue of language of instruction presents major challenges today. Under-represented students are often seen as disadvantaged, under-prepared or in need of remediation. The function of the bridging or foundation programme is often defined as 'getting them up to speed' rather than socializing them into a culture which is new to them. Mphahlele (1994) suggested that such students are over-prepared in the sense that they have been grounded in a certain mode of study at school which is ineffective at tertiary level.

Those tasked with teaching access programmes should therefore consider a new form of enculturation, one which helps students to unlearn secondary-level methods which are inappropriate at tertiary level. It is often forgotten that access students are the cream of the schools from which they come and that they are used to success, albeit in an environment which may have offered them few challenges. In the South African situation, such students are often described as having 'language problems', when in reality they may be fluent in up to seven languages (Rollnick, 2010: 21–22).

They may also face a stigma attached to 'gaining access' to HE through a 'second-chance', or alternative, route. Alienated and marginalized students constantly have to pick their way through the assumptions made by staff of the institutions where they are studying. Institutional processes should be examined to see if they should be changed. When students recognize that they do not fit into the organizational norm, they start trying to find another path to success. The first step is to recognize that they do not agree with the picture of themselves which is imposed on them. Orientation of the access student is extremely important, to the institution, to the 'ground rules' of the discipline and to the student gaining epistemological access.

Students develop their identities through interactions within a community of practice. Being left out can be disempowering. Access students face challenges both in the social and the intellectual spheres, and these can have an impact on their progress. In science, for example, students from disadvantaged backgrounds can develop identities associated only with school science. University instructors in science should not only have knowledge of pedagogical content but also a working understanding of what is happening in classrooms attended by students with different cultural, historical and social backgrounds.

## ▶ Selected University Access Initiatives

South Africa's history led the new democratic government to focus on the needs of the historically excluded groups. Thus programmes were established at all tertiary institutions, with the flagship programmes often being found at prestigious research universities.

One source of variation in university access is the *distance to school*. Students from families situated near a university have the obvious cost-saving alternative of staying at home while attending university, avoiding the added costs associated with leaving home. Those living beyond commuting distance do not have this option and may be less likely to attend university, especially if they are from a low-income family. Universities need to consider the type and level of support they could offer to such students, the extent to which their organizational arrangements and academic cultures are exclusionary and the ways in which they may need to change in order to meet the needs of diverse students. Here we have selected three universities, Cape Town, Stellenbosch and the University of Western Cape, focusing on their mission statements and examining some their access innovations.

## University of Cape Town

### Mission statement

UCT aspires to become a premier academic meeting point between South Africa, the rest of Africa and the world. Taking advantage of expanding global networks and our distinct vantage point in Africa, we are committed through innovative research and scholarship to grappling with the key issues of our natural and social worlds. We strive to provide an environment for our diverse student and staff community that

- ▶ promotes a more equitable and non-racial society;
- ▶ supports redress in regard to past injustices;
- ▶ is affirming and inclusive of all staff and promotes diversity in demographics, skills and backgrounds.

(http://www.uct.ac.za/about/intro/)

The University of Cape Town has set overall enrolment and equity targets in line with this programme, referred to as aspirational targets rather than quotas. All faculties admit specified minimum numbers of eligible African, Chinese, Coloured and Indian students in accordance with their targets. The faculties set the class sizes for the qualification, both for regular programmes and for extended degree and academic development programmes. The minimum requirements for qualification are also set. For an engineering qualification, for example, these would be minimum achievement levels in mathematics and science, as well as the minimum admissions point score (APS). In terms of each qualification or group of qualifications, targets are set to redress enrolment, as well as for each redress category, and for international enrolments for each qualification. UCT offers places to the best applicants in each category, those who have met or exceeded the minimum achievement levels. In addition, UCT's 100 Up project is designed to accelerate the preparation of learners, and efforts are targeted at ensuring that they are provided with the support they need to succeed, and to provide the opportunity to attend an HE institution of their choice (UCT, 2013: 1–2; Rollnick, 2010: 2–3).

The last decade has seen a debate about UCT's race-based admission policy which has been both emotional and divisive. Successive vice-chancellors have failed to resolve this issue. The university's council is reported to be actively investigating better proxies for inequality but to date have been unable to find criteria that are more reliable than race. The arguments against a race-based admission are that it reinforces racial division and may unfairly disadvantage white students from poor backgrounds while giving wealthy black students an unfair advantage. The present vice-chancellor's opinion, based on the university's experience, is that the advantages far outweigh the disadvantages. In the meantime, the UCT admissions policy has been placed on hold (University of Cape Town, 2014).

## Stellenbosch University

### Mission statement

> The raison d´être of the University of Stellenbosch (SU) is to create and sustain, in commitment to the ideal of excellent scholarly and scientific practice, an environment in which knowledge can be discovered, shared, and applied to the benefit of the community.

### Vision

> In a spirit of academic freedom and of the universal quest for truth and knowledge, the university sets itself the aim, through critical and rational thought, of
>
> ▶ pursuing excellence and remaining at the forefront of its chosen focal areas;
> ▶ gaining national and international standing by means of its research outputs; and its production of graduates who are sought after for their well-roundedness and for their creative, critical thinking;

- being relevant to the needs of the community, taking into consideration the needs of South Africa in particular and of Africa and the world in general;
- being enterprising, innovative and self-renewing.

(Stellenbosch University Institutional Intent and Strategy 2013–18, 2013)

The responsibility for widening access to Stellenbosch University, especially to applications from schools which have been historically disadvantaged, rests with each faculty. They do so with the aid of alternative access programmes and extended degree programmes. Candidates are selected according to both academic and non-academic merit. School marks count for 45 per cent; national benchmark tests for 30 per cent; and non-academic merit leadership and community service, rural origin and whether parents are alumni or staff together count for 25 per cent. The top 60 candidates are selected according to their selection mark – irrespective of any other considerations – following which Indian candidates, preferably from the Western and Northern Cape provinces, and African and coloured candidates from all other provinces, are selected. Coloured, Asian and African students who score between 70 per cent and 74.9 per cent are considered for admission to the extended degree programme.

## Extended Degree Programme

An extended degree programme, or EDP, offers students who do not meet all faculty's specific requirements for a particular degree the opportunity to complete a degree programme by adding one year to the minimum time required for that degree. For example, a three-year BSc degree could be extended to four years, or a four-year engineering degree to five years. The extra time is dedicated to foundation modules which offer additional support for students.

Stellenbosch University employs two different models of EDPs. The first is the 'Foundation year' model, which offers foundation modules in the first year. After completing this, the student follows the programme as prescribed for mainstream students. Examples of this model are the science faculty's 'Alternative access programme' and the engineering faculty's 'Foundation year programme'. The second model used by SU is the 'Integration' model. In this, the first year of study is spread over two years, with students supported by foundation modules during these two years.

## University of the Western Cape

### Mission Statement

The University of the Western Cape is a national university, alert to its African and international context as it strives to be a place of quality, a place to grow. It is committed to excellence in teaching, learning and research, to nurturing the cultural diversity of South Africa, and to responding in critical and creative ways to the needs of a society in transition. In particular, it aims to

- assist educationally disadvantaged students gain access to HE and succeed in their studies;
- seek racial and gender equality and contribute to helping the historically marginalized participate fully in the life of the nation. (taken from https://www.uwc.ac.uk/Pages/Mission.aspx)

The university recognized that under-preparedness affected the majority of students. It therefore opted for an academic development model, followed by a teaching and learning strategic plan. It designed a foundation programme which was forward looking, preparing students for the future, as opposed to a bridging one which would focus only on the gaps carried over from high school. Complementing this is an academy for revision and tuition (SMART), a science and maths project aimed at assisting high school learners in their preparation for grade 12, thereby providing them with opportunities to access HE. In particular, UWC targets community-based schools which have shown a potential to be among the best.

## ▶ Conclusion

It seems that the challenge of access to universities is long term and not about to be eradicated, even taking into account the national government's 2030 targets. The present approaches seem superficial, tackling under-preparedness at high school level only. Universities need to address their own teaching and learning for diversity. It would be productive for them to focus on programmes which yielded the best results, without implying that 'one size fits all'. From the three selected universities, the elements which work best in each institution could be studied. These could then be combined into a working guideline for the Western Cape Province. Such a guideline is described below:

- The departments of basic and HE should plan together and introduce a phased-in discussion about facilitating access from early childhood until grade 12. This would ensure that all necessary steps were taken to help learners to excel in school and, by extension, in HE.
- Learning circles could be built where learners were encouraged to work together, facilitating their engagements among themselves, thereby building their confidence levels.

- Teachers and schools need to play a facilitative role, encouraging learners to undertake projects as part of building the self-reliance they will need for HE.
- The competency levels of teachers need to be raised, particularly in language proficiency and understanding of content, to stimulate the confidence of learners.
- The curriculum should be adapted to establish bridging subjects at the intersection between schools and HE.
- University teaching and learning should include an understanding of diversity learning.

# 11 Making Commitment Concrete: Policy and Practice in Access to HE in Ghana

Joseph Budu

### ▶ Background to Higher Education in Ghana

In this chapter, we examine the challenges facing the sector in its drive to increase access The gross enrolment ratio (GER) for higher education (HE) in Ghana is currently around 12 per cent (UNESCO, 2014). This is far below the GER for advanced countries. Since the 2000s, there has been a big drive to increase enrolment in HE in Ghana. The National Council for Tertiary Education (NCTE), the body charged with advising on the development of tertiary education (which includes HE) in Ghana, has set a target GER of 25 per cent for the sector (NCTE, 2013). It appears also that in the midst of the drive towards increasing total enrolments, there have also been concerns about giving equal opportunities for under-represented groups. Such groups include older, mature student entrants as well as those who would otherwise not be able to afford to enter HE. In addition, the issues of rurality, gender inequality and the quality of HE offered loom large in Ghana, and these issues are explored in detail here.

Tertiary education in Ghana has been defined to refer to all education offered after secondary school, usually leading to the award of certificates, diplomas, bachelor's degrees and postgraduate degrees. In order to reach this stage, pupils attend primary school for six years, spend another three years at the junior high school, and if they are successful, go through senior high school for another three years.

The bulk of the students at the tertiary level are in the publicly funded institutions. In Ghana, tertiary education is composed of ten universities, ten polytechnic institutions and a number of professional institutes. The total number of institutions is 58 in all, as outlined in Table 11.1.

A number of private universities and other tertiary education institutions have been established since 2002, although they account for only 5 per cent

**Table 11.1** Type of Tertiary Education Institutions in Ghana

| | Tertiary Education Institutions | | |
|---|---|---|---|
| 1 | Public | Number | % |
| | Universities | 10 | 8.6 |
| | Polytechnics | 10 | 8.6 |
| | Colleges of Education | 38 | 32.8 |
| | Specialized Institutions | 3 | 2.6 |
| 2 | **Accredited Private TE Institutions** | **55** | **47.4** |
| | **Total** | **113** | **100.0** |

Ministry of Education (2013)

of total tertiary enrolments. As of 2013, there were 55 private tertiary institutions accredited by the National Accreditation Board (MoE, 2013).

Admission to bachelor's degree programmes in sector tertiary institutions is mainly based on a student's results from the West African Senior Secondary School Certificate Examination (SSCE) that is administered by the West African Examinations Council. Students who do not meet the competitive departmental requirements and cut-off points, but who do satisfy the minimum entry requirements, may be admitted on a fee-paying basis, whereby they pay a fee higher than what Ghanaian students would normally pay.

Polytechnics were only upgraded to the tertiary level in 1992 through the Polytechnics Law. In 2007, this law was repealed and replaced with the Polytechnics Act, 2007. This law granted autonomy to polytechnics and mandated them to run bachelor of technology (B-Tech) degree programmes (Owusu-Ansah and Poku, 2012). In contrast to universities, polytechnics prepare students for practice-oriented, middle-level professions.

### *Growth in Student Enrolments*

Enrolments at the ten polytechnics in Ghana have shown considerable growth, in particular during the 1990s, with total enrolments increased from 1385 in 1993–94 to 47,294 in 2011–12. The growth of female enrolments has been even more spectacular, growing from 217 in 1993–94 to 14,436 in 2011–12. Male enrolment grew from 1168 in 1993–94 to 32,858 in 2011–12. In spite of the tremendous enrolment growth, gender imbalance still persists, as female enrolment is still only about 25.0 per cent of the total enrolment (NCTE, 2013). The conversion of polytechnics to tertiary institutions in 1992 and the policy of mandating polytechnics to introduce B-Tech degree programmes in the polytechnics in 2007 (which provides an avenue of progression for higher national diploma [HND] graduates) appear to have attracted many more candidates into the polytechnics. It is also true that over the period in question, a lot of investment has gone into the development of physical resources and the academic staff capital of the polytechnics in order to enable them meet their mandates.

Student enrolments at the universities in Ghana have also grown tremendously over the years. Total enrolments increased from 14,278 in 1992–93 to 109,278 in 2011–12. Female enrolments in the universities increased from 3167 in 1992–93 to 35,651 in 2011–12, and male enrolment grew from 11,111 in 1992–93 to 73,627 in 2011–12 (NCTE, 2013). Female enrolment is only about 29.0 per cent of the total student enrolments, compared to the national target of 50 per cent.

A number of reasons account for the relatively low enrolment in the tertiary institutions. The public universities have seen an appreciable expansion of their physical infrastructure financed by allocations from the Ghana Education Trust Fund (GETFund). The GETFund is an innovative funding mechanism that supports budgetary allocations to the education sector from the central government. It is financed by proceeds from a 2.5 percent additional rate on the value-added tax (VAT) in Ghana. But these facilities have still not reached the level where it can cope with the increasing demand for access. In spite of the large number of private institutions, they are not able to attract more students to ease the pressure on the public universities due mainly to the high tuition fees charged in those institutions, coupled with concerns about prestige as well as the breadth of the programmes on offer. A case in point is the dissolution of the Meridian University College (MUC), an accredited private tertiary education which has been receiving mentorship from the University of Cape Coast (UCC). Authorities of MUC cite low student enrolment and financial challenges as the principal reasons for the closure of the institution. At a meeting of MUC, UCC and NAB (National Australia Bank), an agreement was reached for the transfer of the 46 students of MUC to a sister institution – West End University College – to continue their studies (Daily Graphic, 2014).

However, the high rates of attrition earlier down the system are also the predictable causes of low participation in tertiary education. As Atuahene and Owusu-Ansah (2013: 5) argue, drawing on World Bank data in 2008–09:

> For example, during 2008–9, the male to female primary GER was 97% to 92.8% compared with the respective GER of 83.9% and 77% at the

Junior High School, and male to female GER of 36.7% to 30.8% at the Senior High School levels, respectively. Clearly, by the time students graduate from High School, a greater percentage of them would have dropped out.

## ▶ Policy Framework with Regard to Access to Tertiary Education

### *The National Constitution*

The 1992 constitution of the Republic of Ghana has a section on Education, which has a bearing on access to education. Article 25 of the national constitution states:

(1) All persons shall have the right to equal educational opportunities and facilities, and with a view to achieving the full realization of that right –
   a. Basic education shall be free, compulsory and available to all.
   b. Secondary education in its different forms, including technical and vocational education, shall be made generally available and accessible to all by every appropriate means, and in particular, by progressive introduction of free education;
   c. Higher education shall be made equally accessible to all, on the basis of capacity, by every appropriate means and, in particular, by progressive introduction of free education;
   d. Functional literacy shall be encouraged or intensified as far as possible.
   e. The development of a system of schools with adequate facilities at all levels shall be actively pursued.
(2) Every person shall have the right, at his own expense, to establish and maintain a private school or schools at all levels and of such categories and in accordance with such conditions as may be provided by law.

These sections of the national constitution therefore provide the general framework for all educational policies in Ghana. They ingrain equal opportunities for all persons at all levels of education. However, this does not feed through to reality. Although the overall levels of HE participation in Ghana may be low in international terms, there are also distinct differences in participation by social background.

## Who Is Under-represented in HE in Ghana?

Manuh, Gariba and Budu (2007) observed that access to tertiary education in Ghana continues to be quite limited and unquestionably differentiated by socio-economic status, region of origin and types and locations of secondary school. In this section, we provide an overview of the key policies and practices that have been deployed in the past, to support the progression to tertiary education of the groups mentioned above, both at the national and institutional levels.

### Female Students

Gender disparities tend to increase at higher levels of education. Although women's participation in university-based tertiary education is increasing, the percentage of female enrolment becomes lower as one moves up the levels of programmes within the institutions. NCTE figures for public universities indicate that women's participation is highest at the certificate and diploma level, where 46 per cent of students are women, falling to 35 per cent for degrees, and is lowest at postgraduate study, where 29 per cent of Master's students and only 17 per cent of PhD students in Ghana are women (MoE, 2013).

There are many explanations for the gender gap, including low enrolment in basic education and gendered sociocultural practices (Dunne, 2007). Ghana remains a deeply patriarchal society. As Daddieh (2003: 23) argues: '[N]egative parental attitudes and cultural practices have tended to devalue female educational achievements, and thereby undermine their educational participation.' Furthermore, gender is not always examined in combination with socio-economic background, disability and ethnicity (Morley, Leach and Lugg, 2009).

A number of interventions have been adopted, especially at the pre-university stage of education, to improve the chances of young women entering HE. One of the foremost organizations that works at promoting girls' education among the poorest regions of Ghana is CAMFED (Campaign for Girls Education) (https://camfed.org/where-we-work/ghana/). Since 2013, CAMFED has been advancing work to assist girls who are able to progress to the tertiary level, to go through that level as well. The key features of the CAMFED model are described in Table 11.2. The model shows that to affect educational participation a 'whole-community' and a 'whole-person' approach is needed. Support focused in individual areas will not be sufficient.

At the HE level, institutions have adopted various measures aimed at addressing the imbalance in enrolment for females. At the University of Ghana, for example, there is a policy of 'affirmative action' where females who obtain one grade above the normal cut-off point for the non-competitive programmes are offered admission. The cut-off point is usually determined

**Table 11.2** The CAMFED Model

| |
|---|
| ▶ Provision of scholarships and stipends, which are cash and in-kind contributions to girls and/or their families for the purpose of school attendance. |
| ▶ Provision of transportation or boarding facilities as interventions to reduce the distance travelled to school. |
| ▶ Community engagement and sensitization activities involving a wide range of activities promoting positive attitudes and local resource mobilization that support girls in obtaining an education. |
| ▶ Measures aimed at child protection and safety, which include training, codes of conduct and guidelines to ensure girls' safety in the school environment. |
| ▶ Programming for school feeding and other health-related issues. |
| ▶ Recruitment and training of female teachers, assistant teachers and other educators, including the hiring and incentivizing and complementary teaching staff for gender balance. |
| ▶ Curriculum and sensitization for teachers, administrators and school bodies on gender training. |
| ▶ Providing mentoring, tutoring and peer support for girls' development and learning needs through engagement with peers, older women and other adults. |
| ▶ Complementary education as provided through flexible, community-based education, targeting out-of-school youth. |
| ▶ Strengthening governance of entitlements, quality and protection by training school-community oversight committees, strengthening stewardship of resources for girls' education. |

by the number of places available as against the number of applications. At the University of Development Studies Abagre et al. (2013) describe how a bridging programme has been put in place to support the progression of female students into HE. They found that the programme had a positive impact on the academic success of female students who came from lower income and rural backgrounds. They argue for the spread of such projects across institutions in Ghana. However, they also argue that there is a need to improve the level of knowledge regarding such work in the country:

> Even with this, the question of the effective implementation of such a policy by university administrators to ensure the achievement of academic excellence on the part of such female beneficiaries has not been answered. This is because there is lack of adequate information on model programmes being implemented by individual institutions.
>
> (Abagre et al., 2013: 23)

## Students from Less Endowed Schools

Another disadvantaged group are what is described as students from 'less endowed schools'. The Ghana Education Service (GES) has categorized certain schools as less endowed. These are senior high schools in the deprived or rural areas which lack basic facilities such as classrooms, learning materials, and trained as well as experienced teachers. In 2002, out of the about 600 secondary schools in the country, 297 forming about 49.5 per cent were classified as less endowed. This has since not changed, even though the number of senior high schools increased to about 697 in 2009 (Yusif and Ali, 2013). Because academic performance in the SSCE is the main criterion for gaining admission into the universities, access to the universities is highly competitive. Thus given the competitive admission standards, students from the less endowed schools are unable to meet the admission requirements. This is not surprising as one of the major predicators of success in Ghana secondary schools is quality of school attended. As a result, students who normally gain admission to the universities are students from the well-endowed senior high schools.

A range of studies draw upon the available data (which is intermittently available here) to illustrate the extent of divisions here – which in themselves have considerable spatial dimensions, as the distribution of less well-endowed schools is unequal by region. As Atuahene and Owusu-Ansah argue, analyzing data from a range of sources, the educational gini coefficient for tertiary education entry by region varies considerably in the extent of inequality (where 0 reflects complete equality and 1 indicates complete inequality). To illustrate the challenges in particular key occupational areas, Addae-Mensah (2000) found that over 70 per cent of the country's future doctors, scientists, engineers, architects, pharmacists, agriculturists and other professionals emerged from just about 10 per cent of the schools, with almost 50 per cent emerging from less than 4 percent, or only 18 of Ghana's 504 senior secondary schools.

Without any prompting from Central government, some of the universities, both public and private, have adopted measures aimed at dealing with the imbalance in the admission of candidates into tertiary education. One such measure is the admission of candidates from what are known as 'less endowed secondary schools' (LESS).

A comprehensive analysis of the scheme, as operated in the Kwame Nkrumah University of Science and Technology (KNUST), is provided by Yusif and Ali (2013). Every year, the university invites each of these schools to submit the best six candidates – three male and three female. These are screened, and if they make the minimum entry requirements, they are offered admission. It is reported that a total of 1948 students were enrolled in KNUST between 2003 and 2010, out of a total of 2850 offered admission by the university. It is not clear what factors make it impossible for those offered admission to take up the offers, but it is speculated that many of them might not be in a position to bear the cost of the education and therefore opt out.

The University of Ghana took the decision to admit students from less-endowed secondary schools (LESS) in 2004. The first intake of students under the scheme entered in the 2004–05 academic year. The principle behind the scheme is to offer admission to students from less privileged backgrounds who are academically capable but who would otherwise be denied access because of the keen competition. At the University of Ghana, admission is offered to the best candidate from each LESS, provided he or she meets the minimum entry requirements. In very rare cases where there is a tie, both applicants are offered admission. Admission of candidates from the LESS category seeks to correct the disadvantage faced by those candidates who may be less academically prepared only because of geographical location and the resources available to the school.

There are currently 303 schools countrywide which form the LESS. They are mainly located either in rural areas or in economically deprived locations within urban areas. In the absence of quantitative information on the effects of the scheme, some discussions were undertaken in the preparation of this paper with personnel from the University of Ghana who have dealt with the scheme, to sample their views on the operation of the scheme to date.

The views of a number of persons were specifically sought on the scheme as it operates at the University of Ghana. These are all persons who occupy senior management positions at the University of Ghana and who have in the course of their official duty dealt with students directly in one way or another. They all believe the LESS programme is a very good scheme that needs to be continued and expanded to include many more people. In their view, the scheme has been very helpful in making it possible for many candidates, who would otherwise not have made it, to obtain university education.

The University community usually becomes aware of the presence of students from the scheme at graduation and prize award ceremonies that showcase successful students who came in under this policy and have since emerged with very good grades, as well as being very good sportsmen and women. An example of this is one such occasion where the best sportswoman of the year, who had also graduated with a first-class degree, disclosed that she had been admitted under the LESS scheme.

The officials go on to make some suggestions for consideration. They suggest that the current application process, which places the onus on the candidate to apply, should be reviewed to channel the process through the school administration. There is also the suggestion that the University of Ghana should liaise with the other public universities implementing the scheme, so that duplications in the offer of admission could be avoided. Another recommendation is for the introduction of a mentoring system to assist such students to adapt quickly to the HE environment, in order to succeed in receiving good education. To expose more secondary school students to the scheme, it has been suggested that the outreach programmes could be extended to the schools themselves. Other suggestions include encouraging the Students Representative Council (SRC) to make an extra effort to reach out to students with such backgrounds in order to provide support to them; extending the number of schools beyond the GES list; and increasing the number of candidate falling into the category who are offered admission, from the current one to two candidates per school.

## Students with Disabilities

Students with disabilities pose particular challenges to Ghanain HE, not only in terms of gaining physical access to buildings but also in relation to much wider access issues concerning the curriculum, teaching, learning and assessment. For these reasons, they may be seen as a litmus test of the ability of HE to include a diverse range of learners, particularly relevant in light of recent emphasis on initiatives aimed at widening access to HE to under-represented groups.

Students with disabilities in Ghana are, in the main, outside the regular formal educational mainstream. Rather, they are educated in specialized schools such as the school for the blind and deaf, the notion being that they will not fit in the regular schools and should therefore be given special care and attention. Again, teachers at the basic and secondary levels receive little or no training to be able to support the educational needs of students with disabilities, and the facilities in these schools are also not user-friendly for such people. The few who are successfully educated in the specialized schools up to the level they qualify to enrol in HE are rendered 'misfits' because there are no specialized HEIs for the physically challenged in Ghana, where the facilities were designed without the peculiar needs of such students in mind.

In essence, inclusive education has not been given the attention it deserves in the Ghanaian context. A Disability Bill which was expected to address the needs of students with disabilities in Ghana was passed into law in 2006, which, inter alia, mandates institutions and individuals to grant persons with disability access to public places; failure imposes penalties and fines, but very little is done to enforce the law. Articles 6, 7 and 17 of the Act, for example, state:

> The owner or occupier of a place to which the public has access shall provide appropriate facilities that make the place accessible to and available for use by a person with disability. A person who provides service to the

public shall put in place the necessary facilities that make the service available and accessible to a person with disability.... The Minister of Education shall by Legislative Instrument designate schools or institutions in each region which shall provide the necessary facilities and equipment that will enable persons with disability to fully benefit from the school or institution.[1]

(Persons with Disability Act, 2006, http://www.gapagh.org/GHANA%20DISABILITY%20ACT.pdf)

The University of Ghana has an office for students with special needs 'which is to help identify varied needs of students with special needs and provide them with best support services. This is to ensure that students with physical challenges have complete and equitable access to all facets of University life as could be reasonably provided, to enable them achieve optimum academic outcomes' (Modern Ghana, 2009). This has been in existence since 2009, at which time there were 60 such persons being catered for by the office.

*Socio-economic Factors*
To an extent, geography as described above is a proxy for socio-economic disadvantage, but there is a need for specific consideration and analysis here in the Ghanaian context. There is significant evidence that those learners from lower socio-economic groups are less likely to enter HE in Ghana. As Atuahene and Owusu-Ansah (2013: 7) state, 'Data from the Ghana Living Survey indicate that higher education in Ghana is dominated by 67% of individuals from the richest quintile and 10% from the poorest two quintiles.'

This data from the Ghana Living Survey is supported by data included in the 2010 publication from the World Bank, *Education in Ghana: Improving Equity, Efficiency and Accountability of Education Service Delivery.* As the report states:

> Higher Education in Ghana is disproportionately 'consumed' by the richest 20% of the population. Male students from the highest income quintile (Q5) are more than seven times more likely to enter and successfully complete HE than those from the poorest quintile (Q1). The situation is even more precarious for the female category where students come from only the richest 40% of the population.
>
> (World Bank, 2010: 157)

There has been less work done to explore the basis for the disparities in the Ghanaian context. Income differentials will feed through the differences in schooling achievement and then HE progression via the filters of differences in financial and cultural capital (Morley et al., 2007). Addressing the disparities would take long-term work. Providing better financial support for learners who need it is one starting point.

There are schemes at the national as well as institutional levels to assist students who are unable to raise the necessary funds to support their education. Key among these is the provision of student loan support. Such support was established by the Provisional National Defence Council (PNDC) Law of 1992. This scheme was replaced by a market-oriented Student Loan Trust Fund in 2005. The Trust Fund scheme is anchored on the principles of sustainability and scalability. The purpose of the new Student Loan Trust Fund is to provide enhanced support for tertiary education by providing loan facilities to support the maintenance costs of students. The Trust has developed a method of using means testing to establish the extent of financial assistance required by each student, within defined limits. The Trust was to be financed as follows: 10 per cent of all inflows into the GET Fund; tax deductible voluntary contributions; funds mobilized from Ghana's international development partners; loans from the Social Security and the National Insurance Trust; and corporate contributions which are tax deductible to the equivalent of 0.5 per cent of a company's annual profit before tax. However, since the establishment of the Student Loan Trust Fund, the GETFund has become the main source of funding (NCTE, 2013).

At the institutional level, some of the institutions have various schemes for supporting low-income students. The University of Ghana, for example, has a Student Financial Aid Office, which provides an avenue for the university to generate funds through its own budgetary allocations as well as through gifts and donations for the purpose of providing financial aid for students who need such assistance. The Office was established in 2005 in response to the increasing need to provide financial assistance to students of the university. This financial assistance provided is only to cover academic fees and does not include costs of board and lodge. The financial aid may be in the form of a full scholarship, partial scholarship, rescheduling of fee payment and on-campus work-study programme opportunities for students.

*Under-representation Based on Discipline*
It is a national policy that enrolments in the HE institutions should follow a 60:40 ratio for the sciences and humanities, respectively (Ghana MOESS, 2007). However, evidence suggests that the reverse is the case, and many more students are registered in the humanities than in the sciences (Alabi, Alabi and Mohammed, 2013). This is seen in the way most of the private HE institutions offer 'marketable programmes' like business administration, theology and information technology–related programmes. This situation comes about because, contrary to government expectation, it appears that the perception among prospective students is that they are more likely to gain employment within a short time of graduation if they do humanities rather than the sciences (Alabi et al., 2013).

## Conclusions and Views on Challenges for Access to Tertiary Education in Ghana

In this chapter, an effort has been made to describe the context in which access to HE in Ghana may be considered and the challenges being faced. It is clear from the 1992 national constitution and other laws and policies that it is the intention to offer equal opportunities to all citizens in terms of access to HE. As the World Bank stated in 2010:

'Whatever the difficulties, education has become a core priority for Ghana'.
(World Bank, 2010: iii)

It must be stated that two thirds of Ghana's 26 million people are farmers. However, Ghana spends 8 per cent of GDP on education, more than the United Nations' 6 per cent benchmark and more than the United Kingdom's 6.5 per cent. Moreover, almost 90 per cent of Ghanaian children are in school – compared with 64 per cent in Nigeria and 72 per cent in Pakistan (Rustin, 2015). This commitment is not confined to policymakers. It is visible in the behaviour of HE institutions as well. There are bold measures taken by the various institutions to address perceived imbalances in HE participation in favour of under-represented groups, as described above. The situation regarding these groups has been described in the earlier sections: females, persons with special needs (or physical disabilities), those from disadvantaged socio-economic backgrounds and those from LESS. More attention has been paid to the LESS programme, as it provides a unique opportunity to enhance the prospects of persons disadvantaged merely because of the geographical location and the resources available in the schools they attended. From all indications, the scheme, which has operated for about ten years now, has resulted in quite a number of candidates obtaining university education who would otherwise not have benefited. The impact on the candidates themselves, their schools, their families and the larger communities from which they came stands to be encouraged by their achievements both at the university and in life generally.

We suggest that there should be a formal review of schemes such as LESS by the authorities involved, with a view to improving knowledge regarding the more effective programmes and up-scaling those which have the most impact. However, in order for schemes like LESS to achieve optimum results, it is necessary for government to provide the necessary rewards and incentive schemes for the institutions to undertake such ventures. Access for under-representation groups should not be seen as something that must be pursued only after issues with what is considered the 'regular admissions' have been resolved. Although the government in Ghana is committed to enabling more of its learners to enter HE, it needs a pro-active policy approach here. As argued above, Ghana is making significant progress in extending education enrolment for younger pupils, but it also needs to start to build pathways for these learners into HE.

# 12 Evolution or Revolution: The Three Ages of Access in Australia

Margaret Heagney and Fran Ferrier

## ▶ Introduction

The current student equity framework for higher education (HE) in Australia was established in 2009 under the previous Australian government. Located in a 'social inclusion' framework, it emphasizes the responsibility of institutions to contribute to social well-being, but also expresses a strong economic purpose for broadening participation – to ensure the nation has the high-level skills it needs to remain globally competitive.

The framework sets a target of 40 per cent of 25- to 34-years-olds to have a bachelor's degree by 2025, noting that it is not possible to achieve this without altering the social composition of the student body. This requires increased participation among those groups currently under-represented in the HE system, identified as people from regional and remote areas, Indigenous students and students from low socio-economic backgrounds (the bottom quartile of income-earning households).

As we write, it is not at all clear that this framework will continue to shape HE in Australia. The Australian government, elected in 2013, proposed measures that would see public funding for the sector cut by 20 per cent, student fees de-regulated and a further expansion of private provision. Equity scholarships for undergraduate study would be funded from the Higher Education Participation and Partnership Program (HEPPP) (previously used by universities for their outreach and student support programmes). Government support for postgraduate scholarships would be cut.

Modelling indicates the impact of these measures is likely to be greatest on those groups most under-represented in the system (Koshy, Pitman and Phillimore, 2014). It could be argued that the proposed changes would make it harder to achieve the target noted above and could threaten many of the gains already achieved.

Against this background we have chosen in this case study to focus not on a single equity initiative and its outcomes, but on the policy framework that provides the foundation for student equity initiatives in the HE system. Our aim is to highlight those aspects that have been most and least effective in supporting greater student equity and diversity.

To understand how different frameworks have developed and evolved and their impacts, we look back briefly from the present to the 1970s, when the Australian (i.e. federal or national) government assumed financial responsibility for HE from the states. Since this time, successive governments have wielded the 'power of the public purse' to influence institutions to work toward their social and economic objectives.

There have been three main national policy frameworks over this period: expansion of the HE system to increase opportunities; *A Fair Chance for All* – based on a 'target-group' approach; and, mostly recently, a 'demand-driven system' entwining social and economic objectives.

## ▶ Background: Australia's HE System

HE in Australia is provided by public and private universities, branches of overseas universities, some institutions in the vocational education and training (VET) sector and other private providers. Universities are self-accrediting, but other providers may require cooperative arrangements with a university to be able to award degrees.

Universities are the major provider, and the Australian university system is overwhelmingly a public one. Of the 39 universities which are current members of *Universities Australia* (www.universitiesaustralia.edu.au), 37 are public and only two are private. Together they enrol over 1 million students and employ over 100,000 staff.

Australia is a federation of nine states and territories, with most universities established under state legislation. Since the mid 1970s, public universities have been funded by the Australian (Federal or Commonwealth) government. Prior to this, they were funded by the states. In recent years, private institutions have also been eligible to receive some public funding.

Universities increasingly seek to supplement the public funding they receive with income from other sources, such as student fees, research grants and fee-for-service arrangements.

All students pay a tuition fee. Those granted a Commonwealth Supported Place (CSP) are subsidized by the government and thus pay a lower fee, which is capped by the government. Those not granted a CSP pay higher (full-cost) fees. Fees vary according to the field of study, with medicine and dentistry the most expensive. Students are eligible for government loans to cover their tuition fees, and repayment is not required until their income reaches a designated level (around 75% of average weekly earnings). The amount required to be repaid rises with income.

The number of Commonwealth Supported Places is limited and depends on the grants the government provides to the universities.

Some students who do not have family support, or who have low incomes, are also eligible for government-provided income support. Some government scholarships are available, including for research study at postgraduate level.

Although many universities are located in state capital cities, some are located in regional towns and cities, have a commitment to their region and play a role in local economies.

### ▶ Policy Framework 1: Expansion of the System

A larger and more open HE system, offering many new opportunities, was initially part of national recovery and rebuilding in the post-war years, also influenced by heightened idealism about the potential of science to solve global problems in the cold war. This era produced many government-commissioned reviews of HE, leading to a flurry of reports (the Murray report in 1957, the Martin report in 1964, two Partridge reports in 1963 and 1968 and the Williams report in 1979). Many new universities were established, and a whole new post-school sector – colleges of advanced education (CAEs).

New universities took on different roles from the 'sandstones' – those that were long-standing and traditional. Built outside the centres of capital cities and in regional areas, they were expected to build a stronger relationship with local populations and were also less closely tied to traditional professions. CAEs had a stronger technical function. Although not initially degree-granting institutions, this changed in response to demand, and many CAEs became the 'universities of technology' of today.

Scholarships, studentships and bursaries helped to reduce the impact of tuition fees and the costs of studying for some students. Provided mainly by governments and institutions, scholarships were mostly awarded on the basis of academic merit, for example the results of final-year school examinations. Though not designed as an equity initiative, studentships and bursaries offered for study in the fields of teaching and nursing had a greater impact on bringing into the system students from under-represented groups. Responding to concerns about an inadequate number of qualified candidates for the number of jobs available, these provided fairly generous living allowances, making study possible for some students who would otherwise have left school and joined the workforce.

In 1967, of 215 students in the education faculty at Monash University – a new university established in the late 1950s – 144 were studentship holders (History of the faculty, www.monash.edu/education). Biographies of many of Australia's female leaders provide an indication of the importance of studentships in enabling HE study.

In a recent media interview, the chairman of the Australian Securities and Investment Commission (ASIC) spoke about his own experience of the changes in HE during this period:

> I remember when I was in high school ... opportunities to go to university were pretty limited unless you took a studentship ... and became a teacher ... I went to university in '75 so I was really amongst the first of the kids. You suddenly had this influx of working class kids into university ... it was quite an interesting, exciting time ... I felt just privileged.
> (Medcraft, 2014)

In 1974, following the election to power of a progressive political party with a broad social agenda, a more direct initiative was introduced to reduce financial disincentives to HE participation: tuition fees were abolished. The government hoped that this would open up participation, especially among 'working class students' (Maclean 2007).

Today the outcomes of this initiative still remain disputed. Using the available student data, a study (Anderson and Vervoorn, 1983) suggested limited impact, but a growing body of anecdotal evidence now indicates that this measure did have some effect and was particularly important for increasing participation among mature women.

Ultimately though, financial pressures, particularly in the context of demand for further expansion of the system, meant that free tuition could not be sustained, and fees were re-introduced in the 1980s, first as a small administrative charge and then at a level considered commensurate with the private benefit received through participation. The government moved to offset the disincentive impact by creating an 'income-contingent' loans scheme – the Higher Education Contribution Scheme (HECS).

Looking back in 1987 over the period of expansion and experimentation with expansion and fee-free provision, Beswick (1987) summed up the disappointment felt by many that so little change had been achieved, despite strong motivation:

> Despite all the social idealism attached to education in the last decade, the hope that education would lead us to the threshold of a just society

in which inequalities due to personal background and circumstances have been eliminated, higher education remains as much as ever the domain of those in least need of the greater personal opportunity and self-realisation it commonly brings.

It had become clear that a different approach was called for – one that more directly addressed the barriers preventing those in under-represented groups from taking up opportunities in HE.

## ▶ Policy Framework 2: 'A Fair Chance for All' and 'Target Group Initiatives'

In 1990, the Australian government released a paper on the future of HE (Department of Employment, Education and Training, 1990) that would become the primary document shaping thinking and action on student equity for nearly two decades. *A Fair Chance for All – Higher Education That's Within Everyone's Reach* set out the government's ambitions for opening up HE to a broader range of students and embedded it within a social justice framework,

> to ensure that Australians from all groups in society have the opportunity to participate successfully in higher education. This will be achieved by changing the balance of the student population to reflect more closely the composition of society as a whole.
> 
> (Executive Summary, p. 2)

The release of *A Fair Chance for All* was a significant moment in Australian HE, marking the first time a government 'defined an overall national equity objective' (Ramsay, 2006). The following years saw the implementation of a

> robust, well-articulated and clearly understood framework of planning and reporting requirements directed toward the achievement of the overall equity objective.
> 
> (Ramsay, 2006)

The framework identified six groups experiencing relative disadvantage in accessing HE:

- ▶ Indigenous people
- ▶ People from rural and isolated areas
- ▶ People from socio-economically disadvantaged backgrounds
- ▶ People with disabilities
- ▶ People from non-English speaking backgrounds
- ▶ Women, especially in non-traditional areas

**Table 12.1** Operational Definitions of Each Target Group and Indicators for Measuring Progress Were Established by 1994 (the 'Martin Indicators')

| Indicator | Descriptor |
|---|---|
| Access | Commencing equity group students as a percentage of all domestic commencing students |
| Participation | Equity group students as a percentage of all domestic students |
| Apparent Retention | Equity group students re-enrolling in a given year as a proportion of those enrolled in the previous year, less those completing their course. |
| Success | Ratio of SPR (student progress rate, that is, success at passing all units for which the student enrolled) of equity group students to SPR for other students |

In Table 12.1 indicators of success are outlined in relation to this framework. Institutions were required to submit annual Equity Plans and Aboriginal Education Strategies, setting out objectives for the coming year and reporting against those for the previous year. A newly established *Higher Education Equity Program* provided public funds to support their work.

The framework had two important characteristics. Firstly, it established equity in HE as the joint responsibility of government and the institutions:

> The Government believes that achieving a more equitable higher education system needs a joint commitment and a joint effort by the Commonwealth and individual higher education institutions.
> (Department of Employment, Education and Training, 1990: Section 1. National Priorities and Needs, p. 7)

The second was flexibility – with each institution able to identify and work towards its own equity targets, based on local needs and priorities. In a large country with great differences among states and among urban, regional and remote areas, especially in populations, this was welcome.

A third important aspect was that in requiring the collection and reporting of extensive data on students in the target groups, it enabled research and analysis that would provide an evidence base for further refinement and development of equity policies and initiatives.

What was the impact of the new framework? Two years after the release of *A Fair Chance for All*, the government commissioned a comprehensive review of progress (HEC, 1996). Perhaps not surprisingly, given the relatively short time since the framework had been introduced, this reported mixed results. 'Most of the obvious barriers' to participation by disadvantaged groups had been removed, but there was a need for a 'deeper examination' of the reasons why some inequalities persist and for 'more complex solutions' to be found if the goals of *A Fair Chance for All* were to be achieved.

The most under-represented groups in the student population are now people from socio-economically disadvantaged backgrounds and isolated students. Since 1990, access and participation have significantly improved for Aboriginal and Torres Strait Islander students and for people from non-English speaking backgrounds. Women are also now strongly represented in higher education generally but there still remain some fields of study and courses at higher level in which they are particularly under-represented (p. ix.)

The review offered many recommendations to accelerate progress including investigations into 'cross-sectoral' disadvantage (overlaps in the target groups) and the 'mainstreaming' of equity accountability and incentives in institutional processes, for instance that equity planning, monitoring and review be part of mainstream processes for quality improvement and academic quality assurance.

Because of a change of government, the recommendations of this review were sidelined, and student equity planning and reporting arrangements continued unchanged (Ramsay, 2006). However, some of the ideas it presented were influential in the institutions, along with experience with the equity framework and a growing body of student equity research. This led to some changed thinking and action.

Of particular note, 'mainstreaming' of equity became a greater focus of attention, and there were some changes in targeting, with a greater focus on 'central categories' where disadvantage was concentrated. More attention began to be paid also to disadvantaged, outside-the-target-group categories.

Mainstreaming recognized that while student equity remained only an 'add-on', rather than an integral element in institutional policies, processes and planning, it would be difficult to achieve equity and diversity objectives.

Changes in targeting toward 'central categories' was supported by studies demonstrating a high degree of overlap in the membership of the equity target groups and the 'compounding' or intensification of disadvantage, when this occurred. For instance, Dobson, Sharma and Ramsey (1998) had found that more than 80 per cent of low SES students and 60 per cent of rural and isolated students were also members of other equity groups, and

Clarke, Zimmer and Main (1997) noted that low SES was a 'common central element' in the disadvantage experienced by students in other equity categories. Attention to disadvantage outside the equity categories reflected emerging concern that the focus on the designated target groups might have led to neglect of other experiences of disadvantage outside these groups. From our own and others' research, in the late 1990s we wrote that despite its many positive characteristics, as a strategy for improving equity, the identification of target groups tended to provide a simplified picture of the extent and nature of 'disadvantage' and mask diversity within groups. It also set de facto boundaries around equity programmes and activities. A more comprehensive picture emerging from research was that disadvantage extended beyond the boundaries of the target groups and took many forms in addition to under-representation. There were also some differences in disadvantage according to the characteristics of institutions and their local social and economic environments. For instance, in this period we were asked by Monash University to investigate whether there was disadvantage outside the target groups. Our work identified in the university:

> disadvantage that may not be confined to those in the designated categories. These are students with inadequate financial resources, students combining study and work, students with family responsibilities and students who are the first in the family to attend university. Some particular effort could also be made to assist students who experience isolation in the university environment.
> 
> (Ferrier and Heagney, 2001: 66)

We also found that after enrolment the extent and nature of disadvantage experienced by a student could change abruptly and dramatically. For instance, a student might encounter difficulties related to the timetabling of a course, or access to the library, only when an employer demanded a non-negotiable change in working hours. An illness in the family might require a student to fulfil temporary family responsibilities that affected her or his ability to meet assessment requirements. A loss of employment might cause a sudden decline in income that put the purchase of required books beyond the student's reach and made travel to, or between, campuses unaffordable. We suggested that this pointed to a need for new kinds of responses by the institution that would be flexible, dynamic and multifaceted incorporating initiatives at both the local (faculty/campus) and institutional levels.

Although student equity in HE was relatively neglected by Australian governments between 1996 and 2003, institutions continued to submit annual plans and reports which were given only cursory attention (Ramsay,

2006), and other policy changes were made in the system, with implications for broader participation. In particular, changes were introduced to the income-contingent loans scheme which covered students' tuition fees, with new arrangements less favourable to students. Charges were increased and divided into three 'bands' based on likely future earnings rather than course costs, so study in law, medicine, dentistry and veterinary science became much more expensive. Repayment thresholds and rates were also amended so that repayment would begin earlier and be more rapid.

The government also discontinued the annual national equity conference, which had enabled the sharing of ideas and experiences among the institutions and supported more effective initiatives.

This period of neglect came to an end in 2003, when Federal Government Education Minister Nelson released a paper on HE, *Our Universities: Backing Australia's Future*. This contained some reforms to equity arrangements, including an increase in the funds for equity initiatives, but the introduction of 'performance-based' funding and the creation of Commonwealth Learning Scholarships targeted three groups: low socio-economic status, people from rural and isolated areas and Indigenous people. The government also announced a review of the equity framework and re-constituted the 'national equity conference' (Nelson, 2003).

Ramsay (2006) suggests that the review and the national equity conference exposed a gulf between equity practitioners in the institutions and government officials. The practitioners sought 'greater analytical clarity about the nature of educational disadvantage and in particular its clear differentiation from simple quantitative measures of representation', but these issues were ignored. The government had two concerns: to focus equity policy and funding on students experiencing significant disadvantage and to implement new equity performance funding and eligibility criteria. In addition, it was keen to respond to voices in the press about the education of men and boys.

The period that followed was a difficult one for institutions. Ramsay (2006) describes institutions grappling with unclear changes and notes that the following:

- There was no 'gesture towards' reinvigorating national education equity policy or the formulation of a system goal linked to national priorities
- There was no progress to understanding the equity impact of multiple disadvantage and the intersections between different equity characteristics (e.g. age and low SES status)
- All equity funding was directed toward 'needy students'. None was available for innovation, system change or collaborations between sectors and institutions.

► It had become unclear which student groups were regarded as designated equity groups within the framework.

Ferguson (2006) also points to confusion within the institutions arising from internal inconsistencies in the new equity framework:

> Following this review, the funding for equity activities was allocated on the access, success and retention performance of only two groups of students... those from low socio-economic backgrounds and rural and isolated students who are from low socio-economic backgrounds. However, universities are still required to report on their success in attracting and retaining students from three of the original equity groups – students from non-English speaking backgrounds, students with disabilities and Indigenous students.

This period came to an end in 2008 when another change of government led to a wide-ranging *Review of Higher Education* (the Bradley Review) that would ultimately create the most significant change to the equity policy framework since *A Fair Chance for All*. This was the introduction of a 'demand-driven system', bringing together social and economic objectives of HE (Bradley, 2008).

What can be concluded about the impact of the equity policy framework established by *A Fair Chance for All* in 1990?

Analysis by the Bradley review found that there had been some improvement in the participation of students with disabilities and of women, but there was continued under-representation of students from low socio-economic backgrounds and from rural and isolated regions. Students from high and medium socio-economic backgrounds continued to be over-represented compared to their share of the population as a whole. Students from the bottom quartile of income-earning households were only one third as likely to attend university as those from high socio-economic backgrounds.

Across the HE system, the number of students from equity groups increased between 1996 and 2004. However, in the context of very substantial overall growth in student numbers, the rate of participation changed little if at all, except in the case of women and students with disabilities. With students from equity groups achieving success and retention comparable to other students, access remained the 'key issue' (Ferguson, 2006).

We suggest six main impacts of the framework. Firstly, it initially provided a sophisticated and conceptually cohesive system for action and the monitoring of progress – although this lessened over time as governments failed to articulate new system objectives and respond to the recommendations of reviews and growing knowledge of the nature of disadvantage. Secondly, clear articulation of equity objectives provoked action to address under-representation where there may otherwise have been little or none. Thirdly, it led to advances in understanding of the nature of disadvantage and of how this could be countered effectively. Fourthly, all institutions were able to report greater participation by people from target groups. Fifthly, it exposed where progress was weakest and more effort was needed. Lastly, it made available public funding for equity initiatives by the institutions that they were able to target to their own, as well as national priorities. There are probably others that a deeper exploration of the period would reveal.

## ▶ Policy Framework 3: Social Inclusion and a Demand-driven System

Previously the number of student places in HE funded by the government had been limited, with demand exceeding supply. Following the Bradley review, restrictions on bachelor's degree enrolments were gradually lifted and finally completely removed in 2012. This is referred to as the introduction of a 'demand-driven system'.

This significant change had both economic and social objectives. Drawing on concerns about Australia's ability to compete in a global knowledge economy, the review argued that there was a need to increase the proportion of the population with a degree qualification and set a target of 40 per cent of all 25- to 34-year-olds to have a bachelor's level qualification by 2025. However, it also noted that this could only be achieved by raising participation among those currently under-represented in the HE system and thus also set a target of at least 20 per cent of the student populations of all universities to be from low socio-economic backgrounds by 2020 (Bradley, 2008: 30).

The Bradley Review thus laid down a challenge to all institutions, but especially to the 'elite' group, where 'pockets of advantage' persisted:

> Social inclusion must be a core responsibility of all institutions that accept public funding, irrespective of history and circumstances.
> (Bradley, 2008: 33)

The national equity targets to be established were not to be aspirational, but part of each institution's *Mission-based Compacts* with the government, and as such tied to performance-based funding, which itself was to be allocated in proportions hitherto unknown in Australian HE.

Overall, there was to be a stronger focus on 'access', for the review noted that once students from under-represented groups entered HE, they succeeded at rates little different from those of other students (with results stable at this level for a decade).

[I]t is clear that the largest disparities emerge from students' ability and desire to enter university in the first place, not from being unable to cope with their work once there.

(Naylor, Baik and James, 2013: 26)

This finding challenged prevailing myths that the presence of more disadvantaged students in the HE system would lower academic standards and damage Australia's reputation in global education markets. With 'equity students' succeeding at similar rates to other students, equity policy and practice would concentrate, albeit not exclusively, on access and participation (Bradley, 2008: 30). Specific initiatives included increased funding for equity activities by universities and equity funding tied to institutions' performance; increased government income supports for undergraduates and postgraduates and new scholarship arrangements; and investigation of a better measure of low socio-economic status of the individual to replace the widely criticized 'postcode' method.

The review also expressed concerns about the use of final school examination results (Australian Tertiary Admission Rank [ATAR]) as the sole criterion for university entry:

[T]he more widespread use of other approaches to selection and admission with a broader range of criteria in addition to or replacing the ATAR and which recognize structural disadvantage should be trialled.

(Bradley 2008: 38)

*Performance Funding* came online in 2012. Approximately 2.5 per cent of government funding for teaching and learning was earmarked to reward universities for achievement against annual performance targets negotiated with each institution, to encourage them to increase participation and attainment rates in priority areas, especially students with a low socio-economic background.

Together, these measures had the potential to effect major changes to HE, making it more responsive to government social inclusion and economic objectives. Much of the social inclusion 'architecture' recommended by the Bradley Review team drew on research and the experience of equity practitioners over the preceding 15 years. Consequently, their recommendations reflected an informed understanding of the roadblocks to participation and the ways various elements of disadvantage combined to exclude.

## The Higher Education Participation and Partnerships Programme (HEPPP)

The introduction of HEPPP brought with it additional funding (4% of total teaching grants) to support initiatives to increase access and participation by under-represented groups.

Universities could bid for specific funds for partnership activities, such as collaborative outreach programmes with schools and the community sector, to raise aspirations and attainment levels. Activities were expected to engage students early in their schooling, be of long duration and include scholarships, mentoring, curriculum and teaching support.

A *participation* loading based on the number of low socio-economic background students in each university's profile was also introduced to fund intensive supports such as financial assistance, academic support and counselling needed to improve completion and retention rates.

What has been the impact of this framework? Since the implementation of the Bradley Review's recommendations, the total student population in Australian universities has grown significantly, but nearly 80 per cent of the

**Table 12.2** Number of Students in Equity Groups as a Proportion of Domestic Onshore Students and as a Proportion of Australian Population; and Ratio Proportion of These Groups in HE in 2012 to Total National Population 2007 and 2012

| Equity Group | 2007 % | 2012 % | % Australian Population in 2012 | 2012 Participation Ratio |
|---|---|---|---|---|
| Students with a disability | 4.11 | 4.98 | 6.54 | 0.76 |
| Indigenous Students | 1.28 | 1.4 | 2.60 | 0.52 |
| Non-English-speaking | 3.78 | 3.70 | 5.39 | 0.73 |
| Women in Non-Traditional Areas | 18.74 | n/a | 50.6 | n/a |
| Low SES (postcode) | 14.93 | 16.01 | 25 | 0.45* |
| Low SES CD measure | – | 15.97 | 25 | 0.46* |
| Regional | 17.96 | 18.09 | 22.33 | 0.74 |
| Remote | 1.13 | 0.99 | 0.57 | 0.41 |

* Ratio of number of low SES students to high SES students.
Source: Department of Education, Higher Education Student Statistics (2012) Appendix. 5.

growth in commencing students has come from medium and high socio-economic groups. Nevertheless, there have been some small gains for students in under-represented groups. As Table 12.2 above shows the relative share of students from low socio-economic backgrounds has increased by 1 per cent, as has that of students with disabilities (nearly 1%), with lesser gains for Indigenous students (0.12%) and for those from regional areas (0.13%). Participation has not increased for students from remote areas or from non-English-speaking backgrounds.

The substantial growth in student numbers brought about by demand-driven funding resulted in changes to the student demographic. An *Australian Universities* study of student finances found that many of the undergraduates coming on to campus were now older than students in the past and more likely to have children and to be taking on university study with no family back-up and no financial support. In 2012, 46 per cent of full-time undergraduates had no financial help from their family, a rise from 36 per cent in 2006.

The proportion of students who worried about their finances had also risen from 59 per cent in 2006 to 68 per cent in 2013. Although fewer than half of non-Indigenous students had no one else to support them financially, two thirds of Indigenous students were in this situation. More than 80 per cent of full-time undergraduates worked more than 16 hours per week to support themselves, often to the detriment of their studies; 17 per cent regularly went without food or other necessities (Bexley et al., 2013). Debt levels of undergraduates had risen from $28,800 in 2006 to $37,200 in 2012 (Bexley and Maslen, 2014).

There were big changes in the number and scale of university outreach, access and support programmes. Institutions responded to the HEPPP with a large number of individual and collaborative projects.

In 2013, the National Centre for Student Equity in Higher Education (NCSEHE) published 39 case studies of individual institution's programmes to showcase best practice in reaching out to prospective students (outreach), helping them get into university (access) and providing support once enrolled (support), along with programme outcomes. Although many universities had previously been involved in these activities, HEPPP's guidelines and funding model provided incentives to universities to collaborate on a larger scale.

In Queensland, the state's eight public universities joined further education colleges, primary and secondary schools and the State Education Department to form the *Queensland Consortium*. Their *Widening Tertiary Participation* approach, an ongoing aspirations-raising widening-participation strategy, had a vast geographic 'footprint' of 1,852,642 square kms. With a core message of 'Any university, any time', they employed a collaborative model to deliver school outreach and Indigenous engagement activities in disadvantaged schools and communities. In 2013, the Widening Tertiary Participation strategy reached out to approximately 50,000 students in Year 6 to Year 12 in 450 schools throughout the state. Indigenous engagement projects reached 2500 Indigenous school students as well as parents, community members and adults seeking re-entry, including those in correctional facilities. All the projects were evaluated, and the resulting data used to inform ongoing collaboration (Kelly, 2014).

Other features of the Queensland approach included:

- A federated model involving universities delivering programmes tailored to local contexts
- A no-gaps or duplications approach, with each university taking responsibility for partnership activities with a local cluster of disadvantaged schools
- Distribution of grant funds to Consortium universities, based on region size and needs
- Parent and teacher engagement focusing on their influence on aspiration and opportunities
- School outreach activities inclusive of Indigenous people, with a separate Indigenous project to address specific needs of this cohort
- A community engagement approach whereby all Indigenous projects build capacity and are Indigenous led

An increased focus on evaluation has emerged, driven partly by concerns about sustainability, particularly in the context of changes in governments at both national and state levels.

Although it is too early to evaluate many equity initiatives funded by HEPPP, especially the outreach ones currently being delivered to students in the sixth, seventh and eighth years of schooling, there is broad agreement that if these programmes were to continue, there needs to be rigorous evaluation. Researchers Naylor, Baik and James (2013) responded by developing a *Critical Intervention Framework* to guide evaluation and inform future equity activities (p. 7), as there was very little peer-reviewed research or evaluation of the impact and effects of various specific equity activities.

## ▶ The Future: What Kind of Framework?

At the beginning of this chapter, we noted uncertainty in HE due to a range of contentious measures being proposed by the Australian government elected in 2013.

Not long after it came into office, this government commissioned its own review of the demand-driven system (Kemp and Norton, 2014). Reporting in April 2014, the review found that uncapping the number of government-supported student places had been a success and should be retained. There had been a rise of more than 100,000 in student numbers between 2009 and 2013, which included more students from low socio-economic, Indigenous and regional and remote backgrounds. Universities had responded to skills shortages in the labour market by enrolling more students in relevant disciplines. Students' satisfaction with teaching had also increased. New models of partnership between universities, further education and community organizations had evolved, increasing the scope of outreach, and online provision of HE was also reaching new student groups.

However, the review recommended the abolition of the national HE attainment target of 40 percent of 25- to 34-year-olds to have a bachelor's level qualification by 2025, along with the target of low socio-economic background students to have a 20 per cent share of the student population by 2020. It suggested that the attainment goal was unnecessary as it would probably be achieved without the target (it was already at 35% in 2013), but expressed more complex reasons for abandoning the low socio-economic student target. It argued that this failed to pick up students from other disadvantaged and under-represented groups and that collecting the relevant data on students from a low socio-economic background was difficult. In addition, it noted:

> The SES target does not relate to the proportion of people from low SES backgrounds attending university, but only their proportion of the university population.
>
> (Kemp and Norton, 2014: 4)

Other recommendations included the demand-driven system being extended to include postgraduate and sub-bachelor courses and public funding for HE being offered to private providers at 70 per cent of the subsidy given to public institutions.

Possibly the most controversial recommendation was that students contribute more towards the cost of their HE. It proposed that the grant the government pays to the institutions for each student be reduced and that the students' contribution be increased. Controversially, it proposed changes to the income-contingent loans scheme for tuition fees, such as increasing the interest rate on loans from 2.9 to 6 percent.

If these recommendations are to be implemented – either fully or in part – the cohesion of the framework established following the Bradley review will be lost-particularly its coupling of social and economic objectives. What will replace it is far from certain. Most likely, this will downgrade and diminish the focus on student equity and diversity that was re-established in 2008. The policy measures that have been proposed by this government since the review suggest that it is likely to downgrade the social inclusion objectives of HE and give priority to economic objectives.

In this context, it is unlikely to continue to provide the funding for equity initiatives that has been provided in other periods, thus reducing effort throughout the system to address continuing disadvantage.

## ▶ Conclusion

In this chapter, we have briefly explored the three policy frameworks for student equity and diversity in HE adopted in Australia since the 1970s and some of the outcomes they have achieved. Although our exploration has been limited, we have been able to note some successes achieved under each framework, but also the persistence of some issues – especially the continuing under-representation of people from groups with low socio-economic status, those from rural and remote areas and Indigenous people – and the over-representation within student populations of people from middle–high socio-economic backgrounds. This persistence underlines the 'sticky' nature of some problems and that some of the causes and sustaining factors of disadvantage are deeply rooted and strong.

There is evidence that change is achievable, but only through concerted effort and attention. Unfortunately, this appears less likely to occur in the current political cycle than in the past, with the new Australian government giving a lower priority to broadening participation and higher priority to ensuring participation meets national economic goals.

Is any framework better than the others? A framework based on expansion of the system does enable more participation, but not necessarily broader participation. The evidence indicates that this requires more targeted initiatives. A policy framework that is strongly concerned only with promoting more participation is likely to have only a very small impact, at best, on *who* participates. It offers only a poor challenge to privilege.

The two other frameworks have both been able to achieve some success – though less than hoped for – in increasing participation by under-represented groups. The introduction of *A Fair Chance for All* and its target-group approach, backed up by public funding for institutional initiatives, was revolutionary in Australian HE. Until then, specific attention had not been given to under-representation and to addressing the particular kinds of barriers to participation faced by those in under-represented groups. It also for the first time established a system for monitoring and reporting progress in student equity and diversity in the system and at state and institutional levels. Today, over two decades later, the data continue to be a rich resource for equity policymakers, practitioners and researchers.

This framework was especially effective when it had clearly articulated objectives, was internally cohesive and when there was a commitment to it by both governments and institutions that was demonstrated also by public funding to support action. The flexibility it enabled for institutions to be able to respond to local issues and priorities was also an important factor in its success.

However, over time the effectiveness of this framework in driving change became diminished. This occurred for reasons including growing neglect by governments that led to a failure to renew objectives and emerging concerns among equity practitioners and researchers about some aspects of the understandings on which the framework was constructed – particularly the use of 'under-representation' as a proxy for disadvantage. It was also challenged by the development of understanding of 'multiple membership' of target groups and its implications.

The introduction of the demand-driven framework was also revolutionary. For the first time it removed restrictions on the number of people the government would support to participate in HE, and it entwined the economic and social objectives of HE so that the achievement of one (expanded participation to meet national skill needs) was recognized as possible only through the simultaneous achievement of the other (greater participation by under-represented groups).

The introduction of this framework renewed attention to student equity and diversity in a way that had not occurred since the introduction of *A Fair Chance for All*. It also benefited from the understanding – developed from the experience and using data from the previous era – that students from all groups progressed at similar rates once in the system. Therefore, access was the key issue and should be the main focus of attention.

Ultimately, it is unhelpful to attempt to compare these three frameworks as completely separate entities. Each did not develop in a vacuum, but evolved from what was there before, benefiting from a greater understanding of the issues and how they are best addressed. In the current era of uncertainty it is our hope that this process of evolution and knowledge development, leading to more effective approaches to addressing issues of advantage and disadvantage in HE, will continue.

## ▶ Acknowledgement

We are grateful to Geoffrey Mitchell, Project Manager of Widening Participation Tertiary Education and Training, Department of Education, Training and Employment, Brisbane, for providing information and advice on the Queensland Consortium.

# 13 Conclusions: The Age of Access

The case studies in this volume illustrate that who participates in HE is not a peripheral issue for HE itself, nor for the individual countries examined. It is part of how these countries understand themselves in the twenty-first century. The rest of the chapter unpicks this relationship between access and national identity, focusing on four themes emerging from the case studies in this book. It will be argued that a nuanced, holistic and connected discourse which locates equity within a broader set of challenges facing countries themselves and HE systems within/across them is required. What Clancy describes as the legitimized categories for access to HE differ across countries. Nor are they static. They appear to be ones that evolve and are shaped by wider socio-economic forces. The approaches (and commitment) of policymakers and practitioners to inequalities in access also contrast across countries and continents. But these differences are not ones that can be easily mapped against levels of economic development. Who provides the HE that will allow access to be expanded is clearly a pressing issue for those countries who are attempting to grow their systems – in Asia and Africa especially. However, this is not an issue confined to this part of the world. We see in North America and Europe, as well, the entrance of new kinds of provider into the system, providing challenges to how the development of established systems can be done in an equitable way. The chapter concludes by developing an approach to understanding access and equity in HE in the international context based around the concept of nationhood.

▶ **For Whom Should Access Be Widened?**

The case studies clearly bring out the distinctive nature of the 'legitimized categories' where access to HE is concerned in each country. The first thing to emphasize is that it is categories we are speaking of here, as opposed to one category. No one country can have their access story reduced to participation in HE, or not of one group. How these categories become the legitimized ones is rooted in social, economic and political histories. They can be shaped by events. The end of apartheid in South Africa signalled the transformation in the composition of the HE population in that country. The shifting equity frameworks since the 1970s in Australia has changed the relationship between these categories over time. In the United Kingdom, although the levels of participation seem as yet relatively unaffected, the increase in tuition fees in England in 2012 has changed significantly the landscape against which access to HE work is delivered. These categories are durable, however. In the case of the Chinese, despite the economic growth that the country has enjoyed in the last 20 years and the subsequent transformations in Chinese society, in a country so vast, geography maintains its hold as the primary way in which differences in HE participation are constructed.

## ▶ The Commitment of Policymakers to Widening Access and What Politicization Means

There are demonstrable commitments by policymakers to addressing inequalities in HE participation evident in the chapters in this book. These commitments come in different forms. In the United Kingdom, India, Germany, the United States, South Africa, Australia and Ghana in particular, there are examples of projects and initiatives supported by the government to address directly the goal of greater equity in HE. This commitment is not confined, however, to specific programmes. The problem with programme investment is that it can be peripheral and separated from the mainstream priorities of government. In both Finland and Ghana, a commitment to equity in education is enshrined in the respective constitutions of the different countries. In India, China and Colombia, HE participation appears in national development plans, whereas in the United States, the United Kingdom and South Africa the respective chapters show conclusively that HE participation is a mainstream political issue.

However, looking across the countries, there is also a sense of unease where the commitment of policymakers is concerned. There is evidence that the rhetoric or policy commitments are not always being met by action. In a number of cases, authors point to the difficulties in securing long-term commitment to this issue from policymakers. Diana Wickham's chapter on Canada illustrates what happens when commitment to the access and equity agenda shifts has happened after the end of the Millennium Scholarship Foundation and investment declines. Manasi Navani talks of how in India, the 'considerable tokenism in the nature of the schemes available that explicitly address equity issues' (Chapter 8, this book, p. 119). In the Australian case, this unease is expressed in grave worries that the progress made since the 1970s may be undone by political change. As Heagney and Ferrier conclude:

> In the current era of uncertainty it is our hope that this process of evolution and knowledge development, leading to more effective

approaches to addressing issues of advantage and disadvantage in HE, will continue.

(Chapter 12, this book, p. 181)

Even in Finland, long held up as a beacon of social equity and educational opportunity, there are questions to be asked regarding the commitment of policymakers to access and equity in HE. The most obvious one is why, in a country with such a deep commitment to education and equity in education, is it that no data on participation in HE by socio-economic group are systematically collected at the national level?

On the basis of the chapters in the book, access appears to be a deeply politicized issue. This politicization is pivotal to understanding inequalities in HE participation and how to effect these. There is less across the chapters, however, regarding how to deal with this politicization and in particular the tacit commitment of policymakers which several viewed as so problematic. Much of the existing literature gives a prominent role to politicization in the context of access to HE, but it is mainly constructed in the context of how policymakers approach the issue. It is a 'top-down' interpretation of politicization (Altbach, Reisberg and Rumbley, 2009; Goastellec, 2010; Santiago et al., 2008). The chapters here, in the main, echo this approach. There is little on how those working in access and equity can be engaged in this politicization as partners or, preferably, equal partners. If the weaknesses in real commitment from politicians are to be addressed, then concerted action by the 'access community' itself will be essential. Who is part of this community, however, and who should be part of it needs to be debated. Although those working directly on access/equity in HE would form the core of such a community, there may be other groups such as employers who could form an important part. There also needs to be both national and international vehicles to coalesce such communities and give their ideas shape and purpose. Further work is required here to explore in more detail how the politicization of access and equity could manifest itself in this way across countries.

### ▶ Access, Activity and Action

The chapters in this volume highlight the range of activities and initiatives being undertaken by policymakers, institutions and practitioners to make participation in HE more equitable. The chapter on the United States features considerable detail on how inequalities in access and equity in HE are addressed in practical terms. This is unsurprising, given the long history of work to support HE progression among low-income groups that stretches back to the 1960s. In his chapter, Kamatuka develops the concept of 'college ready' to underpin sustained pre-HE activity with learners before they reach HE. The Montes Gutiérrez and Abad chapter on Colombia details most thoroughly a particular approach to addressing HE inequality. The Children's University EAFIT in Medellin is part of the global children's university movement located in over 40 countries. It works with children from age seven years old and has a sustained, systematic approach to support progression into HE. The activities described in these chapters and in Germany with the MINT-Kolleg, Rent-a-student and ArbeiterKind.de, or in India with the Equal Opportunity Cells, or in the United Kingdom supported by the various forms of outcome agreements between government and HE institutions (HEIs) draw on the view that there are differences in cultural or social capital between learners from different groups that need to be addressed to enable to those from particular equity groups to be supported to enter HE.

The approaches documented in the book broadly support the ideas of cultural capital from Bourdieu deployed by a number of writers from the United States and the United Kingdom to explain difference in HE participation (Archer, Hollingworth and Halsall, 2003; Horvat, 2001, 2003; Reay, David and Ball, 2005). Such differences in cultural capital manifest themselves in what Bourdieu describes as habitus. Archer (2007) describes habitus as

> an amalgamation of the past and the present that mediates current and future engagement with the world, shaping what is perceived as ab/normal, un/desirable and im/possible'.
>
> (Archer et al., 2007: 220)

Habitus is deeply rooted in the culture of particular groups in society (Bourdieu, 1992). For middle-class groups, their habitus fits easily with the education system, whereas for those from working-class groups there is a friction which manifests itself in the view that education is always somehow unnatural for 'the likes of us'. Bourdieu's ideas have been heavily criticized by some. Many prefer to locate social reproduction of inequality less in the realm of cultural difference and more in terms of the responses that different groups make to the situations they face, structured by experiences they have available to them rather than in differences in cultural endowments (Atherton and Roberts, 2011). Furthermore, in the context of this book Bourdieu has a one-dimensional approach to inequality, focusing on social class as opposed to the multifaceted nature of inequality as described here.

Nevertheless, the work into social reproduction of educational inequality shows differences in HE participation are rooted in much wider forms of social and economic inequalities. They go beyond removing individual barriers to HE entry, such as a lack of knowledge of the student finance system (Gorard et al., 2006; Heath, Fuller and Paton, 2008), and they begin very early on in life. This relationship has been documented before. Research undertaken by the European Union and by the OECD points to the basis for difference in HE participation being found in inequalities constructed far earlier in educational careers (Commission of the European Communities, 2006; d'Addio, 2007). Nevertheless, this book highlights the validity of social reproduction as a guiding principle for action to drive greater equity in HE drawing on a more diverse group of countries than has been attempted before. It also points to the potential for further work to explore how the relationship between social reproduction and HE participation differs across the world though. If habitus is what shapes engagement with HE, how does that habitus differ between Ghana and Colombia, for example? Or between South Africa and Australia? Moreover, where do the interactions between legitimized categories, not just within but between countries, differ then? This kind of detailed exploration will hopefully indicate the potential for exchange of practice in the field. Most excitingly, it could be the springboard for the development of new cross-country activities to address inequalities in HE access.

## ▶ Who Can Provide Access?

While the different case studies focus mainly on the demand side of access and equity, they are not ignorant of the importance of supply. There are two major themes evident here. Firstly, there is the division between 'academic' and 'technical' HE. This division is most evident in Finland and Germany where this binary divide is entrenched in their education systems. But it is also evident among the other countries as well – in particular India, the United Kingdom and the United States. The expansion of HE systems may threaten or bolster such systemic divides. The tendency for those from equity groups to be found more commonly in the 'technical' parts of the system merits further examination. The extent to which such over-representation is a good or bad thing is at the crux of the issue here. In the India and also US chapters, the failure of the labour market to keep pace with the HE system was highlighted. The evidence shows that globally there is an apparent greater demand for more university graduates, but in many countries graduate unemployment is unacceptably high. This becomes, then, not just an issue of who provides access, but what is provided.

The second major theme is the prevalence of private HE. The chapter by Crosling, Cheng and Lopes on Malaysia argues strongly that private HE providers can make a positive contribution to the growth of participation in Asia. They point to the impressive expansion of HE participation in Malaysia and the increase in the number of private HE providers from under ten in the 1970s to over 500 by the 2010s.

Manasi is less convinced of the merits of private provision in the Indian context. As she states, 'The underlying assumption that increases in the number of private (and foreign) institutions will increase substantially the educational opportunities in HE is not based on any empirical evidence and the rhetoric of equity with the upsurge of privatization is circumspect'. The role of private providers is unlikely however to fade away. The Ghananian chapter shows how private providers constitute nearly half of all tertiary institutions in that country.

It is not only in developing systems where private providers are growing, nor is it just in such countries where there is concern about the implications of this growth. As Kamatuka argues in Chapter 2, on the United States: 'Another disturbing barrier of access to HE in the United States is the increasing targeting of low-income and first-generation college students, by for-profit institutions of higher learning.' In Australia and the United Kingdom as well, the shift to the political right has ushered in the prospect (and in England anyway the reality) of new sorts of HE providers bringing uncertain implications for access and equity.

The changing nature of national HE systems is not the focus of this book. As argued in the introductory chapter, the evidence appears to suggest that HE participation will grow considerably over the course of this century. As this growth occurs, and as the systems are put in place to cope with increased demand (and to stimulate it), the challenge is how to put the needs of learners from diverse and marginalized backgrounds at the centre of this process. To the extent that these case studies deepen understanding of policies and practices related to these learners, they then provide a good starting point for a sustained dialogue regarding HE systems and equitable access. The necessity of this dialogue is based in the extent of the challenge where equitable access is concerned. It is not one that will be addressed by either defending the status quo where the provision of HE is concerned in an individual country, or opening the doors to new providers. Mergner, Mishra and Orr, in their chapter on Germany, summarize the problem excellently. Germany is one of the strongest economic nations in the world, with a much-admired education and training system. But Mergner, Mishra and Orr argue that

> Germany therefore can be seen as a higher education system making efforts to become more inclusive on all system levels. At the same time, the fact that the social selectivity of German higher education has existed for so long shows that opening access to underrepresented groups also requires a change of mindset to complement the new policies, regulations, and initiatives.

## ▶ Access and Nationhood

The more holistic and nuanced discourse on HE equity which this book makes the case for can be summarized as a 'nationhood' approach. This approach means understanding of access and equity needs to be grounded firmly in the broader social, political and cultural narrative of the individual country. It requires researchers and theorists to attempt to position access and equity within these evolving narratives first, before attempting to examine the mechanics of higher educational systems such as financial support arrangements, admissions systems and so on. The 'mechanics' of the system matter, and it is essential they are understood. But in themselves they depend on the context which produces them and the social and cultural norms which frame the importance of HE participation in a particular country. As Liu and Su argue when they begin their chapter on China:

> With a long history of Confucian culture, China is a country that values education. It is China's national policy to prioritize the development of education and in the era of mass higher education, it becomes the wish of every young man and woman to receive higher education.

The four themes described above interact together to form the basis of the access–nationhood relationship. Who the 'legitimized categories' are goes to the heart of the question of interrelationships between groups within particular societies. These relationships are what both challenge and support notions of national identity. These categories are what Hüsamettin and Ünal (2013) describe as 'others' in the context of identity formation. The durability of national identities is related directly to the ability of nations to reconcile the relationships between groups within the population. South Africa's ability to do this, post-apartheid, is what has enabled the country to remain as one entity, for example, while many others have been unable to do this and in recent years have fractured into smaller territories across the world. In the access and equity context, Kamatuka's quote from Chapter 2 captures best the relationship between access, other and nation:

> The late fifties and the early sixties witnessed a shift of paradigm by practitioners and policy makers. The nation started to pay attention to those Americans who were denied access to higher education. These were, and continue to be, the low-income and first-generation college students. They represent the American national tapestry: They are White, African-American, Latino, Asian, Alaskan, Hawaiian Native and Native American.

The politicization of access is the visible manifestation of its relationship to nationhood. In five of the countries in the book, the authors relate a commitment to more equitable access to education to the constitution of the respective nations. Commitments to equitable access are being used to perform the key function in translating the broad vision expressed in such documents into more concrete objectives. However, constitutional commitment in itself, though important, becomes relevant when it is given day-to-day energy through political rhetoric and debate.

The public nature of the rhetoric on HE participation therefore also takes on an important role. The policies pursued by governments with regard to access and equity in HE described in this book are often high-profile ones – they often connect HE with the broader body politic in ways that other aspects of what HE does do not do. They also act to illustrate to those outside the country the aspirations for the nation. Rusciano describes two parts to national identity: the *Selbstbild* part and the *Fremdbild* part. As he explains:

> [T]he construction of national identity derives in part from a negotiation between a nation's *Selbstbild* (or the nation's national consciousness, or the image the citizens have of their country) and a nation's *Fremdbild* (or the nation's perceived or actual international image in world opinion).
>
> (Rusciano, 2003: 361)

Access and equity in HE related to both Selbstbild and Fremdbild. It is a feature of how countries express moral characteristics by acting as a public marker of 'fairness' to both those inside and outside the country. This 'nationhood' approach to looking at access to HE in the global comparative context advocates approaching understanding inequalities in HE participation from a different angle. The connection between economic development of a particular country and access remains axiomatic. Increasing global competitiveness remains a (and sometimes *the*) motivation for governments to invest in increasing participation in HE. But *why* a particular government chooses to give HE participation in this role in aiding global competitiveness, and the prominence it may give it in doing this, can only be understood through a more thorough analysis of the relationship between access and nationhood.

To further illustrate the connection between access and equity in HE and deeper cultural mores, as illustrated above in the discussion of social reproduction on how different countries attempted to ameliorate inequalities in HE participation, showed some real consistencies in practice across the developed and developing world. But the nature of the work undertaken brings us back to deeper, broader questions of social and cultural division. The approaches described in the book were not primarily about the mechanics of the system, that is, changing admissions practices, teaching and learning or financial support. They were attempts to challenge dominant cultural norms and address the impact of historical inequality and injustice on marginalized groups.

Finally, differentials in HE provision can also be understood through the nationhood approach. It can be argued that in many countries the growth in private provision has been the consequence of necessity as there have been insufficient public resources to fund expansion. But the way in which private provision has been introduced and has developed differs across countries. These differences are part of a bigger struggle for countries as they try to navigate the relationship between state and market in the early twenty-first century. As was argued in Chapter 8 on India and also Chapter 11 on Ghana, who provides HE relates to what HE is for and its meaning. The case studies illustrate how, across the developed and developing world, tensions were apparent regarding the extent to which the private sector should encroach on what is seen by so many as an inherently public sector endeavour. This places HE in the context of the broader debate regarding the role of the market per se in any individual country and what public services should and should not be marketized in the early twenty-first century (Sandel, 2012).

▶ **The Age of Access?**

In 2015, UNESCO for the first time recognized access to lifelong learning for all as one of its new development goals up to 2030.

> Increased equitable access to quality education for children, youth and adults should be provided for all from early childhood to higher education.
> (UNESCO, 2015)

This move from UNESCO has the potential to further advance the importance of access and equity in HE for national governments and HE institutions. The chapters in this book show both the potential that exists to move toward this goal, but the challenges as well. They show that the contours of inequality in HE participation are not just a function of differences across countries by wealth, political system, HE structures or student finance systems. Neither are they just an addendum to inequalities that exist within a country's educational system. Nor can they merely be seen as a reflection of deep historical schisms within a society. Who participates in HE in a more globalized, more knowledge-driven world is a statement about the kind of country you are and the kind of country you want to be.

The nationhood approach needs further development, both theoretically and empirically. It must also be recognized that when one looks globally, this sample of countries could justifiably be described as unique where access and equity in HE is concerned. It occupies a much more advanced position in policy and practice in these countries compared to many in the world. As Atherton and Whitty (2016) show in their global overview of the data available, where participation by social background is concerned, the majority of countries are not collecting good information on the inequalities in their HE systems. This lack of data is a good indicator of the extent to which countries take access and equity in HE seriously.

Developing the nationhood approach also implies extending the scope of enquiry beyond equity as participation, to equity as outcome. Across the countries examined, big differences existed between participation in types of institution and big concerns existed regarding the kind of jobs that would exist for graduates from different backgrounds. Analysing inequalities within the system will be as much the future of access work as understanding who gains entry to HE. But these inequalities can also potentially be better understood by the development of the 'nationhood' approach.

This book shows that who goes to and succeeds in HE is becoming increasingly important to countries across the world. If, as many argue, the age of access is just beginning, then we will need the tools to understand how to make this access as equitable as possible. This book provides some of these tools.

# References

## Introduction

Asian Development Bank (ADB) (2012a) *Access without Equity? Finding a Better Balance in Higher Education in Asia* (Philippines: Asian Development Bank).

Asian Development Bank (ADB) (2012b) *Private Higher Education Across Asia Expanding Access, Searching for Quality* (Philippines: Asian Development Bank).

Bloom, D., D. Canning and K. Chan (2005) *Higher Education and Economic Development in Africa* (Washington, DC: World Bank).

Brown, P, D. Ashton, H. Lauder and G. Theron (2008) *Towards a High Skilled Workforce*, ESRC Funded Centre on Skills, Knowledge and Economic Performance, Cardiff and Oxford Universities.

Brunner, J. J., P. Santiago, C. García Gaudilla, J. Gerlach and L. Velho (2006) *Thematic Review of Tertiary Education* (Paris: Organisation for Economic Co-operation and Development).

Clancy, P. and G. Goastellec (2007) 'Exploring Access and Equity in Higher Education: Policy and Performance in a Comparative Perspective', *Higher Education Quarterly*, 61(2), pp. 136–54.

Cowen, T. (2013) *Average Is Over: Powering America Beyond the Age of the Great Stagnation* (New York: E.P. Dutton).

Department of Business, Innovation and Skills (BIS) (2014) The Benefits of Higher Education Participation for Individuals and Society: Key Findings and Reports "The Quadrants" (London: BIS).

European Commission/EACEA/Eurydice (2014) *Modernisation of Higher Education in Europe: Access, Retention and Employability 2014*, Eurydice Report. (Luxembourg: Publications Office of the European Union).

Grubb, N. W., R. Sweet, M. Gallagher and O. Tuomi (2006) *Korea: Country Note* (Paris: Organisation for Economic Co-operation and Development).

Kirkland, J, (2015) 'A Pyramid without a Higher Education Roof?', *University World News*, 20 March 2015.

Koucký, J. and A. Bartušek (2010) *Who Gets a Degree? Access to Tertiary Education in Europe 1950–2009*, OECD IMHE 2010 General Conference Paris, 13–15 September.

McKinsey Global Institute (2012) *The World at Work: Jobs, Pay and Skills for 3.5 Billion People* (New York: McKinsey & Company).

Meyer, H., E. P. St. John, M. Chankseliani and L. Uribe (2013) *Fairness in Access to Higher Education in a Global Perspective* (Rotterdam: Sense Publishers).

Mphahlele, M. K. (1940 Access, equity and redress in science academic development programmes: Critical Issues and concerns. In S.Levy (ed) Projects speak for themselves (pp. 49–54) Johannesburg: S. Levy.

Murray, N. and C. Klinger (2013) *Aspirations, Access and Attainment: International Perspectives on Widening Participation and an Agenda for Change* (London: Routledge).

Organisation for Economic Co-operation and Development (OECD) (2011) *Education at a Glance* (Paris: OECD).

Organisation for Economic Co-operation and Development (OECD) (2014) *Education at a Glance* (Paris: OECD).

Orr, D., A. Usher and J. Wespel (2014) *Do Changes in Cost-sharing Have an Impact on the Behaviour of Students and Higher Education Institutions?* (Brussels: European Commission).

Santiago, P., K. Tremblay, E. Basri and E. Arnal (2008) *Tertiary Education for the Knowledge Society, Vol. 2: Special Features: Equity, Innovation, Labour Market, Internationalisation* (Paris: OECD).

Shavit, Y., Arum, R. and Gamoran, A. (eds) (2007) 'Stratification in Higher Education: A Comparative Study', in *Studies in Social Inequality Series* (Stanford, CA: Stanford University Press).

Shavit, Y. and H.-P. Blossfeld (1993) *Persistent Inequality: Changing Educational Attainment in 13 Countries* (Boulder, CO: Westview Press).

Tapper, T. and D. Palfreyman (2005) *Understanding Mass Higher Education: Comparative Perspectives on Access* (Oxon: RoutledgeFalmer Press).

Thomas, L. and J. Quinn (2003) *International Insights into Widening Participation: Supporting the Success of Under-represented Groups in Tertiary Education: Final Report* (Stoke-on-Trent: Institute for Access Studies, Staffordshire University).

Tremblay, K. and P. Mangeol (2014) 'OECD Perspectives: Higher Education Key to a More Fulfilling Career and Life', available at http://qualityoflifeobserver.com/content/oecd-perspectives-higher-education-key-more-fulfilling-career-and-life (accessed 23 November 2014).

Trow, M. A. (1973) 'Problems in the Transition from Elite to Mass Higher Education', in *Policies for Higher Education* (Berkeley, CA: Carnegie Commission on Higher Education).

Trow, M. A. (2005) 'Reflections on the Transition from Elite to Mass to Universal Access', in J.J.F. Forest and P. G. Altbach (eds) *International Handbook of Higher Education* (Dordrecht: Kluwer).

United Nations (2000) 'United Nations Millennium Declaration', available at http://www.un.org/en/ga/search/view_doc.asp?symbol=A/RES/55/2 (accessed 25 November 2014).

United Nations Educational, Scientific and Cultural Organization (UNESCO) (2012) *World Atlas of Gender Equality in Education* (Paris: OECD).

Usher, A. (2004) *A New Measuring Stick: Is Access to Higher Education in Canada More Equitable?* Toronto (ON: Educational Policy Institute).

Usher, A. and J. Medow (2010) *Global Higher Education Rankings 2010 Affordability and Accessibility in Comparative Perspective* (Toronto, Ontario: Higher Education Strategy Associates).

Wolf, A. (2002) *Does Education Matter?* (London: Penguin Books).

## Chapter 1

Aboriginal Affairs and Northern Development Canada (AANDC) (2015a) 'Grants and Contributions to Support First Nations and Inuit Post-Secondary Education Advancement', available at http://www.aadnc-aandc.gc.ca (accessed 21 May 2015).

Aboriginal Affairs and Northern Development Canada (AANDC) (2015b) 'Introduction of Bill C-33: The First Nations Control of First Nations Education Act', available at https://www.aadnc-aandc.gc.ca/ (accessed 21 May 2015).

Alberta Advanced Education (2006) *A Learning Alberta: Final Report of the Steering Committee*, May (Alberta: Alberta Advanced Education).

Alexander, C. and S. Mobasher Fard (2011) *Postsecondary Is the Best Investment* (Canada: TD Economics).

Birgeneau, Robert (2001) *A Troubling Disparity: Narrowing the Student-faculty Visible Minority Gap*, University of Toronto (former) President's message, available at http://www.magazine.utoronto.ca/presidents-message/visible-minority-gap-universities/ (accessed 21 May 2015).

# References

Canadian Alliance of Student Organizations (CASA) (2013) 'Setting the Access Agenda', available at http://casa-acae.com/setting-the-access-agenda/ (accessed 21 May 2015).

Council of Ministers of Education, Canada (CMEC) (2015) Learn 2020 (Toronto: CMEC).

Council of the Federation (2006) 'Competing for Tomorrrow: A Strategy for Post-Secondary Education and Skills Development in Canada', July, available at http://www.canadaspremiers.ca/ (accessed 21 May 2015).

Canadian Council on Learning (2006) *Report on Learning in Canada 2006, Canadian Postsecondary Education: A Positive Record – An Uncertain Future* (Ottawa, Canada).

Canadian Council on Learning (2011) *What Is the Future of Learning in Canada?* (Ottawa: Canada).

Canadian Information Centre for International Credentials (CICIC) (2015) 'An Overview of Education in Canada', available at http://www.cicic.ca/421/an-overview.canada (accessed 21 May 2015).

College Student Alliance (2009) 'Breaking Barriers', available at http://collegestudent alliance.ca/ (accessed 21 May 2015).

Community Foundations of Canada (2006) 'Leadership for Canada's Changing Communities', available at http://www.cprn.org/ (accessed 21 May 2015).

Council of Ministers of Education (CMEC) (1995) 'Pan-Canadian Protocol on the Transferability of University Credits', available at http://www.cmec.ca/ (accessed 21 May 2015).

Council of Ministers of Education, Canada (CMEC) (2015) 'Education in Canada: An Overview', available at http://www.cmec.ca/299/Education-in-Canada-An-Overview/index.html#02 (accessed 21 May 2015).

Council of Ontario Universities (2006) 'Progress Report: University Access, Accountability and Quality in the Reaching Higher Plan', November 2006, available at http://cou.on.ca/ (accessed 21 May 2015).

Drummond, D. and E. K. Rosenbluth (2013) *The Debate on First Nations Education Funding: Mind the Gap*, Working Paper 49, December 2013, School of Policy Studies, Queens University.

Finnie, R., S. Childs and A. Wismer (2011) *Access to Postsecondary Education: How Ontario Compares* (Toronto: Higher Education Quality Council of Ontario).

Finnie, R., S. Childs and A. Wismer (2011) *Under-Represented Groups in Post-Secondary Education in Ontario: Evidence from the Youth in Transition Survey* (Toronto: Higher Education Quality Council of Ontario).

Finnie, R, S. Childs and F. Martinello (2014) 'Postsecondary Student Persistence and Pathways: Evidence from the YITS-A In Canada', Education Policy Research Initiative (EPRI), available at https://www.ruor.uottawa.ca/bitstream/10393/31972/1/YITS-A%20 Persistence%20Paper.pdf (accessed 21 May 2015).

Finnie, R. and R. Mueller (2012) 'Access to Post-Secondary Education among the First and Second Generation Children of Canadians Immigrants', available at http://www.yorku.ca/pathways/literature/Access/finnie.mueller.immigrants.june.2008.pdf (accessed 21 May 2015).

Fisher, D., K. Rubenson, J. Bernatchez, R. Robert Clift, G. Jones, J. Lee, M. MacIvor, et al. (2006) *Canadian Federal Policy and Postsecondary Education* (Vancouver: Centre for Policy Studies in Higher Education [CHET], University of British Columbia).

Garcia, A. and T. Pritchard (2013) *Fall Policy Papers: A Comprehensive Access Strategy* (Ontario: The Ontario Undergraduate Student Alliance [OUSA]).

Giroux, Dominic (2012) 'Closing the Gap in First Nations Education', *Policy Options*, 33(7), August, available at http://policyoptions.irpp.org/ (accessed 21 May 2015).

Government of Canada (2012) 'Audit of Specified Purpose Account of the Canada Millennium Scholarship Foundation – January 2012', available at http://www.esdc.gc.ca/eng/publicationsl (accessed 21 May 2015).

Government of New Brunswick (2008) *Be Inspired. Be Ready, Be Better. The Action Plan to Transform Post-Secondary Education in New Brunswick*, June.
Government of Newfoundland and Labrador, Department of Advanced Education and Skills (2005) 'White Paper on Post-Secondary Education', available at http://www.aes.gov.nl.ca/postsecondary/skillstaskforce/whitepaper.html (accessed 21 May 2015).
Government of Ontario (2006) 'McGuinty Government Invests in Opportunities for First Generation Students in 2005/06', available at http://news.ontario.ca/ (accessed 21 May 2015).
Jones, G. and C. Field (2013) *A Review of System-Led Policy Initiatives* (Ontario Institute for Studies in Education (OISE), University of Toronto).
Kirby, D. (2007) 'Reviewing Canadian Post-Secondary Education: Post-Secondary Policy in Post-Industrial Canada', *Canadian Journal of Educational Administration and Policy (CJEAP)*, 65(3): 1–24.
Lang, D. (2013) 'Incentives in Financing Higher Education', in C. Amrhein and B. Baron (eds) *Building Success in a Global University* (Lemmens Medien, Bonn-Berlin).
Ministry of Advanced Education – British Columbia and the Aboriginal Post-Secondary Education and Training Partners (2013) *Aboriginal Post-Secondary Education and Training Policy Framework and Action Plan: Report Out for 2013*, available at http://www.aved.gov.bc.ca/ (accessed 21 May 2015).
National Post (2009) 'Canada Not as Smart as It Thought It Was', 19 October 2009, available at http://www.pressreader.com/canada/national-post-latest-edition/20091017/281526517116717/TextView (accessed 21 May 2015).
OECD (2012) *Education at a Glance: OECD Indicators* (Paris: OECD).
Office of the Auditor General of Canada (2011) 'June Status Report of the Auditor General of Canada, Chapter 4: Programs for First Nations on Reserves', available at http://www.oag-bvg.gc.ca/ (accessed 21 May 2015).
Parkin, A. and N. Baldwin (2009) 'Persistence in Post-Secondary Education in Canada: The Latest Research', available at http://www.yorku.ca/.
Plant, G. (2007) *Campus 2020: Thinking Ahead. Access & Excellence – The Campus 2020 Plan for British Columbia's Post-Secondary Education System*, April 2007, available at http://www.aved.gov.bc.ca/ (accessed 21 May 2015).
Rae, B. (2005) *Ontario: A Leader in Learning. Report and Recommendations*, February 2005 (Ontario: Ministry of Training, Colleges and Universities).
Sattler, P. (2010) *From Postsecondary Application to the Labour Market: the Pathways of Under-represented Groups* (Toronto: Higher Education Quality Council of Ontario).
Service Regional d'Admission du Montréal Métropolitain (SRAM) (2015) 'What Are Cégeps?', available at https://sram.qc.ca/international-student/what-are-cegeps (accessed 21 May 2015).
Statistics Canada (2011a) *Immigration and Ethnocultural Diversity in Canada*, available at http://www12.statcan.gc.ca/ (accessed 21 May 2015).
Statistics Canada (2011b) 'The Educational Attainment of Aboriginal Peoples in Canada', available at http://www12.statcan.gc.ca/ (accessed 21 May 2015).
Statistics Canada (2011c) 'Canada Year Book 2011', available at http://www.statcan.gc.ca/ (accessed 21 May 2015).
Statistics Canada (2014a) 'Canadian Postsecondary Enrolments and Graduates, 2012/2013', available at http://www.statcan.gc.ca/ (accessed 21 May 2015).
Statistics Canada (2014b) 'Definitions, Data Sources and Methods: Aboriginal Identity of a Person', available at http://www.statcan.gc.ca/ (accessed 21 May 2015).
Statistics Canada (2015) 'Undergraduate Tuition Fees for Full-Time Canadian Students by Discipline, By Province', available at http://www.statcan.gc.ca/ (accessed 21 May 2015).

Tucker, M. S. (2011) *Standing on the Shoulders of Giants: An American Agenda for Education Reform* (Washington: National Centre on Education and the Economy).
Ungerleider, C. (2008) *Evaluation of the Ontario Ministry of Education's Student Success / Learning to 18 Strategy Final Report*, Canadian Council on Learning, September 2008 Canadian Council on Learning, available at https://www.edu.gov.on.ca/eng/ (accessed 21 May 2015).
United Way of Greater Toronto, 'Community of Practice on Youth Educational Attainment Partnerships', available at http://www.unitedwaytoronto.com/community-of-practice (accessed 21 May 2015).
Universities Canada (2009) *Trends in Higher Education* (Ottawa: The Association of Universities and Colleges of Canada).

## Chapter 2

Abdul-Amin, J. (2014) '50 Years Later: TRIO Programs Paving Pathways to Success', Diverse Education, 21 August 2014, available at http://diverseeducation.com/article/66495/.
ACT (2012) 'Staying on Target: The Importance of Monitoring Student Progress toward College and Career Readiness', Act Research and Policy, Research Brief, June, available at https://forms.act.org/research/policymakers/pdf/Staying-on-Target.pdf.
ACT and COE (2013) The Condition of College and Career Readiness, Washington: ACT and COE.
Bowen (2009) From p. 9.
Bowen, W. G., M. M. Chingos and M. S. McPherson (2009) *Crossing the Finish Line: Completing College at America's Public Universities* (Princeton, NJ: Princeton University Press).
Brubacher, J. S. and W. Rudy (1976) *Higher Education in Transition: A History of American Colleges and Universities*, 3rd edn (Piscataway, NJ: Transaction Publishers).
Center for Educational Opportunity Programs (CEOP) (2014) Unpublished data of the University of Kansas Achievement and Assessment Institute Center for Educational Opportunity Programs (CEOP), University of Kansas, Lawrence, KS.
Consortium of Chicago School Research at the University of Chicago (2010) From p. 4.
Council for Opportunity in Education, (2014) *Upward Bound, First U.S. Program to Help Students Escape Poverty through Higher Education, Celebrates 50 Years*, June, press release.
Ford, P. L. (1962) The New-England Primer. *Classics In Education No. 13*, 2nd printing (New York: Teachers College, Columbia University).
Gray-Little, B. (2014) *Educating Leaders. The Chancellor's Message*, April.
Groutt, J. (2003) *Milestones of TRIO History Part I*. National TRIO Clearinghouse.
Haycock, K., (2013). *The Federal Pell Grant Program: What Truly Is Unsustainable*. The Pell Institute for the Study of Opportunity in Higher Education, Reflections on Pell.
Hinojos, B. (2014) *To the Stars, through Difficulties*. Keynote Speech: Delivered at the University of Kansas McNair Scholars Banquet.
Kahlenberg, R. D. (2013) *The Federal Pell Grant Program: Higher Education's Brown v. Board of Education*, The Pell Institute for the Study of Opportunity in Higher Education, Reflections on Pell.
Long, B. T. (2013) *Addressing the Academic Barriers to Higher Education. Supporting Disadvantaged Youth*, The Hamilton Project, Brookings Institution.
Lumina Foundation (2012) *A Stronger Nation Through Higher Education, A Special Report*, March.

Mathematica Policy Research (2006). From p. 6.
Mitchem, A. L. (2010) *Forbes Magazine*, October 26.
Mitchem, A. L. (2013) *An Advocate for Access Reflects on Decades of Political Battles*. Chronicle of Higher Education, 4 October 2013.
Mortenson, T. (2013) *The Federal Pell Grant Program: Alternative Futures*, The Pell Institute for the Study of Opportunity in Higher Education, Reflections on Pell.
Nagaoka, J., M. Roderick, V. Coca and E. Moeller (2008) *From High School to the Future: Potholes on the Road to College*.
Roderick, M, J. Nagaoka and V. Coca (2009). 'College Readiness for All: The Challenge for Urban High Schools', *The Future Of Children*, 19(1), 185–210.
Roderick, M., J. Nagaoka, V. Coca, E. Moeller and E. Allensworth (2010) *Rising to Meet Obama's Challenge: What the Crisis in Educational Attainment Means for Urban High Schools*, School of Social Service Administration and Consortium on Chicago School Research at the University of Chicago Urban Education Institute.
Swail, W. S. (2014) *A White House Summit on College Opportunity*.
The Pell Institute (2011) Developing 20/20 Vision on the 2020 Degree Attainment Goal: The Threat of Income-Based Inequality in Education, Washington: Pell Institute.
Tinto, V. (2008) Access without Support Is Not Opportunity In Inside Higher Education, 9th June 2008 https://www.insidehighered.com/views/2008/06/09/access-without-support-not-opportunity
US National Archives and Records Administration, August 4, 2014.
U.S. Department of Education. (1997). National Center for Education Statistics [NCES]. The Condition of Education. Retrieved from http://nces.ed.gov/pubs97/97388.pdf
White House Task Force on Middle Class Families: Barriers to Higher Education. (2014). (retrieved from https://www.whitehouse.gov/assets/documents/MCTF_staff_report_barriers_to_college_FINAL.pdf)
Yang, H., Kezar, A. (2009). Financial Education in TRIO programs. An Institutional Policy Brief, Washington: The Pell Institute.

## Chapter 3

Caballero, C. and L. Herrera (2013) 'El financiamiento de la educación superior en Colombia'. in L. E. Orozco (ed.) *La educación superior: retos y perspectivas* (Bogotá DC: Universidad de los Andes), pp. 121–80.
Departamento Administrativo Nacional de Estadística (DANE) (2012) *Estadísticas por tema*, available at http://www.dane.gov.co/index.php/acerca-del-dane/114-top-menu/acerca-del-dane/4031-generalidades (accessed 22 February 2014).
Götz, P. and M. Seifert (2010) 'Monitoring Children's Universities', in *The EUCU.NET White Book. A Reference Guide on Children's Universities* (Vienna: European Children's Universities Network – EUCU.NET), pp. 49–51.
Instituto Colombiano para el Fomento de la Educación Superior (ICFES) (1985) *Estadísticas de la Educación Superior 1985* (Bogotá: ICFES).
Instituto Colombiano para el Fomento de la Educación Superior (ICFES) (1992) *Estadísticas de la Educación Superior Resumen Anual 1992* (Bogotá: ICFES).
Instituto Colombiano para el Fomento de la Educación Superior (ICFES) (2002) *Estadísticas de la Educación Superior Resumen Anual 2002* (Bogotá: ICFES).
Instituto Colombiano para el Fomento de la Educación Superior (ICFES) (2012) 'Resultados de la prueba Saber 11', available at http://www.icfesinteractivo.gov.co/resultadosSaber/sniee_ind_resul.htm (accessed 10 April 2014).

Ministerio de Educación Nacional (MEN) (2012) *Estadísticas de Educación – Glosario 2014*, available at http://menweb.mineducacion.gov.co/seguimiento/estadisticas/glosario.html (accessed 23 January 2014).
MEN and SNIES (1992). From page 1.
OCFES (2002). From page 1.
Organisation for Economic and Co-operation Development (OECD) and The World Bank (2012) *Reviews of National Policies for Education: Tertiary Education in Colombia 2012* (Paris: OECD), available at http://dx.doi.org/10.1787/9789264180697-en (accessed 10 January 2014).
Sistema para la Prevensión de la Deserción de la Educación Superior (SPADIE) (2014) *Estadísticas de Deserción*, available at http://spadies.mineducacion.gov.co/spadies/consultas_predefinidas.html?2 (accessed 5 March 2014).

## Chapter 4

Arum, R., A. Gamoran and Y. Shavit (2007) 'More Inclusion Than Diversion. Expansion, Differentiation, and Market Structure in Higher Education', in Y. Shavit, R. Arum and A. Gamoran (eds) *Stratification in Higher Education. A Comparative Study* (Stanford: Stanford University Press), pp. 1–35.
Autorengruppe Bildungsberichterstattung (2012a) *Bildung in Deutschland 2012* [Education in Germany 2012] (Bielefeld: W. Bertelsmann).
Autorengruppe Bildungsberichterstattung (2012b) *Tabelle F1 Hochschulzugang und Studienaufnahme. Ergänzende Tabellen/Abbildungen im Internet* [Excel sheet], available at http://www.bildungsbericht.de/zeigen.html?seite=10218.
Bundesministerium für Bildung und Forschung (BMBF) (2008) ANKOM – Crediting of Vocational Competencies for Higher Education Programme. *Status of Recognition of Non-formal and Informal Learning in Germany* (Bonn: BMBF), pp. 47–49.
Bundesministerium für Bildung und Forschung (BMBF) (2014). *Wettbewerb 'Aufstieg durch Bildung: offene Hochschulen'* [Competition 'advancement through education: opened higher education institutions'], available at http://www.bmbf.de/de/17592.php.
Burckhart, H. (2014). *Umsetzung der Europäischen Studienreform – Strategische Handlungsempfehlungen* [Implementation of the European Higher Education Reform – Strategic Recommendations for Actions], available at http://www.hrk-nexus.de/uploads/media/Praesentation-Burckhart.pdf.
Duru-Bellat, M., A. Kieffer and D. Reimer (2008). 'Patterns of Social Inequalities in Access to Higher Education in France and Germany', *International Journal of Comparative Sociology*, 49: 347–68.
European Commission (2010) *Europe 2020: A European Strategy for Smart, Sustainable and Inclusive Growth* (Brussels: European Commission).
European Commission (2011) *Supporting Growth and Jobs – An Agenda for the Modernisation of Europe's Higher Education Systems* (Luxembourg: European Union), available at http://ec.europa.eu/education/library/policy/modernisation_en.pdf.
European Commission, and Eurydice (2011) *Modernisation of Higher Education in Europe: Funding and the Social Dimension* (Brussels: EACEA), available at http://eacea.ec.europa.eu/education/eurydice/documents/thematic_reports/131en.pdf.
European Union (2013) *Country Report Germany: Developing the Adult Learning –Opening Higher Education to Adults* (Brussels: European Union), pp. 135–79.
Hochschulrektorenkonferenz (HRK) (2013). *Europäische Studienreform; Empfehlung der 15. Mitgliederversammlung der Hochschulrektorenkonferenz Karlsruhe, 19.11.2013* [European study reform: Recommendations of the 15th meeting of members of the German Rectors'

Conference in Karlsruhe, on 19th November, 2013], available at http://www.hrk.de/uploads/tx_szconvention/Empfehlung_Europaeische_Studienreform_19112013.pdf.

Hochschulrektorenkonferenz (HRK) (2014a) *The European Higher Education area*, available at http://www.hrk.de/hrk-international/european-higher-education-policy/.

Hochschulrektorenkonferenz (HRK) (2014b) *Higher Education Institutions*, available at https://www.hochschulkompass.de/en/higher-education-institutions.html.

Hochschulrektorenkonferenz (HRK) (2014c) *Gute Beispiele und Konzepte – Good practice*, available at http://www.hrk-nexus.de/material/gute-beispiele-und-konzepte-good-practice/.

Hochschulrektorenkonferenz (HRK) (2014d). *Studieren ohne Abitur: Wachstumstrend setzt sich fort* [Study without high school diploma: Growth trend continues], available at http://www.hrk-nexus.de/aktuelles/news/detailansicht/meldung/studieren-ohne-abitur-wachstumstrend-setzt-sich-fort-3410/.

Hochschulrektorenkonferenz (HRK) and Deutscher Industrie- und Handelskammertag (DIHK) (2008) *Für mehr Durchlässigkeit zwischen beruflicher Bildung und Hochschulbildung*. [For a better transition between vocational education and higher education. A joint declaration of the German Chambers of Industry and Commerce DIHK and German Rectors' Conference HRK], available at http://www.hrk.de/uploads/media/HRK_DIHK_Erklaerung_2008_02.pdf.

Kaulisch, M., and J. Huisman (2007) *Higher Education in Germany* (The Netherlands: Centre for Higher Education Policy Studies).

Kultusministerkonferenz (KMK) (2009) *Hochschulzugang für beruflich qualifizierte Bewerber ohne schulische Hochschulzugangsberechtigung* [Higher education access for people with vocational training but no formal access qualification], available at http://www.kmk.org/fileadmin/veroeffentlichungen_beschluesse/2009/2009_03_06-Hochschulzugang-erful-qualifizierte-Bewerber.pdf.

Kultusministerkonferenz (KMK) (2010) *Nationale Strategien zur sozialen Dimension des Bologna-Prozesses* [National strategies for the social dimension of the Bologna process], available at http://www.kmk.org/fileadmin/pdf/Wissenschaft/BE_081010_Nat Bericht_TeilII_SozialeDimension_endg.pdf.

Koucky, J., A. Bartusek and J. Kovarovick (2010) *Who Gets a Degree? Access to Higher Education in Europe 1950–2009* (Prague: Charles University), available at http://www.strediskovzdelavacipolitiky.info/download/Whogetsadegree.pdf.

Leicht-Scholten, C. (2013) *Hochschule öffne dich, oder: Wie Vielfalt und Chancengerechtigkeit Hochschulen stärken* [Open Higher Education Institution or how diversity and equality of chances can strengthen higher education institutions], in Heinrich-Böll-Stiftung (ed.) *Öffnung der Hochschule* [Opening of higher education institutions] (Berlin: Heinrich-Böll-Stiftung), pp. 47–51.

Mayer, K. U., W. Mueller and R. Pollak (2003) *Institutional Change and Inequalities of Access in German Higher Education*. [Paper presented at the First Workshop of the International Comparative Project on Higher Education: Expansion, Institutional Forms and Equality of Opportunity] Prague, 7–9 June 2002.

Nickel, S., and S. Duong (2012) *Studieren ohne Abitur: Monitoring der Entwicklung in Bund, Ländern und Hochschulen* [Studying without an Abitur – Monitoring the development at federal, state and institutional level] (Gütersloh: CHE).

Organisation for Economic Co-operation and Development (OECD) (2012) *Germany Country Notes: Results from PISA 2012*, available at http://www.oecd.org/pisa/keyfindings/PISA-2012-results-germany.pdf.

Organisation for Economic Co-operation and Development (OECD) (2014) *Germany, Keeping the Edge: Competitiveness for Inclusive Growth*, available at http://www.oecd.org/about/publishing/Better-policies-germany.pdf.

Orr, D. (2012) 'Widening Access to Higher Education – What Can EUROSTUDENT Say About the New Challenges Emerging for Teaching and Learning?' in A. Curaj,

P. Scott, L. Vlăsceanu, and L. Wilson (eds) *European Higher Education at the Crossroads. Between the Bologna Process and National Reforms* (New York: Springer), pp. 173–90).

Orr, D., C. Gwosc and N. Netz (2011) *Social and Economic Conditions of Student Life in Europe. Synopsis of indicators. Final Report. Eurostudent IV 2008–2011* (Bielefeld: W. Bertelsmann Verlag).

Orr, D., and E. Hovdhaugen (2014) '"Second-chance" Routes into Higher Education: Sweden, Norway and Germany Compared', *International Journal of Lifelong Education*, 33(1): 45–61.

Orr, D., and M. Riechers (2010) *Organisation des Hochschulzugangs im Vergleich von sieben europäischen Ländern* [Organisation of higher education access in comparison of seven European countries]. HIS GmbH, available at http://www.his.de/pdf/pub_fh/fh-201011.pdf.

Peer Learning for the Social Dimension (PL4SD) (2014) *Rent a Student*, available at http://www.pl4sd.eu/index.php/measure?measure=289.

Reimer, D., and R. Pollak (2010) Educational Expansion and Its Consequences for Vertical and Horizontal Inequalities in Access to Higher Education in West Germany, *European Sociological Review*, 26(4): 415–30.

Rothe, G. (2008) *Berufliche Bildung in Deutschland. Das EU-Reformprogramm 'Lissabon 2000' als Heraus-forderung für den Ausbau neuer Wege beruflicher Qualifizierung im lebenslangen Lernen* [Vocational training in Germany – The EU-Reform programme Lisbon 2000 as challenge for the design of new paths of vocational training in lifelong learning] (Karlsruhe: Universitätsverlag).

Statistisches Bundesamt (2014) *Studierende an Hochschulen – Vorbericht Wintersemester 2013/2014 (Fachserie 11 Reihe 4.1)* [Students at universities preliminary report winter term 2013/2014] (Wiesbaden: Statistisches Bundesamt).

Ulbricht, L. (2012) *'Öffnen die Länder ihre Hochschulen? Annahmen über den dritten Bildungsweg auf dem Prüfstand'* [Are German states opening their higher education institutions? Testing assumptions on the third educational path], *Die Hochschule*, 2012, 154–68.

Urbatsch, K. (2013) *Studierende der ersten Generation andeutschenHochschulengewinnen und fördern* [Winning and supporting first-generation students at German higher education institutions], in Heinrich-Böll-Stiftung (ed.), *Öffnung der Hochschule* [Opening of higher education institutions] (pp. 22–26]. (Berlin: Heinrich-Böll-Stiftung).

Wolter, A. (2012) 'Germany: From Individual Talent to Institutional Permeability: Changing Policies for Non-traditional Access Routes in German Higher Education', in M. Slowey and H. G. Schuetze (eds) *Global Perspectives on Higher Education and Lifelong Learners* (New York: Routledge).

## Chapter 5

Brown, P., H. Lauder and D. Ashton (2011) *The Global Auction: The Broken Promises of Education, Jobs, and Incomes* (Oxford: Oxford University Press).

Kivinen, O., S. Ahola and J. Hedman (2001) 'Expanding Education and Improving Odds? Participation in Higher Education in Finland in the 1980s and 1990s', *Acta Sociologica*, 44(2): 171–81, available at http://asj.sagepub.com/content/44/2/171.abstract.

Kooij, Y. (2015) *European Higher Education Policy and the Social Dimension: A Comparative Study of the Bologna Process* (London: Palgrave Macmillan).

Lafont, P. and M. Pariat (2012) *Review of the Recognition of Prior Learning in Member States in Europe* (Brussels: European Commission).

Lähteenmäki-Smith, K. (2011) *Finland Promoting Social Inclusion of Roma A Study of National Policies* (Brussels: European Commission).
Ministry of Education, Finland (2005) *OECD Thematic Review of Tertiary Education Country Background Report for Finland* (Finland: MoE).
Ministry of Education and Culture Finland (2012) *Finnish Education in a Nutshell* (Finland: Ministry of Education and Culture).
Ministry of Education, Finland (2013) *Education System in Finland*, available at http://www.minedu.fi/OPM/Koulutus/koulutusjaerjestelmae/?lang=en.
Official Statistics of Finland (OSF) (2015) 'University Education', ISSN=2324-0148. (Helsinki: Statistics Finland) [referred: 20.10.2015], available at http://www.stat.fi/til/yop/kas_en.html.
Organisation for Economic Co-operation and Development (OECD) (2011) 'Lessons from PISA for the United States, Strong Performers and Successful Reformers in Education', OECD Publishing, available at http://dx.doi.org/10.1787/9789264096660-en.
Organisation for Economic Co-operation and Development (OECD) (2013) *Education Policy Outlook: Finland* (Paris: OECD).
Organisation for Economic Co-operation and Development (OECD) (2015), Education Policy Outlook 2015: Making Reforms Happen, OECD Publishing, available at http://dx.doi.org/10.1787/9789264225442-en.
Regional Council of Lapland (2013) *Lapland in Figures 2012–13, Regional Council of Lapland*.
Roemer, J. E. (2000) 'Equality of Opportunity', in K. Arrow, S. Bowles and S. Durlauf (eds) *Meritocracy and Economic Inequality* (Princeton: Princeton University Press), pp. 17–32.
UNESCO (2013) *UNESCO Handbook on Education Policy Analysis and Programming* (Bangkok: UNESCO).
United Nations (2013) *Inequality Matters Report of the World Social Situation* (New York: United Nations).

## Chapter 6

Atherton, G. (2012) Access HE: Can Collaborative Outreach Work Continue in London after Aimhigher? *Widening Participation and Lifelong Learning*, 13(Special Issue): 93–99.
Attwood, R. (2011) 'You Mean Offa Is Toothless? The Reason for Policy Chaos', *Times Higher Education*, 24 February 2011.
Benn, R. and R. Burton (1995) 'Access and Targeting: An Exploration of a Contradiction', *International Journal of Lifelong Education*, 14(6): 444–58.
Committee on Higher Education (1963) *Report of the Committee Appointed by the Prime Minister under the Chairmanship of Lord Robbins 1961–1963* (The Robbins Report), Cmnd 2154, London, HMSO, 23 September.
Court, S. (2001) 'Date with Destiny', *The Guardian*, 13 February, available at https://www.theguardian.com/education/2001/feb/13/highereducation.uk3.
Department of Business, Innovation and Skills (BIS) (2011) Guidance to the Director of Fair Access Issued by Secretary of State for Business, Innovation and Skills and Minister for Universities and Science February 2011 (London: Department of Business, Innovation and Skills [BIS]).
Department of Business, Innovation and Skills (BIS) (2014) National Strategy for Access and Student Success in Higher Education Published by the Department for Business, Innovation and Skills (London: Department of Business, Innovation and Skills [BIS]).

Department for Employment and Learning Northern Ireland (DELNI) (2010) *Review of Widening Participation Funded Initiatives*, available at http://www.delni.gov.uk/review-of-widening-participation-funded-initiatives-final.pdf.

Fergus, L. (2014) 'Every One of Northern Ireland's Top Five Schools Is a Catholic Grammar', *Belfast Telegraph*, 11 May 2015, available at http://www.belfasttelegraph.co.uk/news/education/every-one-of-northern-irelands-top-five-schools-is-a-catholic-grammar-30140937.html.

Gallacher, J. and D. Raffe (2011) 'Higher Education Policy in Post-devolution UK: More Convergence Than Divergence?', *Journal of Education Policy*, 27(4): 467–90.

Giddens, A. (1998) *Beyond Left and Right: The Future of Radical Politics* (Cambridge: Polity Press).

Hamilton, A. (2010) *Widening Participation in Higher Education – Department for Employment and Learning. Tullyglass House Hotel, Ballymena – 19 May 2010*, available at http://www.delni.gov.uk/index/further-and-higher-education/higher-education/role-structure-he-division/he-policy/he-widening-participation.htm (accessed March 2012).

HEA (2009). From p. 8.

HEFCE/OFFA (2013) *National Strategy for Access and Student Success: Interim Report to the Department for Business, Innovation and Skills* (Bristol: HEFCE).

Higher Education Funding Council for England (HEFCE) (2011) From p. 11.

Higher Education Funding Council for England (HEFCE) (2015) *Outcomes of Student Opportunity allocation and National Scholarship Programme Monitoring for 2013–14*, (Bristol: HEFCE).

Higher Education Funding Council for Wales (HEFCW) (2011) *Reaching Wider Strategies 2011–12 to 2013–14: Supplementary Guidance* (Cardiff: HEFCW).

Higher Education Funding Council for Wales (2015) *Fee Plan Guidance 2016/17* (Cardiff: HEFCWE), available at https://www.hefcw.ac.uk/documents/publications/circulars/circulars_2015/W15 05HE Fee Plan Guidance 2016 17.pdf.

Hill, M. and S. Hatt (2012) *Review of Widening Access and Reaching Higher Strategies in Wales* (York: Higher Education Academy).

Johnson, S. (2014) 'Alex Salmond Unveils Tuition Fees Tribute as He Resigns', *The Telegraph*, 18 November 2014.

Lothian Equal Access Programme for Schools (LEAPS) (2011) Annual Report, available at http//www.leapsonline.org/annual-report.html.

McGoldrick, J. (2005) *Learning For All. Edinburgh. SFEFC/SHEFC Widening Participation Review Group, Scottish Funding Council*, available at http://www.sfc.ac.uk/publications/pubs_other_sfcarchive/learning_for_all_pu blication_september_2005.pdf (accessed September 2012).

Morgan, J. (2015) 'Aimhigher Revisited? New National Outreach Project Launched', *Times Higher Education*, 8 January 2015, available at http://www.timeshighereducation.co.uk/news/aimhigher-revisited-new-national-outreach-project-launched/2017856.article.

National Committee of Inquiry into Higher Education (Dearing Report) (1997) *Report 6 Widening Participation in Higher Education for Students from Lower Socio-economic Groups and Students with Disabilities* (London: Her Majesty's Stationery Office).

Nolan, P (2014) *Northern Ireland Peace Monitoring Report Number Three* (Northern Ireland: Community Relations Council).

Osborne, B. and I. Shuttleworth (2004), 'Widening Access to Higher Education in the UK: Questioning the Geographic Approach', *Higher Education Management and Policy*, 16(1): 101–18.

Pratt, J. (1997) *The Polytechnic Experiment 1965–1992* (London: Milton Keynes: Society for Research into Higher Education and Open University Press).

Purvis, D. (2011) *Educational Disadvantage and the Protestant Working Class: A Call to Action*, available at http://www.amazingbrains.co.uk/static/uploads/media/pdfs/A-Call-to-Action-FINAL-March2011_0.pdf.
Secretary of State for Education (2001) From p. 10.
Scottish Funding Council (SFC) (2009) *Widening Participation in Scotland: Case Studies from the Wider Access Regional Forums* (Edinburgh: SFC).
Scottish Funding Council (SFC) (2011) *Schools for Higher Education Programme*, available at http://www.sfc.ac.uk/SchoolsforHigherEdcuationProgramme/SchoolsforHigherEducationProgramme.aspx (accessed February 2012).
Scottish Funding Council (SFC) (2015) *Learning for All: Fifth Measures for Success* (Edinburgh: SFC).
Thomas, L. (2012) *Building Student Engagement and Belonging in Higher Education at a Time of Change: Final Report from the What Works? Student Retention and Success Programme* (London: Paul Hamlyn Foundation).
Universities and Colleges Admission Service (UCAS) (2014) *End of Cycle Report 2014* (Bristol: UCAS_/
Universities Scotland (2014) *Delivering for Scotland: The Third Round of Outcome Agreements for Higher Education* (Edinburgh: Universities Scotland).
Universities UK (2013) *The Power of Part-time: Review of Part-time and Mature Higher Education* (London: Universities UK).
Watts, A. G. (2013) 'False Dawns, Bleak Sunset: The Coalition Government's Policies on Career Guidance', *British Journal of Guidance & Counselling*, 41(4): 442–53.
Weedon, E. (2014) *Working Paper 1: Widening Participation to Higher Education of Underrepresented Groups in Scotland: The Challenges of Using Performance Indicators* (Edinburgh: University of Edinburgh: CREID).

## Chapter 7

Asian Development Bank (2012) *Access Without Equity? Finding a Better Balance for Higher Education in Asia* (The Philippines: Asian Development Bank).
Brown, G. (2005) 'Making Ethnic Citizens: The Politics and Practice of Education in Malaysia', Centre for Research on Inequality, Human Security and Ethnicity (Oxford: University of Oxford).
Buchbinder, H. (1993) 'The Market-oriented University and the Changing Role of Knowledge', *Higher Education*, 26: 331–47.
Cheng, M. W. (1997) *A Study of a Business Education Twinning Programme at a Private College in Petaling Jaya*, Master's of Education thesis, Kuala Lumpur, University of Malaya.
Cheng, M. W. (2005) *A Study of a Work-based Learning Partnership within the Malaysian Context, Using a Financial Institution as Case Study*, Master's of Arts thesis, United Kingdom: Middlesex University.
Coleman, D. (2003) 'Quality Assurance in Transnational Education' *Journal of Studies in International Education*, 7: 354–78.
Crosling, G., Martin, K. (2004) 'Student Diversity and Group Work: A Positive Combination for Curriculum Internationalization', in E. Manalo and G.Wong-Toi, (eds), *Communication Skills in University Education: International Dimensions* (Auckland, Pearson Educational).
Crosling, G., R. Edwards and W. Schroder (2008) 'Internationalizing the Curriculum: The Implementation Experience in a Faculty of Business and Economics', *Journal of Higher Education Policy and Management*, 30(2): 107–21.

Crosling, G., M. Nair and S. Vaithilingam (2014) 'A Creative Learning Ecosystem, Quality of Education and Innovative Capacity: A Perspective from Higher Education', *Studies in Higher Education*, published online 8 April 2014, available at http://www.tandfonline.com/doi/abs/10.1080/03075079.2014.881342.

Economic Planning Unit, Prime Minister's Department, Malaysia (2010) 'New Economic Policy', available at http://www.epu.gov.my/en/dasar-ekonomi-baru (accessed 24 November 2014).

Edwards, R., G. Crosling, S. Lavazeric-Petrovic and P. O'Neill (2003) 'Curriculum Internationalisation: Meaning and Implementation', *Higher Education Research and Development*, 22(2): 183–92.

Edwards, R., G. Crosling and N. C. Lim (2014) 'Organizational Structure for International Universities: Implications for Campus Autonomy, Academic Freedom, Collegiality, and Conflict', *Journal of Studies in International Education*, 18 May: 180–94.

Fernandez-Chung, R. M. (2006). *A Study of the Impact of Education and Immigration Policies on the Recruitment of Foreign Students to PHEIs in Malaysia*, PhD thesis, University of Leicester, Leicester.

Hudzik, J. K. (2011) *Comprehensive Internationalization: From Concept to Action*, NAFSA Association of International Educators, available at http://www.nafsa.org/uploadedfiles/nafsa_home/resource_library_assets/publications_library/2011_comprehen_internationalization.pdf (accessed 13 June 2014),

Karram, G. (2014) 'Australian-style Training for Leadership Makes Waves', *University World News*, 30 May 2014, available at http://www.universityworldnews.com/article.php?story=20140527161909570 (accessed 12 June 2014.

Leask, B. (2014) 'Emerging Agreement on Internationalising the Curriculum', *University World News*, June 11, available at http://www.universityworldnews.com/article.php?story=20121017163121188 (accessed 11 June 2014).

Lee, M.N.N. (1999a) 'Corporatization, Privatization, and Internationalization of Higher Education in Malaysia', in P. G. Altbach (ed.), *Private Prometheus: Private HE and Development in the 21st Century* (Westport, CT: Greenwood Press), pp. 137–59.

Lee, M.N.N. (1999b). *Private Higher Education in Malaysia* (Penang: School of Educational Studies, Universiti Sains Malaysia).

Lopes, R. (2014) Interview with Directors of Australian-type Pre-university Programmes at Private Higher Education Institutions, Malaysia (Unpublished).

Ministry of Education, Malaysia (2007) 'National Higher Education Strategic Plan', available at http://www.moe.gov.my/en/pelan-strategik-pengajian-tinggi-negara (accessed 24 November 2014).

Ministry of Education, Malaysia (2013) *Indikator Pengajian Tinggi Malaysia 2011–2012*, Kementarian Pinadaken Malaysia, available at https://www.mohe.gov.my/ms/muat-turun/awam/statistik/2012/79-indikator-pengajian-tinggi-malaysia-2011-2012/file (accessed 12 June 2014).

Ministry of Education, Malaysia (2014) Meeting of Minister of Education II and Chief Executives of Private Higher Education Institutions, Seri Pacific Hotel, Kuala Lumpur, 12 May.

Morshidi, S. (2006) 'Transnational Higher Education in Malaysia: Balancing Benefits and Concerns through Regulations', in F. Huang (ed.) *Transnational Higher Education in Asia and the Pacific Region* (Hiroshima: Hiroshima University), p. 169.

Morshidi, S. (2009) 'Trends in International Higher Education and Regionalism: Issues and Challenges for Malaysia', in K. Kuroda (ed.) *Education and Asian Regional Integration Research Group, GIARI* (Penang: Universiti Sains Malaysia).

PEMANDU (2010) *Economic Transformation Programme: A Roadmap for Malaysia*. Prime Minister's Department Malaysia, available at http://etp.pemandu.gov.my/Invest_in_Malaysia-@-Malaysia's Transformation.aspx (accessed 24 November 2014).

Rao, S. (2009) 'Globalisation, Affirmative Action and Higher Education Reforms in Malaysia: A Tightrope Walk between Equality and Excellence', *Asian Economic Papers*, 10(1): 160–63.
Symaco, L. (2010) 'Higher Education and Equity in Malaysia', *The International Journal of Educational and Psychological Assessment*, 5(2): 265–72.
Tan, A. M. (2002) *Malaysian Private Higher Education: Globalisation, Privatisation, Transformation and Marketplaces* (London: Asean Academic Press).
Tham, S Y. (2011) 'Exploring Access and Equity in Malaysia's Private Higher Education', ADBI Working Paper (Tokyo: Asian Development Bank Institute).
W.A.M.W. Muda (2008). 'The Malaysian National Higher Education Action Plan: Redefining Autonomy and Academic Freedom Under the APEX Experiment', paper presented at the *ASAIHL Conference, University Autonomy: Interpretation and Variation*, Universiti Sains Malaysia, 12–14 December 2008.

## Chapter 8

Basant, R. and G. Sen (2010) 'Who Participates in Higher Education in India? Rethinking the Role of Affirmative Action', *Economic & Political Weekly*, 45(39): 62–70.
Chattopadhyay, S. (2009) 'The Market in Higher Education: Concern for Equity and Quality', *Economic and Political Weekly*, 44(29): 53-61.
Deshpande, S. (2013) 'Introduction' in S. Deshpande and U. Zachariah (eds) *Beyond Inclusion* (New Delhi: Routledge).
Deshpande, S. and Y. Yadav (2006) 'Meeting the Challenges of Mandal II', *The Hindu*, 22 May, available at http://www.hindu.com/2006/05/22/stories/2006052202261100.htm.
Government of India (2010) *Report of the Committee to Advise on Renovation and Rejuvenation of Higher Education* (New Delhi: Government of India).
John, M. (2012) 'Gender and Higher Education in Times of Reform', *Contemporary Education Dialogue*, 9(2): 197–221.
Ministry of Human Resource Development (MHRD) (1986) *National Policy on Education* (New Delhi: Government of India, MHRD, Department of Education).
Ministry of Human Resource Development (MHRD) (2013) *Rashtriya ucchatar shiksha abhiyan: The National HE Mission* (New Delhi: Government of India, MHRD), available at http://mhrd.gov.in/sites/upload_files/mhrd/files/upload_document/RUSA_final090913.pdf.
National Knowledge Commission (2009) *National Knowledge Commission: Report to the Nation (2006–2009)* (New Delhi: Government of India, National Knowledge Commission).
Planning Commission (2012) *The Twelfth Five Year Plan (2012–17): Social Sectors, Vol. 3*. (New Delhi: Government of India), available at http://planningcommission.gov.in/plans/planrel/12thplan/pdf/vol_3.pdf.
Sundaram, K. (2007) *Fair Access to Higher Education Re-visited: Some Results for Social and Religious Groups from NSS 61st Round Employment Unemployment Survey, 2004–05: Working Paper No. 163* (New Delhi: Centre for Development Economics, Delhi School of Economics).
Tilak, J.B.G. (2007) 'Knowledge Commission and Higher Education', *Economic and Political Weekly*, 42(8): 630–33.
Tilak, J.B.G. (2012) 'Higher Education Policy in India in Transition', *Economic and Political Weekly*, 47(13): 36–40.
University Grants Commission (UGC) 2008. *Higher Education in India – Issues Related to Expansion, Inclusiveness, Quality and Finance* (New Delhi: UGC).
University Grants Commission (UGC) (2013) *Higher Education in India at a Glance* (New Delhi: UGC).

## Chapter 9

Beihang University (2015) 'The Enrolment Guide of Rural Students', available at http://zsjyc.buaa.edu.cn/ZSWeb/News/Go/6be492625aef40b9b6c9e52a0545ff95 (accessed June 2015).

Branigan, T. (2010) 'China Census Could Be First to Record True Population', *The Guardian*, 1 November 2010.

Chen, X. (2012) 'Who Is More Likely to Enter Better Colleges: An Empirical Evidence of the Distribution Of China Higher Education Opportunity of Different Quality', *Journal of Higher Education*, 2: 20–29.

China Disabled Persons' Association (CDPA) (2012) 'The Number of Persons with Disabilities by the End of 2010, by Category and Degree Of Disabilities', available at http://www.cdpf.org.cn/sjzx/cjrgk/201206/t20120626_387581.shtml (accessed June 2015).

Gou, R. (2005) 'Equality in Access to Higher Education Being Assessed from the Opportunities between Urban and Rural Students', *Educational Development Research*, 6: 29–31.

Liu, Y. et al. (2009) 'Selection of Elites: Views from Social Status, Geographical Variation, and Capital Gaining – Case Study on Farmers' Children Who Get Admitted into Peking University (1978–2005)', *Tsinghua Journal of Education*, 5: 42–59.

Ministry of Education of the PRC (MoE) (2012a) '2011 Statistical Bulletin of National Education Development', available at http://www.moe.edu.cn/publicfiles/business/htmlfiles/moe/moe_633/201407/171144.html (accessed June 2015).

Ministry of Education of the PRC (MoE) (2012b) 'The Cooperative Program of Supporting the Enrolment in Mid-western Regions', available at http://www.moe.edu.cn/publicfiles/business/htmlfiles/moe/s6811/201209/141512.html (accessed June 2015).

Ministry of Education of the PRC (MoE) (2014) '2013 Statistical Bulletin of National Education Development', available at http://www.moe.edu.cn/publicfiles/business/htmlfiles/moe/moe_633/201407/171144.html (accessed June 2015).

Ministry of Education of the PRC (MoE) (2015a) 'The Notice for Key Universities to Recruit Rural Students in 2015', available at http://www.moe.edu.cn/publicfiles/business/htmlfiles/moe/s7063/201504/185578.html (accessed June 2015).

Ministry of Education of the PRC (MoE) (2015b) 'The Regulation on the Administration of Participation of the Students with Disabilities in the National College Entrance Examination in 2015', available at http://www.moe.edu.cn/publicfiles/business/htmlfiles/moe/B21_xxgk/201503/184885.html (accessed June 2015).

Mu, Y. C. (2013) *Educational Statistics Yearbook of China 2012* (Beijing: People's Education Press).

Mu, Y. C. (2014) *Educational Statistics Yearbook of China 2013* (Beijing: People's Education Press), pp. 14, 15, 16, 17.

National Bureau of Statistics (2011) 'Bulletin of the Sixth National Population Census Data in 2010, No. 1)', available at http://www.stats.gov.cn/tjsj/tjgb/rkpcgb/qgrkpcgb/201104/t20110428_30327.html (accessed June 2015).

Peking University (2015) *The Enrolment Guide of the Dream-building Project*, available at http://www.gotopku.cn/index/detail/596.html (accessed June 2015).

The State Council of the PRC (TSC) (2014) *Implementation Suggestions for Deepening the Reform of Examination and Enrolment System*, available at http://www.moe.edu.cn/publicfiles/business/htmlfiles/moe/moe_1778/201409/174543.html (accessed June 2015).

Tsinghua University (2015) *The Enrolment Guide of the 'Self-improvement Project'*, available at http://www.tsinghua.edu.cn/publish/bzw/7527/2015/20150415110338991 99746 9/20150415110338991997469_.html (accessed June 2015).

Zhao, F. H. (2007) 'Large-scale Public Survey on National College Entrance Examination System Shows Generally a Positive Attitude by the Public', *Science and Technology Daily*, 24 July.

## Chapter 10

Bitzer, E. M. (2010) 'Some Myths on Equity and Access in Higher Education', *South African Journal of Higher Education*, 24(2): 301–2, 304.

Council on Higher Education (CHE) (2013) *A Proposal for Undergraduate Curriculum Reform in South Africa: The Case for a Flexible Curriculum Structure* (Pretoria: CHE), p. 41.

Department of Education, South Africa (2001) *Draft National Plan for Higher Education in South Africa* (Pretoria: DoE).

Department of Higher Education and Training (DHET) (2013) *White Paper for Post-school Education and Training: Building an Expanded, Effective and Integrated Post-school System*, pp. 7–8, 28, 30–33, 36.

Extension of University Education Act, Act No. 45 of 1959, Group Areas Act. Act No 41 of 1950, available at www.nelsonmandela.org/omalley/index.php/site//061v01850.htm.

http://www.nelsonmandela.org/omalley/index.php/site/9/./061v01850

Higher Education South Africa (2010) Higher Education Commitment to Facilitate Increased Access to and Affordability of Higher Education, press release, 28 January, available at http://stbweb02.stb.sun.ac.za/ctl/extended.

Kennedy-Dubourdieu, E. (ed.) (2006) *Race and Inequality: World Perspectives on Affirmative Action* (Farnham: Ashgate).

Lehohla, P.J (2013). 'Mid-year Population Estimates, Statistics (South Africa)', available at http://www.southafrica.info/about/people/population.htm.

Magopeni, N. and L. Tshiwula (2010) 'The Realities of Dealing with South Africa's Past: A Diversity in Higher Education', paper presented at the Tenth International Conference on Diversity in Organizations, Communities and Nations, Queen's University Belfast, Northern Ireland, 19–21 July.

Morrow, W. (1994) 'Entitlement and Achievement in Education', *Studies in Philosophy and Education*, 13: 33–47.

Mphahele (1994) From p. 10.

Ntshoe, I. (2011) 'The Political Economy of Public-private Good of Open, Distance, Higher Education Institutions in South Africa', *Acta Academia*, 43(3): 84–106.

Reddy, K. (2012) 'Students as Consumers: The Implications of the Consumer Protection Act for Higher Education Institutions in South Africa', *South African Journal of Higher Education*, 26(3): 586–605.

Report of the Ministerial Committee for the Review of the Funding of Universities, October 2013.

Rollnick, M. (2010) 'Identifying Potential for Equitable Access to Tertiary Level Science: Digging for Gold and the Anglophone World', *Springer Science+Business Media B.V.* pp. 2–3, 21–22.

Sedgwick, R. (2004) 'Institutions of Higher Education in South Africa after the Mergers', *World Education News and Reviews*, 17(3), available at http://www.wes.org/ewenr/04may/Feature.htm (accessed 27 August 2011).

Soudien, C. (2007) 'Diversity and Higher Education in South Africa', paper presented at a Diversity Conference, University of the Western Cape.
Stellenbosch University (2013) *Stellenbosch University Institutional Intent and Strategy 2013–2018* (Stellenbosch: Stellenbosch University), available at http://www.sun.ac.za/english/management/src/Documents/Archive/Institutional%20Intent%20and%20Strategy%202013-2018.pdf.
The Constitution of the Republic of South Africa, Act 108 (1996) (Pretoria: Government Printers).
University of Cape Town (2014) 'Guidelines for Admission to UCT in 2014 for Holders of a National Senior Certificate', available at http://www.uct.ac.za/downloads/uct.ac.za/apply/apps/undergrad/uctadmis_guidelines_2014.pdf.

## Chapter 11

Abagre, C. I., F. Issahaku and M. Bukari (2013) 'Promoting Affirmative Action in Higher Education: A Case Study of the University for Development Studies Bridging Programme', *Journal of Education and Practice*, 4(9), available at www.iiste.org ISSN 2222-1735 (paper) ISSN 2222-288X.
Addae-Mensah, I. (2000) 'Education in Ghana: A Tool for Social Mobility or Social Stratification?' Delivered at the J. B. Danquah Memorial Lectures (Accra: Ghana Academy of Arts and Sciences).
Alabi, G., J. Alabi and I. Mohammed (2013) 'Congruence between National Policy for Science and Humanities Enrolment Ratio and Labour Market Demand in Ghana, *Educational Research and Reviews*, 8(10): 708–19.
Anonymous (n.d.) Persons with Disability Act, 2006 Act 71, accessed at http://www.gapagh.org/GHANA%20DISABILITY%20ACT.pdf (accessed 23 August 2014).
Atuahene, F. and A. Owusu-Ansah (2013) 'A Descriptive Assessment of Higher Education Access, Participation, Equity, and Disparity in Ghana', *Sage Journals*, 23 July, DOI: 10.1177/2158244013497725,
Daddieh, C. K. (2003) *Gender Issues in Ghanaian Higher Education* (Occasional Paper No. 36) (Accra, Ghana: The Institute of Economic Affairs).
Daily Graphic (23 August 2014) 'Lifeline for MUC Students', available at http://graphic.com.gh/news/education/29391-lifeline-for-muc-students.html (accessed 23 August 2014).
Dunne, M. (2007) 'Schools and the Production of Gendered Identities: Insights from Ghana and Botswana', in Commonwealth Secretariat, *Commonwealth Education Partnership 2007* (London, Nexus Strategic Partnerships) pp. 26–30.
Ghana Ministry of Education, Science and Sports (MoESS) (2007) 'Education Reform 2007 at a Glance' (Accra, Ghana:
Kirkland, J. (2015) 'A Pyramid without a Higher Education Roof?', *University World News*, 20 March 2015.
Manuh, T., S. Gariba and J. Budu (2007) *Change and Transformation in Ghana's Publicly Funded Universities. Partnership for Higher Education in Africa* (Oxford, UK: James Currey and Accra, Ghana: Woeli Publishing Services).
Ministry of Education (MoE) (2013) 'Education Sector Performance Report', Ministry of Education, Republic of Ghana.
Modern Ghana (2009) 'UG Students with Special Needs Get Support Office', 25 March 2009, available at http://www.modernghana.com/news/208159/1/ug-students-with-special-needs-get-support-office.html.

Morley L., F. Leach and R. Lugg (2009) 'Democratising Higher Education in Ghana and Tanzania: Opportunity Structures and Social Inequalities', *International Journal of Educational Development*, 29: 56–64.

Morley L., F. Leach, R. Lugg, J. Opare E. Bhalalusesa, L. D. Forde and R. Mwaipopo (2007) *Widening Participation in Higher Education in Ghana and Tanzania: Developing an Equity Scorecard* (An ESRC/DfID Poverty Reduction Programme Funded Research Project), available at http://r4d.dfid.gov.uk/PDF/Outputs/ESRC_DFID/60335-working_paper_1.pdf.

NCTE (2013) *Statistics on Tertiary Education in Ghana: Ministry of Education: Performance Report* (Accra, Ghana: MoESS).

Owusu-Ansah, W, and K. Poku (2012) 'Entrepreneurship Education, a Panacea to Graduate Unemployment in Ghana?', *International Journal of Humanities and Social Science*, 2(15) August: 211.

Rustin, S. (2015) 'Almost 90% of Ghana's Children Are Now in School', *Guardian*, 7 April 2015, available at http://www.theguardian.com/education/2015/apr/07/ghana-global-education-campaign-young-ambassadors-visit-ghanaian-school.

United Nations Educational, Scientific and Cultural Organization Institute for Statistics (UNESCO) (2014) *Global Education Digest 2014: Comparing Education Statistics across the World* (Montreal, Quebec, Canada: UNESCO).

World Bank (2010) *Education in Ghana: Improving Equity, Efficiency and Accountability of Education Service Delivery*, Africa education country status report, Washington World Bank, available at http://documents.worldbank.org/curated/en/2010/02/17932091/education-ghana-improving-equity-efficiency-accountability-education-service-delivery.

Yusif et al. (2011) From p. 7.

Yusif, H. M. and B. Ali (2013) 'Academic Performance of Less Endowed High School Students in the Kwame Nkrumah University of Science of Technology' *Journal of Science and Technology*, 33(2): 104–17.

## Chapter 12

Anderson, D. S. and A. E. Vervoorn (1983) *Access to Privilege: Patterns of Participation in Australian Post-Secondary Education* (Canberra: Australian National University Press).

Australian Government (2009) *Transforming Australia's Higher Education System* (Canberra: Commonwealth of Australia).

Beswick, D. (1987) 'Trends in Australian Higher Education Research. A General Review', in J. P. Keeves (ed.) *Australian Education: Review of Recent Research* (Sydney: Allen and Unwin), pp. 205–38.

Bexley, E. and G. Maslen (2014) 'Student Poverty Increasing by Degrees', *The Age*, July 22: 14.

Bexley, E., S. Daroesman, S. Arkoudis and R. James (2013) *University Student Finances in 2012: A Study of the Financial Circumstances of Domestic and International Students in Australia's Universities* (Parkville: Centre for the Study of Higher Education, The University of Melbourne and Universities Australia).

Bradley, D. (Chair) (2008) *Review of Australian Higher Education: Final Report* (Canberra: Commonwealth of Australia).

Clarke, J., B. Zimmer and R. Main (1997) *Under Representation in Australian Higher Education by the Socio-economically Disadvantaged: Review of Trends and Issues, and the Implications for University Planning and Practice*, Australasian Association of Institutional Research (AAIR) 8th International Conference, Adelaide: November 26–28.

Department of Education, *Higher Education Student Statistics, 2012 Appendix 5*, available at https://education.gov.au/selected-higher-education-statistics-2012-student-data Appendix 5 (accessed 28 July 2014).

Department of Employment, Education and Training (1990) *A Fair Chance for All: Higher Education That's within Everyone's Reach* (Canberra: Australian Government Publishing Service).

Dobson, I., R. Sharma and E. Ramsay (1998) *Designated Equity Groups in Australian Universities: Performance of Commencing Undergraduates in Selected Course Types 1996* (Canberra: Australian Vice-Chancellors' Committee).

Evolution Media Group. (2014, July 2). Press release: ASIC Chairman Greg Medcraft on the Bottom Line, available at http://www.gcmag.com.au/greg-medcraft-speaks-challenges-running-asic.

Ferguson, K., 2006. *Fair Chance for All: Can This Value Survive in Today's Higher Education Sector?* Institutional Management in Higher Education (IMHE) conference, Organisation for Economic Co-operation and Development (OECD), Paris.

Ferrier F. and M. Heagney (2000) 'Dealing with the Dynamics of Disadvantage: Options for Equity Planning in Higher Education Institutions', *Widening Participation and Lifelong Learning*, 2(1): 5–14.

Ferrier F. and M. Heagney (2001) 'Re-thinking Equity for Students at Monash University', *Journal of Institutional Research in Australasia*, 10(2): 50–68.

Higher Education Council (HEC) (1996) *Equality, Diversity and Excellence: Advancing the National Higher Education Framework* (Canberra: Australian Government Publishing Service).

Kelly, M. (2014) 'Social Justice and Universities: Policy, Partnerships and Politics'. *Curtin Corners* Conference, National Centre for Student Equity in Higher Education (NCSEHE) (Perth: Curtin University), March 14.

Kemp, D. and A. Norton (2014) *Review of the Demand Driven Funding System Report* (Canberra: Commonwealth of Australia).

Koshy, P., T. Pitman and J. Phillimore (2014) *The Effect of the 2014–15 Federal Budget's Higher Education Proposals on Students: A Focus on Low-income Graduates,* (Perth: National Centre for Student Equity in Higher Education (NCSEHE) and Curtin University).

Maclean, R., ed. (2007) *Learning and Teaching for the 21st Century: Festschrift for Professor Phillip Hughes* (New York: Springer).

Marginson, S. (1999) 'Young People's Participation in Higher Education', in *Australia's Youth: Reality and Risk* (Sydney: Dusseldorp Skills Forum), pp. 87–102.

Martin, L. M. (1994) *Equity and General Performance Indicators in Higher Education*, Vol. 1: Equity Indicators (Canberra: Australian Government Printing Service).

National Centre for Student Equity in Higher Education (NCSEHE) (2013) *Access and Participation in Higher Education – Outreach, Access, Support* (Perth: Curtin University).

Naylor, R., C. Baik and R. James (2013) *Developing a Critical Interventions Framework for Advancing Equity in Australian Higher Education* (Parkville: Centre for the Study of Higher Education, The University of Melbourne).

Nelson, B. (2003) *Our Universities: Backing Australia's Future* (Canberra: Commonwealth of Australia).

Queensland Consortium (2014) *Widening Tertiary Participation 2013 Progress Report*, unpublished report submitted to the Queensland Department of Education

Ramsay, E. (2006) Higher Education Equity, Yesterday, Today (and Tomorrow): Equal Opportunity Practitioners in Higher Education Australasia (EOPHEA), *Strategic Connections* conference proceedings (Brisbane: Queensland University of Technology, Continuing Professional Education).

Ramsay, E., D. Tranter, S. Charlton and R. Sumner (1998) *Higher Education Access and Equity for Low SES School Leavers: A Case Study* (Canberra: Evaluation and Investigation Program, Department of Education, Training and Youth Affairs [DETYA]).

Robinson, B. (2014) *Senate: Approve Higher Education Package with Amendments*, media release (Canberra: Universities Australia), 28 August.

## Chapter 13

Altbach, P. G., L. Reisberg and E. Rumbley (2009) *Trends in Global Higher Education: Tracking an Academic Revolution A Report Prepared for the UNESCO 2009 World Conference on HE* (Paris: UNECSO).
Archer, L., M. Hutchings and A. Ross (2003) *Higher Education and Social Class: Issues of Exclusion and Inclusion* (London: Routledge Falmer).
Archer, L., S. Hollingworth and A. Halsall (2007) '"University's Not for Me — I'm a Nike Person": Urban, Working-Class Young People's Negotiations of "Style", Identity and Educational Engagement', *Sociology*, 41(2): 219–37.
Atherton, G. and K. Roberts (2011) Career Development among Young People in Britain Today: Poverty of Aspiration or Poverty of Opportunity? *International Journal of Education Administration and Policy Studies*, 3(5): 59–67.
Atherton, G. and G. Whitty (2016) *Drawing the Global Access Map* (London: Pearson).
Bourdieu, P. (1992) *Language and Symbolic Power*, Cambridge: Polity Press Commission of the European Communities (2006), —Efficiency and Equity in European Education and Training Systems||, Commission Staff Working Document, SEC(2006) 1096, Brussels.
d'Addio, A. C. (2007) 'Intergenerational Transmission of Disadvantage: Mobility or Immobility across Generations? A Review of the Evidence for OECD Countries', OECD Social Employment and Migration Working Papers, No. 52, OECD.
Goastellec, G. (2010) 'From Empiry to Theory: The Social Construction of Inequalities', in Goastellec G. (eds) (2010) *Understanding Inequalities in and by Higher Education* (Rotterdam: Global Perspectives on Higher Education, Sense Publisher), pp. 123–31.
Gorard, S, N. Adnett, H. May, K. Slack, E. Smith and L. Thomas (2006) *Review of Widening Participation Research: Addressing the Barriers to Participation in Higher Education* (Bristol: HEFCE).
Heath, S., A. Fuller and K. Paton (2008) 'Network-Based Ambivalence and Educational Decision-making: A Case Study of Non-Participation in Higher Education', *Research Papers in Education*, 23(2): 219–29.
Horvat, E. (2001) Understanding Equity and Access in Higher Education: The Potential Contribution of Pierre Bourdieu', in William G. Tierney (ed.) *Higher Education Handbook of Theory and Research* (New York: Agathon Press), pp. 195–238.
Horvat, E. (2003) 'The Interactive Effects of Race and Class in Educational Research: Theoretical Insights from the Work of Pierre Bourdieu', *Penn GCE Perspectives on Urban Education*, 2(1): 1–25.
Hüsamettin, I. and F. Ünal (2013) 'The Construction of National Identity in Modern Times: Theoretical Perspective', *International Journal of Humanities and Social Science*, 3(11); June 2013.
Reay, D., M. David and S. Ball (2005) *Degrees of Choice: Social Class, Race and Gender in Higher Education* (Stoke on Trent: Trentham Books).
Rusciano, F. L. (2003) 'The Construction of National Identity: A 23-Nation Study', *Political Research Quarterly*, 56(3): 361–66.
Sandel, M. (2012) *What Money Can't Buy: The Moral Limits of Markets* (New York: Farrar, Straus and Giroux).
Santiago, P., K. Tremblay, E. Basri and E. Arnal (2008) *Tertiary Education for the Knowledge Society*, Vol. 2., *Special Features: Equity, Innovation, Labour Market, Internationalisation* (Paris: Office of Economic Cooperation and Development).
UNESCO (2015) *Concept Note on the Post-2015 Education Agenda* (Paris: UNESCO).

# Index

*A Fair Chance for All – Higher Education That's Within Everyone's Reach* 168–74, 180, 181
Abagre et al. 156
Aboriginal Affairs and Northern Development Canada (AANDC) 16, 18
Aboriginal students 15–18, 22, 170
academic under-preparation 33, 45
access to higher education (HE)
 and academic under-preparation 33
 access agreements 82, 88
 access–nationhood relationship 188–90, 191
 Australia 183
 Canada 13, 19, 22–5, 26–7, 183
 Colombia 43–7, 49, 185
 and culture 189–90
 and equity 8–9, 139, 189
 fairness in 6
 Finland 73–6, 184
 formal/epistemological 137, 145
 Germany 55–7, 187
 Ghana 154–63
 India 109–10, 183
 Malaysia 95–105
 meaning of 7
 Ontario model of inclusive access 22–5, 26–7
 politicization of 189
 South Africa 143–9
 and support 33
 United Kingdom 77, 88
 United States 29, 31–2, 38–41, 184
Access to Success, Northern Ireland 81
*Access without Equity? Finding a Better Balance in Higher Education in Asia* 5
accountability, Canada 23
*Action Plan to Transform Post-Secondary Education in New Brunswick, The* 20
activist student movements, Canada 27
Addae-Mensah, I. 157
admissions system, Finland 72
adult learners
 England 86, 90
 Malaysia 105
 second-chance learners in Germany 58, 59, 60, 63, 64, 67
 University of Kansas 40
Advancement through Education initiative, Germany 60–1
advocacy, Canada 18, 26
affirmative action
 Ghana 155–6
 India 113–16
AHOT project, Finland 73
Aimhigher programme, UK 87, 90
Alberta, post-secondary education in 20
Ali, B. 157
American degree transfer programme, Malaysia 104
ANKOM, Germany 61
apartheid era, South Africa 137–9
application process, engaging parents in 39–40
Arbeiterkind.de initiative, Germany 60, 65
Asia, and participation in HE 5
Asian Development Bank 5
Asmal, Kader 141
Assembly of First Nations, Canada 18
Atuahene, F. 153, 157, 160
Auditor General's Status Report 2011, Canada 16
Australia
 access to HE 183
 branch campuses in Malaysia 104, 105
 demand-driven systems 174–5, 177, 178–9
 disadvantaged groups in higher education 168–9, 170, 171
 equity 164, 169–73
 the future 178–80
 HE in 164–6
 higher education participation and partnerships programme (HEPPP) 176–8

participation in higher education 174
policy framework 1: expansion of the system 166–8
policy framework 2: 'a fair chance for all'/'target group initiatives' 168–74
policy framework 3: social inclusion/demand-driven system 174–5
Australian Tertiary Admission Rank (ATAR) 175

Baden-Württemberg initiative 61–4
Bantu Education Act, Act No. 47 of 1953, South Africa 138
barriers to access and success in higher education
 Colombia 44–6, 48
 United States 33, 35, 37
Bartušek, A. 4
Basant, R. 115
Beihang University 132
Beijing Normal University 132
*Berufsschulen* 56
Beswick, D. 167–8
Blossveld, H. -P. 4
Blue Chair campaign, Ontario 25–6
Bologna Declaration 1999 55
Bologna Process 58–9, 62, 66
Bourdieu, P. 185
Bowen et al. 37
Bradley Review, Australia 173, 174, 176
branch campuses, Malaysia 104–5
Breaking Barriers: A Strategy for Equal Access to Higher Education, Ontario 26
British Columbia, post-secondary education in 20
Brown et al. 1, 76
*Brown v. Board of Education of Topeka* 30
Bumiputera people 95, 97, 98, 103, 105, 107

Campaign for Girls Education (CAMFED), Ghana 155–6
*Campus 20/20*, British Colombia 20
Canada
 access to HE in 13, 19, 183
 equity 183
 HE system 13–15
 Ontario model of inclusive access 22–5
 participation in higher education 15–17, 27–8
 policies and practices supporting HE progression 17–22
 post-secondary participation 15–17, 27–8
Canada Millennium Scholarship Foundation (CMSF) 18, 26, 28
Canadian Alliance of Student Associations (CASA) 27
Canadian Council on Learning (CCL) 18
careers advice, England 90
caste system, India 111–12, 113, 115
categories, legitimized 182–3
CÉGEP system, Canada 14, 17
Center for Educational Opportunity Programs (CEOP), University of Kansas 34, 38–41
Chattopadhyay, S. 120
Children's Universities 46–7, 185
Children's University EAFIT, Colombia 46–54, 185
China
 disadvantaged/under-represented groups 125–8, 128–34, 136
 Gaokao and proposition 122–4, 130, 134–5, 136
 HE entry in 121–4
 legal basis of access policy of HE 128
 new challenges/directions in access to HE in 134–6
 policies/practices 121, 127–8, 135
civil rights movement, United States 31
Clancy, P. 7, 8, 182
Clarke et al. 171
class issues
 Germany 57, 60, 64
 India 114 *see also* caste system
collaboration strategies 24, 101
college application process, engaging parents in 39–40
college degrees, in the US 37
college fit 32, 33–6, 39
college graduation, United States 37–8
College Student Alliance (CSA), Ontario 26
colleges of advanced education (CAEs), Australia 166
Colombia, access to HE in 43–7, 49, 185
Committee to Advise on Renovation and Rejuvenation of Higher Education, India 116
Commonwealth Learning Scholarships, Australia 172

Commonwealth Supported Places (CSP), Australia 165, 166
Communities First areas, Wales 84–5
community investments, Ontario 24–5
compliance agreements, UK 92
Compulsory Education Law 1986, China 128
constitutions
   Canadian 13
   Finnish 68–9
   Ghanaian 154
   Indian 111, 113
   South African 137, 144
   United States 30
context, and access to education 7
Cooperative Programme of Supporting the Enrolment in Mid-western Regions, China 129
Core Curriculum for Pre-School Education (2000), Finland 70
corporate-sponsored (CSR) programmes, Malaysia 102–3, 108
Council of Educators of Toronto (CET) 24
Council of Ministers of Education (CMEC), Canada 19, 20
Council of the Federation, Canada 19, 28
Crediting of Vocational Competences for Higher Education Study Programmes (ANKOM), Germany 61
*Critical Intervention Framework* 178
cultural capital 185
cultural minorities *see* minorities
culture(s)
   and access to education 189–90
   college 35–6, 39
   college-going 32
   and female participation in HE 155
   and habitus 185
curricula, pre-school education in Finland 70

Daddieh, C. K. 155
data collection systems, UK 92
Dearing Review 87
Dearing, Ron 87
debt levels, of students 36, 91
degree transfer programme, Malaysia 104
demand-driven systems, Australia 174–5, 177, 178–9

demand, for HE in Colombia 44
Department of Higher Education and Training's (DHET), South Africa 142, 143
deprivation, UK 84 *see also* poverty
Deshpande, S. 114–15
disabilities
   participation rates in Australia 173, 177
   students with in China 126–7, 134
   students with in Ghana 159–60
Disability Bill 2006, Ghana 159–60
disadvantaged groups in higher education *see also individual groups; i.e disabilities; minority groups; rural areas etc.*
   Australia 168–9, 170, 171
   China 125–8, 128–34, 136
discrimination, India 111, 113
distance learning 22, 74–5
diversity
   Canada 14–15
   China 125–7
   of students 66
   teaching and learning for 149–50
Dobson et al. 170
Dream-building Project, Peking University 131
dropout rates
   Colombia 45–6
   Finland 70
   Ghana 154
   South Africa 139
   United States 33, 35
dropping out, students at risk of 62, 63
Duncan, Arne 30

e-learning, Canada 22
EAFIT, Colombia 46–54, 185
early childhood education and care (ECEC), Finland 70
earnings, and education 1, 31
economic development
   China 125
   and education 95, 98, 143, 189
   Malaysia 99
Economic Opportunity Act 1964, US 30
Economic Transformation Policy (PEMANDU), Malaysia 97, 108

Economic Transformation Programme
  (ETP), Malaysia   99–100, 108
economy
  China   125
  Malaysia   94, 95
education
  China   121
  Colombia   43–4
  and earnings   1, 31
  and economic development   95, 98,
    143, 189
  effectiveness of   68 *see also* outcomes;
    success for learners
  further education in Scotland   82–3
  and globalization   76, 106, 108
  goals of   74
  higher education (HE) *see* higher
    education (HE)
  and innovation   69
  post-secondary *see* post-secondary
    education
  primary education   1
  purpose of   2
  tertiary education *see* tertiary education
Education at a Glance reports   7
*Education in Ghana: Improving Equity,*
  *Efficiency and Accountability of*
  *Education Service Delivery*   160
Education Law 1995, China   128
Education Summit 2008, Germany   59
educational achievement gaps, Aboriginal
  students in Canada   16
Educational Equity Index (EEI)   5
educational qualifications, as a positional
  good   2
Educational Talent Search, US   30,
  34–5
effectiveness, of education   68 *see also*
  outcomes; success for learners
employment *see also* unemployment
  and choice of discipline studied   161
  and educational participation   1–2
  lower-skilled work   1
Employment and Social Development
  Canada (ESDC)   17
engagement
  of parents in the application
    process   39–40
  of students   39, 41
England *see also* United Kingdom
  access to HE in   88

participation in HE by social
  background   86–92
English language, as global *lingua*
  *franca*   106
enrolment for higher education
  China   124
  Colombia   44
  Ghana   151, 152–4
  South Africa   142
epistemological access   137, 145
equal opportunity cells (EOCs),
  India   115–16
equity
  and access to education   8–9, 139, 189
  Australia   164, 169–73
  Canada   183
  Colombia   44
  and expansion in HE   4
  Finland   68–76, 184
  in HE   2
  India   110, 116–18, 183
  United Kingdom   87, 89
equity framework for higher education
  (HE), Australia   164
equity in higher education (HE),
  Canada   183
ethnic groups/minorities *see also*
  minorities
  China   126, 128–9, 129–30, 136
  Malaysia   94–5, 95–6, 97, 105–6,
    107–8
Europe, inequalities in access to tertiary
  education   4
European higher education system   55
European Social Fund   73
EUROSTUDENT reports   57
extended degree programme (EDP),
  Stellenbosch University   148
Extension of Universities Act, Act No. 45
  1959, South Africa   139
extra-curricular activities, and
  low-income/first-generation
  students   36, 39

*Fachhochschulen*   56
*Fair Chance for All – Higher Education*
  *That's Within Everyone's Reach, A*
  168–74, 180, 181
fairness, in access   6
Federal Ministry of Education and
  Research (BMBF), Germany   60, 61

Federal State initiatives, Germany 60–4
Federal Student Aid (FAFSA), US 35, 39
Ferguson, K. 173
Ferrier, F. 183–4
Field, C. 21
finance *see also* funding; tuition fees
  educational system financing in Canada 17–18
  financial aid in Finland 71, 72
  financial aid in Ghana 161
Finland
  access to HE 73–6, 184
  education system 69–72
  equity in HE 68–76, 184
  and innovation in access to HE 73–6
  and participation in HE 3, 5, 71
Finnie et al. 15
first-generation students
  defined 29
  and extra-curricular activities 36, 39
  Germany 64, 65
  India 119
  United States 32, 33
Five-year Plan documents, India 117, 118, 119
foundation programmes, Malaysia 102–5
funding *see also* finance; tuition fees
  Australia 164, 165, 166–7, 172–3, 174, 175, 176, 177
  Finland 70–1
  Germany 61–2, 66
  Ghana 151, 153, 160–1
  India 115, 117, 119
  Malaysia 95, 98
  Ontario 23
  and performance indicators 21
  Scotland 82, 83, 93
  South Africa 138, 142, 143
  United Kingdom 79, 82–3, 85, 89, 93
  United States 30, 36–7, 38
  Wales 85
further education, Scotland 82–3

Gaining Early Awareness and Readiness for Undergraduate Programs (GEAR UP), University of Kansas 34
Gallacher, J. and Raffe, D. 92
Gaokao, China 122–4, 130, 134–5, 136
gender *see also* women
  and participation in HE 3
  and student enrolments in Ghana 152–3, 155–6, 160

Germany
  access to HE 55–7, 187
  innovation in practice 60–5
  participation in HE 3
  policy programmes/initiatives for widening access to HE 58–60, 68
  under-represented groups in HE 57–8
Ghana
  access to tertiary education 154–61
  challenges for access to tertiary education 161–3
  HE in 151–4
  less endowed schools 157, 158, 162
  under-represented groups 155–61, 162–3
Ghana Education Service (GES) 157
Ghana Education Trust Fund (GETFund) 153, 161
Giddens, Anthony 87
global analysis, of post-secondary participation 6–7
global financial crisis 103
*Global Higher Education Rankings 2010* 5
globalization, and education 76, 106, 108
goals, of education 74
Goastellec, G. 7, 8
graduate endowments, Scotland 82
graduate unemployment/underemployment, England 90 *see also* unemployment
graduation rates, United States 33
grants *see also* tuition fees
  Australia 179
  China 133–4
  Finland 72
Gray-Little, B. 41
Group Areas Act No. 41 1950, South Africa 138

habitus 185, 186
Harvest of Hope Leadership Academy programs, US 38
Haycock, K. 31
Heagney, M. 183–4
Higher Education Contribution Scheme (HECS), Australia 167
Higher Education Equity Program, Australia 169
Higher Education Funding Council for Wales (HEFCW) 85

higher education (HE) *see also* post-secondary education; tertiary education
  academic/technical  186
  Australia  164
  progression  32, 90–1
  student body in Canada  14–15
  who participates in?  2–6
higher education participation and partnerships programme (HEPPP), Australia  176–8
Higher Education Quality Council of Ontario (HEQCO)  23, 27
Higher Education South Africa (HESA)  142
Hindu Varna System  111
household registration, China  125–6
Hudzik, J. K.  97
human capital development, Malaysia  97

identity(ies)
  Aboriginal in Canada  16
  national  188–90
  of untouchables  111
immigrants, Canada  15, 16
*Implementation Suggestions for Deepening the Reform of Examination and Enrolment System*, China  135
in-service professional development programmes, Malaysia  105
*Increasing Access to HE: A Review of System-Level Policy Initiatives*, Canada  21
India
  access to HE  109–10, 183
  challenges  118–20
  equitable expansion  116–18
  equity in HE  110, 183
  HE system  109
  participation in HE  109, 110–12, 115
  State, access and affirmative action  113–16
indigenous cultural minorities *see also* minorities
  Australia  177, 178, 179, 180
  Finland  75
individual narratives, and access to education  8
inequalities
  in access to tertiary education  4
  change in character of  4
  China  122, 125–7

Colombia  44–6
  and education systems  55
  Germany  57, 66
  Ghana  157
  and HE participation  186
  India  109, 110–12, 113–14, 116–17, 119–20
  in participation in HE  2–3
  and participation in higher education  2–3, 186
  and policymakers  183–4
  and politicization  184
  social reproduction of  185–6
  South Africa  144–5
  United States  30, 32, 41
infrastructure, Ghana  153
innovation
  and access to HE in Finland  73–6
  and access to HE in Malaysia  100–5
  and education  69
  in practice, Germany  60–5
institutions
  Finland  70
  for-profit in the US  37
  India  116–18
  numbers of by country in the UK  77–8
  post-secondary institutions (PSIs), Canada  14, 17–18
  private HE in Malaysia  100
  ranking of in China  123
  tertiary education in Ghana  151–2
international pre-university programmes, Malaysia  100–2
internationalization of higher education, Malaysia  99, 101

Johnson, Lyndon Baines  30
Jones, G.  21

Kivinen et al.  72
Klinger, C.  6, 9
knowledge
  China  121
  student's relationship with  50–1
Koucký, J.  4
Kwame Nkrumah University of Science and Technology (KNUST), Ghana  157–8

Lang, D.  21
language
  English as global *lingua franca*  106

language (*Continued*)
  Finnish 75
  issues in South Africa 145
leadership, governmental in Canada 22
leadership skills, for students 41
*Learn Canada 2020* 20
*Learning Alberta Report, A* 20
*Learning for All*, Scotland 84
less endowed secondary schools (LESS), Ghana 157, 158, 162
liberalization of higher education, Malaysia 98–9
lifelong learning
  Finland 73
  UNESCO development goal 190
Lisbon Agenda 2000 55
literacy rates, South Africa 138
loans
  Australia 166, 167, 172, 179
  Canada 17
  China 133, 134
  Finland 72
  Ghana 161
  Malaysia 99, 103
  South Africa 142
local foundation programmes, Malaysia 102–5
low-income students
  best practice in extending access to 38–41
  Colombia 45–6
  defined 29
  and extra-curricular activities 36, 39
  United States 32, 33, 37, 38–41
low socio-economic groups
  Australia 173, 174, 175, 177, 179, 180
  China 127, 133–4
  England 91
Lumina Foundation 2010 Big Goal, US 37

Malaysia
  access to post-secondary education 95–100
  innovation in access to HE 100–5
  international pre-university programmes 100–2
  internationalization of HE 99, 100
  liberalization of HE 98–9
  local foundation programmes 102–5
  nation-building 98
  participation in higher education 96, 97
  post-independence Malaysia 98–100
  post-secondary education 94–5
  student enrolments 96
Malaysian Ministry of Education (MoE) 95, 98, 99
Malaysian Qualifications Agency (MQA) 102
Mangeol, P. 1
Manuh et al. 155
maximally maintained inequality (MMI) 4
McKinsey Global Institute 1
McNair Scholars Program, University of Kansas 35–6
means testing, Finland 72
Medellin, Children's University EAFIT 47–54, 185
Medow, J. 5
mentoring
  less endowed secondary schools (LESS), Ghana 159
  and low-income/first-generation students 40, 65
Meridian University College (MUC), Ghana 153
merit scholarships, India 115
Meyer et al. 6
Mid-western applicants, China 128–9
Mid-western Regions, China 135
migrant students, China 125–6, 132–3
Millennium Development Goals 1
Ministry of Education (MoE), China 122, 124, 129, 131, 135
Ministry of Education (MoE), Finland 72
minorities *see also* ethnic groups/minorities
  Australia 177, 178, 179, 180
  Canada 14–18, 22
  China 126
  Finland 75
MINT-Kolleg model 63–4
Mitchem, A. L. 31, 37
monitoring, of students and support 41
Morrill Land Grant Acts of 1862/1890, US 30
Mortenson, T. 36
Mphahlele, M. K. 145
Murray, N. 6, 9

Nagaoka et al. 32
nation-building, Malaysia 98

National Centre for Student Equity in Higher Education (NCSEHE), Australia  177
National College Entrance Examination, China  126, 129
National Council for Tertiary Education (NCTE), Ghana  151
National Development Plan for Colombia 2010–14  53
National Development Plan, South Africa  142
National Endeavour Fellowship, China  133
National High Education Strategic Plan (NHESP) 2020, Malaysia  99, 102, 104, 108
National Knowledge Commission (NKC), India  115
National Networks of Collaborative Outreach (NNCO) programme, England  90
*National Outline of the Long and Mid-term Plan for Education Development and Reform 2010–2020*, China  129, 134
National Policy on Education 1986, India  113
National Student Financial Aid Scheme (NSFAS), South Africa  142
National Training Service (SENA), Colombia  45
nationhood, and access to education  188–90, 191
Natives Act, Act No. 67 of 1952, South Africa  138
Naylor et al.  178
New Economic Policy 1970, Malaysia  98
*New Measuring Stick: Is Access to Higher Education in Canada More Equitable?, A*  5
Newfoundland and Labrador, post-secondary education in  20
Nordic welfare states  69, 71
Northern Ireland, participation in HE by social background  80–2, 93
*Notice for Key Universities to Recruit Rural Students in 2015*, China  131
*Notice of Holding Minority Classes in National Key Universities*, China  130

Obama, Barack  37
Office for Fair Access (OFFA), England  88

older learners, England 90 *see also* adult learners
100 Up project, University of Cape Town  147
*Ontario – A Leader in Learning, Report and Recommendations*  23
Ontario, post-secondary education in  20
Ontario Student Assistance Program  23
Ontario Student Trustees Association (OSTA)  26
Ontario Undergraduate Student Alliance (OUSA)  25–6, 27
Open University, Finland  74–5
*Opinions on Children of Migrant Workers Attending the National College Entrance Examination after Compulsory Education*, China  132
Orang Asli people  108
Organisation of Economic Cooperation and Development (OECD)  1, 2–3, 7, 45
Orr et al.  7–8
other backward classes (OBCs), India  111–12, 113, 115
*Our Universities: Backing Australia's Future*  172
outcomes, for students in Malaysia  97, 105–7 *see also* effectiveness; success for learners
outreach  92, 177
overseas study, and Malaysians  98
Owusu-Ansah, A.  153, 157, 160

Palfreyman, D.  6
parental educational achievement  35
parents
 engagement in application process  39–40
 socio-economic background of  57
participation in higher education *see also* student enrolments
 Australia  174
 Canada  15–17, 27–8
 Finland  3, 5, 71
 Germany  3
 global analysis of  6–7
 India  109, 110–12, 115
 and inequalities  2–3, 186
 Malaysia  96, 97
 and socio-economic background  2, 3–4, 5, 7, 72, 79–86, 154
 South Africa  144

partnership activities
  Australia   176
  and pre-college programs   38–9
  Wales   84–5
Pathways to Education, Toronto   25, 27
Peking University, Dream-building Project   131
Pell Grant Program, US   36
People's Republic of China Household Registration Ordinance 1958   125–6
performance, educational in Canada   28
performance funding, Australia   175
performance indicators, Canada   21
*Plessy v. Ferguson*   30
POLAR measure of disadvantage   79, 91
policy(ies)
  Australia   166–75, 180
  Canada   17–22
  China   121, 127–8, 135
  Finland   69, 70, 71, 75–6
  Germany   58–60, 68
  Ghana   154–61
  India   113–16, 117, 119
  Malaysia   95, 97, 98, 99, 107
  South Africa   141–3
policymakers, addressing inequalities in HE participation   183–4
policymaking   68
politicization
  of access   189
  and inequalities   184
polytechnics   86, 152–3
Polytechnics Act 2007, Ghana   152
Population Registration Act 1950, South Africa   138
post-secondary education *see also* higher education (HE); tertiary education
  access to   8–9
  Malaysia   94–5
  participation in   1
  participation in Canada   15–17, 27–8
  private provision of *see* private provision of post-secondary education
*Post-Secondary Education Review*, Ontario   20, 23
post-secondary institutions (PSIs),
  Canada   14, 17–18 *see also* institutions
poverty
  and access to HE in China   131, 136
  and access to HE in the US   29–31

practices supporting HE progression, Canada   17–22
pre-college programs, and partnerships   38–9
pre-university programmes
  China   129–30
  Malaysia   100–2
Preparatory Instruction and Guidance for VET (Ammattistartti) programme, Finland   70
preparatory programmes, Malaysia   100–2
primary education, participation in   1
prior learning, Finland   73
Private High Educational Institutions Act (PHEIA), Malaysia   99, 104
private provision of post-secondary education
  Asia   186–7
  Ghana   187
  India   109–10, 187
  Malaysia   96, 98–9, 100, 101, 106, 107–8
privatization, India   119–20
professional development programmes, Malaysia   105
progression for learners, England   90–1
Project for Minority's High-level Administrative Talents, China   128–9
proposition, China   122–4
Provisional National Defence Council (PNDC) Law 1992, Ghana   161
psychological barriers, to accessing higher education   45–6
Public Private Partnership (PPP), India   119
public universities, Canada   14

qualifications, as a positional good   2
Quebec, tuition fees   17
Queensland Consortium   177–8
quota systems
  China   124
  Malaysia   98
  reservation quotas in India   113, 114

racial segregation, US   30
Rae Report, Ontario   20, 23
Ramsay, E.   172
*Reaching Higher Strategy (2005–2010)*, Ontario   23, 24
Reaching Wider partnerships, Wales   84–5

reforms, structural in Canada   21
*Regulation of Enrolment for Regular HE Institutions*, China   130
Regulation of Preparatory Course and Classes of Minority Groups and Minority Classes for Regular HE Institutions, China   129–30
*Regulation on the Administration of Participation of the Students with Disabilities in the National College Entrance Examination*, China   134
regulatory regimes   76
religion, and HE in India   110–11
remedial education, low-income/first-generation students   37–8
Rent a Student initiative, Germany   60, 64
reservation quotas, India   113, 114
*Review of Higher Education*, Australia *see* Bradley Review, Australia
*Revitalization Plan of Higher Education in Mid-western Regions (2012–2020)*, China   129
RMSA (*Rashtriya Madhyamik Shiksha Abhiyan*)   117
Roderick et al.   33
Rollnick, M.   137
Roma people, Finland   75
Ronald E. McNair Post-Baccalaureate Achievement Program, US   36, 40
rural areas
  Australia   173, 177, 179, 180
  Canada   16, 22
  China   126, 127, 130–2, 136
  Colombia   53
  Finland   71
  Ghana   157, 158, 162
  India   112
  South Africa   139, 142, 143
rural–urban divide, India   112, 113
RUSA (*Rashtriya Uchhatar Shiksha Abhiyan*)   117–19
Rusciano, F. L.   189

Salmon, Alex   83
Sami people   75
Santiago et al.   7
scheduled castes (SCs), India   111–12, 113, 115
scheduled tribes (STs), India   111–12, 113, 115

scholarships
  Australia   172
  China   133–4
  India   115
Schools for Higher Education Programme, Scotland   83
Scotland, participation in HE by social background   82–4, 93
second-chance learners, Germany   58, 59, 60, 63, 64, 67
Self-improvement Project, Tsinghua University   131–2
Sen, G.   115
'separate but equal' doctrine, US   30
Serviceman's Readjustment Act 1945, US (GI Bill)   30
Shavit et al.   4
Shavit, Y.   4
skills, needed for college access/success   33
social background, and participation in HE in the UK   84–5, 89, 93
social class, in the UK   93
social dimension, of European HE   55
social exclusion, India   113
social inclusion, Australia   174–5
social inequality, Germany   66 *see also* inequalities
social origins, and choice of HE   56–7
social reproduction of inequalities   185–6
socio-economic factors
  Germany   57
  Ghana   160–1
  and participation in HE   2, 3–4, 5, 7, 72, 79–86, 154
  United Kingdom   93
South Africa
  access progress   144–5
  apartheid era   137–9
  government interventions   141
  models of post-school interventions   140
  myths about access to HE   143–4
  policies/practices supporting progression to HE   141–3
  supply chain from secondary schooling   139–40
  university access initiatives   146–9
Special Services for Disadvantaged Students, US   30
spending on education, Ghana   161 *see also* funding

Standing Conference of Education and Culture Ministers 2009, Germany 59–60, 61, 66
State Higher Education Councils, India 118
Stellenbosch University, access initiative 147–8
Step Up programme, University of Ulster 82
structural reforms, Canada 21
student enrolments *see also* participation rates in higher education
  India 109, 110, 112
  Malaysia 96
student life cycle 91
Student Loan Trust Fund, Ghana 161
student loans *see also* tuition fees
  Australia 166, 167, 172, 179
  Canada 17
  China 133, 134
  Finland 72
  Ghana 161
  Malaysia 99, 103
  South Africa 142
Student Success/Learning to 18 (SS/L 18) Strategy, Canada 23
Student Support Services Program, US 30, 40
student voice, Ontario 25–6
students
  of colour in South Africa 140
  debt levels of 36, 91
  with disabilities in China 126–7, 134
  with disabilities in Ghana 159–60
  diversity of 66
  engagement of 39, 41
  financial aid for in Finland 71, 72
  leadership skills for 41
  numbers of by country in the UK 77–9
  outcomes for in Malaysia 97, 105–7
  at risk of dropping out 62, 63
  rural in China 130–2
  transnational 99
  views of the Children's University EAFIT 49–50
studentships, Australia 166–7
Study Models of Individual Speeds initiative, Germany 60, 61–4
success for learners *see also* effectiveness, of education; outcomes
  England 90–1
  Malaysia 96–7

summer schools, Finland 74
Summer University System, Finland 74–5
Sundaram, K. 113
Sunway College/University 103, 104, 105, 108
support
  and access to HE 33
  and low-income/first-generation students 40–1
  programmes in Australia 177
  for students in India 115

Tapper, T. 6
teachers, Finland 69–70
tertiary education *see also* higher education (HE); post-secondary education
  Australia 177–8
  Canada 15
  Finland 71
  Ghana 151–2, 153–63
  inequalities in access to 4
  participation in 3
Tham, S. Y. 96, 98
Thomas, L. 9
Tilak, J. B. G. 119–20
Tinto, V. 33
Toronto District School Board (TDSB) 23
Torres Strait Islander students 170
transnational HE (TNHE) options, Malaysia 104
transnational students 99
Tremblay, K. 1
TRIO programs, US 30–1, 33, 34, 35, 39, 40
Trow, M. A. 8
Tsinghua University, Self-improvement Project 131–2
tuition fees
  Australia 164, 165–6, 166–7, 172, 177, 179
  Canada 17
  Colombia 45
  Finland 74
  Ghana 152, 153, 161
  Malaysia 98, 99
  and participation in HE 7–8
  Scotland 82, 83
  South Africa 138, 142
  United Kingdom 79, 82, 83, 88
  United States 35, 36–7, 38
twinning arrangements, Malaysia 101, 103–4

under-representation, based on discipline in Ghana  161
under-represented groups
  Australia  176–7, 180–1
  Canada  23
  China  125–7, 128–34
  Germany  57–8
  Ghana  155–61, 162–3
*Understanding Mass Higher Education*  6
unemployment *see also* employment
  Aboriginal population in Canada  17
  graduate  90
United Kingdom
  access to HE  77
  branch campuses in Malaysia  104, 105
  compliance agreements  92
  data collection systems  92
  equity  87, 89
  HE in  77–9, 93
  outreach work  92
  participation in HE by social background  79–86
  social class in the  93
United Nations Educational, Scientific and Cultural Organization (UNESCO)  3, 190
United Nations, Millennium Development Goals  1
United States
  access to HE  29, 184
  barriers to access and success in HE  31–2
  best practice in extending access to low-income students  38–41
  college fit  33–6
  college graduation  37–8
  Constitution of the US  30
  financing of college education  36–7
  population holding college degrees/credentials  37
  poverty and access to HE  29–31
United Way of Greater Toronto's Community of Practice on Youth Educational Attainment Partnerships  24, 25
Universities and Colleges Admissions Service (UCAS), UK  79–80
university degrees, Aboriginal students in Canada  16

University Grants Commission (UGC), India  115
University of Bremen  60, 64
University of Cape Coast (UCC), Ghana  153
University of Cape Town  146–7
University of Development Studies, Ghana  156
University of Ghana  155–6, 157, 160, 161
University of Kansas  34, 35–6, 38–41
University of the Third Age, Finland  74
University of the Western Cape  148–9
University of Ulster  82
university preparatory programmes, Malaysia  100–2
untouchables, identity of  111
Upward Bound, US  30
urban diversity strategy, Toronto  23
urban-rural divide, China  126, 127
Usher, A.  5

vocational education and training (VET), Germany  55–6, 57–8, 61

Wales, participation in HE by social background  84–5, 93
War on Poverty, US  30
well-being, and post-secondary education  1, 5
West African Senior Secondary School Certificate Examination (SSCE)  152, 157
*White Paper on Public Post-Secondary Education*, Newfoundland and Labrador  20
'Who Gets a Degree? Access to Tertiary Education in Europe 1950–2009'  4
widening access regional forums (WARFs), Scotland  83
Widening Tertiary Participation strategy, Australia  178
women *see also* gender
  Australia  167
  and participation in HE  3
  participation rates in Australia  173
  student enrolments in Ghana  152–3, 155–6, 160
  students in Canada  14
  tertiary education in Finland  71

working-class families, Germany  57, 60, 64
*World Atlas of Gender Equality in Education*  3
World Bank  3, 45, 160, 161

Yadav, Y.  114–15
Youth Guarantee (2013), Finland  70
Youth in Transition Survey  15
Yusif, H. M.  157